BUCKNELL REVIEW

Phenomenology,
Structuralism, Semiology

STATEMENT OF POLICY

Bucknell Review is a scholarly interdisciplinary journal. Each issue will be devoted to a major theme or movement in the humanities or sciences, or to two or three closely related topics. The editors invite heterodox, orthodox, and speculative ideas and welcome manuscripts from any enterprising scholar in the humanities and sciences.

BUCKNELL REVIEW
A Scholarly Journal of Letters, Arts and Sciences

Editor
HARRY R. GARVIN

Special Associate Editor This Issue
PATRICK BRADY

Associate Editors
IRVING H. BUCHEN
ROBERT E. BUTTS
WILLIAM CADBURY
K. WARD HOOKER
MICHAEL D. PAYNE
JEROME RICHFIELD
ARTHUR JOSEPH SLAVIN
MARIA LUISA STRINGA
CALVIN G. THAYER
JOHN WHEATCROFT

Assistant to the Editor
DOROTHY L. BAUMWOLL

Contributors should send manuscripts with a self-addressed, stamped envelope to the Editor, Bucknell University, Lewisburg, Pennsylvania 17837. Subscription, $12.00 per volume of two issues; single copy, $7.50.

BUCKNELL REVIEW

Phenomenology, Structuralism, Semiology

Edited by
HARRY R. GARVIN

LEWISBURG
BUCKNELL UNIVERSITY PRESS
LONDON: ASSOCIATED UNIVERSITY PRESSES

Associated University Presses, Inc.
Cranbury, New Jersey 08512

Associated University Presses
108 New Bond Street
London W1Y OQX, England

Library of Congress Cataloging in Publication Data

Main entry under title:

Phenomenology, structuralism, semiology.
(Bucknell review ; [v. 1])
Includes bibliographical references.
1. Phenomenology—Addresses, essays, lectures.
2. Structuralism—Addresses, essays, lectures.
3. Semiotics—Addresses, essays, lectures.
I. Garvin, Harry Raphael, 1916–
II. Series: Bucknell review (Lewisburg Pa.)
B829.5.p48 1975   149'.9   75-29734
ISBN 0-8387-1880-9

April, 1976

Printed in the United States of America

Contents

PHENOMENOLOGY, STRUCTURALISM, SEMIOLOGY

Preface

With this first issue of our "book-journal," *Bucknell Review* is launching a major enterprise in order to assume a larger role in providing for the changing needs of the scholarly world. A systematic effort is being made to increase the number of our readers nationally and internationally. We have hopes that the book-journal will make possible a unique adventure for a scholarly interdisciplinary review.

Specialists, professors, students—here and abroad—have growing desires to keep abreast of intellectual developments in the enlarging scholarly domain, to keep in touch with the next steps in the arts and sciences. There are relatively few interdisciplinary journals appealing to intellectuals seriously interested in both the sciences and the humanities; and not one, to our knowledge, has the distinctive scholarly emphasis of *Bucknell Review*. We do not compete with commercial or deeply specialized journals.

Each issue will be devoted to a major theme or movement in the humanities or sciences, or to two or three closely related topics. (Every number will about double the pages of recent issues of the *Review*.) The editors take pleasure in the intellectual openness of the *Review* to speculative, orthodox, and heterodox ideas, and they welcome manuscripts from any enterprising scholar in the humanities and sciences.

Future issues of *Bucknell Review* will explore such topics as: Literature and the Arts; New Frontiers in Humanistic Studies; New Steps in Philosophy of the Social Sciences; Interactions of History and Literature; Shakespeare and Contemporary Critical Theory; Romanticism, Modernism, and Post-Modernism.

We invite manuscripts on specific subjects that we can fit into these and related general topics. Furthermore, we invite offers to do a scholarly review-article for one of these topics, or to become a guest editor for a particular issue of the *Review*.

With rare and mocking exceptions, the editors of the *Review* have succeeded in coming to a decision on a manuscript within four weeks.

We now wish to accelerate and intensify the appeal of *Bucknell Review* to the humanistic and scholarly interests of all intellectuals.

Harry R. Garvin, Editor

Notes on Contributors

PATRICK BRADY: Teaches at Rice University. Published a book-length study of Zola and completed manuscripts for four books plus numerous articles in European and American critical journals. Special interests are in French and comparative literature, theory and methodology of literary criticism, relationships among the arts, the development of the novel.

MADELEINE WRIGHT: Teaches at University of Wisconsin. Special interest in twentieth-century novel, and particularly the French. Has also published on comparative linguistics and on semantics.

THOMAS PISON: Special interests are in Romanticism, autobiography, and modern poetry and philosophy. Work in progress: the autobiographical structure of the narrative poem.

DENNIS M. WELCH: Teaches at Gonzaga University. Articles on Milton, Blake, Robert Lowell; poems in small magazines. Specialist in the Romantic Age.

WILLIAM J. FILSTEAD: Assistant Professor of Sociology and Director of Research in the Department of Psychiatry, Northwestern University Medical School. Principal interests are in medical sociology, evaluation research and qualitative research methods. Editor of collections of essays and author of numerous articles in professional and scholarly journals. Work in progress: monograph on the rise and fall of a therapeutic community and the development of conceptual models to describe the identification, definition, intervention and resolution of a variety of personal problems.

RICHARD GILLIS: Teaches at Russell Sage College. Main interests are in history of political philosophy and in the philosophy of the social sciences in general. Work in progress: a critique of empirical social science.

GENE BERNSTEIN: Teaches at the University of Notre Dame. Special interests are in Keats, structuralism, Romantic mythopoesis.

RENÉ GIRARD: Distinguished Professor, State University of New York, Buffalo. Author of *Mensonge romantique et vérité romanesque* (translated in many languages, and in English as *Deceit, Desire and the Novel*) ; *Dostoïevski: Du double à l'unité; La Violence et le sacré*. Numerous articles and reviews in American and European journals. A

9

number of essays are scheduled to be published, as well as English and Spanish translations of his *La Violence et le sacré*.

JAMES R. BENNETT: Teaches at the University of Arkansas and co-edits *Style*, which he founded in 1967. He has edited *Prose Style: A Historical Approach Through Studies* (1972) and is the author of articles in *Keats-Shelley Journal, D. H. Lawrence Review, South Atlantic Bulletin*, and other journals. His special area of teaching is nineteenth-century English literature.

SUSAN WITTIG: Teaches at the University of Texas at Austin. Special interests are in literary theory, medieval literature, translation.

LUDWIG VON BERTALANFFY: The late Professor von Bertalanffy was a pioneer in the theory of organismic biology and the founder of general systems theory. Author of twelve books (appearing in eight languages) and some 250 scientific papers.

ERIK SCHWIMMER: Teaches at the University of Toronto. Author of books on the Maori and Orokaiva peoples. Editor of *Journal of Symbolic Anthropology*. Work in progress: "Study of Regional Communication Systems in Papua and the Problem of Social Boundaries"; translation, editing, analysis of Orokaiva myth collection: "The Origin of Social Exchange in Orokaiva Mythology"; an analysis of New Zealand Maori community of Latter-Day Saints: "Valley of Atonement: A Study of Indoctrination."

DOUGLAS J. STEWART: Teaches at Brandeis University. Has published many articles on philosophy, myth, historiography, and drama (ancient and modern) ; forthcoming essays on "Aeneas the Politician" and "Falstaff the Centaur." Work in progress: monograph on the myth of Aphrodite.

RICHARD S. CALDWELL: Teaches at the University of Texas at Austin. Publications on Greek tragedy, psychoanalysis and classical studies, a translation of Aeschylus's *Supplices*. Work in progress: psychoanalysis and mythology, and a commentary on Apollodorus's *Bibliotheca*.

BUCKNELL REVIEW

Phenomenology, Structuralism, Semiology

Phenomenology, Structuralism, Semiology

Patrick Brady
Rice University

ESSENTIALLY, structuralism was the avant-garde of critical theory and practice (more theory than practice) during the past decade; that of the coming decade may well be semiotics, which came of age in Milan in June, 1974, with the founding of the International Society for Semiotic Studies. This is therefore an appropriate moment at which to review the achievements of phenomenology and structuralism and their role in preparing the emergence of the new science, which is destined to inherit many of the aspirations of the parent movements.

The Sixties ended in a flurry of book-length reviews of modern French criticism. Some came from American scholars like Laurent LeSage (*The French New Criticism* [University Park: Pennsylvania State Univ. Press, 1967]) and Wallace Fowlie (*The French Critic: 1549–1967* [Carbondale, Ill.: Southern Illinois Univ. Press, 1968], which dismisses pre-twentieth-century criticism in the first thirteen pages). Other books grouped essays in which the French looked at themselves, under the editorial guidance of practicing critics like Georges Poulet (*Les Chemins actuels de la critique* [Paris: Union Générale d'Editions, 1968]) and Philippe Sollers (*"Tel Quel": Théorie d'ensemble* [Paris: Seuil, 1968]). It is hardly surprising that these reviews and collections spawned by the heroic decade of structuralist analysis gave a large place to this new school of criticism: its inclusion is explicit in Fowlie (pp. 130–50), implicit in the other volumes,

13

where it is represented by Barthes, Foucault, Girard, Genette, Goldmann.[1] The *Tel Quel* volume also makes room for such harbingers of change as Derrida and Kristeva—and indeed the story of the last five years is in large part the story of the impact of such thinkers as these on the structuralist movement.

As the Seventies opened, "classical" structuralist analysis was still being applied in masterly fashion by virtuosi like Michael Riffaterre and Gérard Genette, but the termination of Lévi-Strauss's great four-volume work *Mythologiques* (*L'Homme nu* [Paris: Plon, 1971] constitutes volume IV) closed an era. Levi-Strauss himself confirmed this impression by taking advantage of the opportunity to review the work of Goldmann, Lacan, and Piaget in relation to his own. After being attacked in the late Sixties by Derrida and others, structuralism in the Seventies has experienced several new developments: it has been either bypassed for other concerns (such as new theories of schizophrenia: Deleuze, Girard), modified by genetic theory (drawing on Chomsky, Piaget, or Goldmann), or transformed into semiotics (Kristeva, Lotman, Uspensky). In sketching these developments of the last few years, I shall of course be obliged to limit myself to the salient points.

Earlier modes of criticism continued to survive, of course: existentialism produced perhaps its greatest critical effort in Jean-Paul Sartre's massive work on Flaubert, *L'Idiot de la famille*, in three volumes (Paris: Gallimard, 1971–72), and phenomenologists like Jean Starobinski and Jean Rousset of the so-called "Geneva school" continued to write in their established vein—witness the former's *La Relation critique* (Paris: Gallimard, 1970) and the latter's *Narcisse romancier* (Paris: Corti, 1973). But the structuralists—and their successors—were now occupying the foreground of critical activity and interest. The original four Titans of the structuralist adventure—the ethnologist Claude Lévi-Strauss, the psychoanalyst Jacques Lacan, the philosopher of history Michel Foucault, and the Marxist theorist Louis Althusser—were succeeded by four technically oriented analysts of prose fiction (originally grouped together in a now famous issue of *Communications* [No. 8, 1966]): Roland Barthes, A. J. Greimas, Tzvetan Todorov, and Claude Bremond. These produced notable work in the Seventies, developing and refining their previous investigations into the nature of narrative

---

[1] In the Poulet volume, structuralism is explicitly examined, under the disguise of "formalist criticism," in the essay by Dominique Noguez.

structures: Barthes: *S/Z* (Paris: Seuil, 1970), Greimas: *Du sens* (Paris: Seuil, 1970), Todorov: *Poétique de la prose* (Paris: Seuil, 1971), Bremond: *Logique du récit* (Paris: Seuil, 1973). While each scholar has developed along his own lines, that team spirit first established by Barthes in *Communications* 8, where he attempted to integrate the work of all four into a coherent ensemble of complementary contributions, may still be detected. This is particularly true of the work of Bremond, where a serious attempt is made not only to relate his work to that of Greimas and Todorov (and of the American Alan Dundes) but also to recall their common debt to the pioneering research of Vladimir Propp.

This French school of structuralist analysis was vigorously evaluated in 1969 (as was the Lévi-Strauss-Jakobson study of Baudelaire's *Les Chats* in 1966) by Michael Riffaterre, in essays later included in his volume entitled *Essais de stylistique structurale* (Paris: Flammarion, 1971). While essentially sympathetic to their efforts, this critic finds a general discordance between the structuralists' theory and their practice, a discordance he attributes chiefly to neglect of the condition of "perceptibility" (used, however, by their forebears, the Russian Formalists). To justify his reservations, Riffaterre quotes the work of Ricardou, Sollers, Pleynet, and—to a lesser extent—Barthes, all of whom he criticizes (quite convincingly), especially for overinterpretation. He reproaches the authors of the famous essay on *Les Chats* (1962) with neglecting to distinguish between active ("marked") and inactive elements of the poem, and insists that a distinction be made between language, which is a mere vehicle of information, and style, which is constituted by the emphasis used by the author to draw attention to certain parts of his message. The stylistic context is seen as a linguistic pattern broken by an unpredictable element productive of contrast: microcontext and contrast together constitute the stylistic effect, which thus involves deviation from its context, not from a norm. Great rigour is displayed both in the formulation of these principles and certain ancillary concepts and in their application to specific texts. Riffaterre affirms even more explicitly (or at least more adamantly) than Barthes that the structuralist model used to analyse a text must be adapted to the unique character of each particular text; and his demand that the reading of a text be always progressive (sequential) in character coincides with that of Derrida in "Force et signification."

Another important contribution to structuralist theory and practice is that of Gérard Genette, whose collections of essays entitled *Figures* (Paris: Seuil, 1966) and *Figures* II (Paris: Seuil, 1969) have recently been followed by *Figures* III (Paris: Seuil, 1972). In this last volume he differs from Riffaterre in calling for a criticism not linked to the unique character of particular works, and follows Foucault (*L'Archéologie du savoir* [Paris: Gallimard, 1969]) in proposing a sophisticated conception of period style research. Genette intervenes in the controversy concerning the relationship between metaphor and metonymy, disagreeing with Jakobson's polarisation of these two principles. Actually, his detection of metonymy at the heart of many metaphors in Proust's *Recherche* (of which he provides an exemplary analysis) solves a period style problem associated with Proust (to which Genette does not advert), namely that concerning the paradoxical coexistence in the *Recherche* (as in Verlaine) of tendencies both impressionist (metonymic) and symbolist (metaphorical). The immanent perspective, however, is threatened by Genette's willingness to read the *Recherche* as autobiography, and even to see a value in not deciding whether it is autobiography or fiction: while two such readings may perhaps be envisaged separately, surely only confusion and loss of rigour can result from their being mingled. The doubts (concerning the immanence of Genette's approach) awakened by this attitude are confirmed by his recourse to quotations from Proust's correspondence to throw light on the *Recherche*.

While structuralism continues to flourish, there is also a strong current of post-structuralism, detectable especially since the publication of two major works by Jacques Derrida: *L'Ecriture et la différence* (Paris: Seuil, 1967) and *De la grammatologie* (Paris: Edit. du Minuit, 1967). A central preoccupation here is the concept of *parole*. Structuralism offers two interrelated types of distinction involving this concept. The more basic is the Saussurean distinction between *parole* and *langue*: the latter term is used for the synchronic system constituted by a language, while *parole* is the syntagmatic use of elements drawn from the *langue*. For Jacques Lacan (*Ecrits* [Paris: Seuil, 1966]), *langue,* which is absorbed by a child during the years preceding speech (when it is still "non-speaking": *in-fans*), constitutes the child's unconscious, and alienates the child from immediate reality by setting up a filter through which all reality is later seen. Elements from this mediating unconscious are organized syntagmatically in conscious use of language, which is *parole*—necessarily false because it is dependent on *langue* and because it is affected by self-other awareness. However, *parole* is only one of two basic types of syntagma which draw on *langue;* the other is *écriture.* The distinction between *écriture* and *parole* has emerged from the research in which the concept of *écriture* was extracted from Rousseau by Lévi-Strauss and further explored by Derrida. Derrida now attacked Lévi-Strauss for having, when he distinguished *écriture* from *parole,* given the impression that the alienated character of *écriture* is not present in *parole;* it is essential, wrote Derrida, to further distinguish between *parole vide* (false, and related to *écriture*) and *parole pleine.* These reflections were to exert considerable influence in the following years. Equally important is the insistence on the dynamic progression of a work ("force et signification") as opposed to mere formal configuration as denounced by Derrida in the work of Jean Rousset ("forme et signification"); less convincing, perhaps, is Derrida's affirmation that Rousset's method is structuralist (indeed, "ultra-structuralist")—and that in fact all literary criticism is necessarily structuralist in character. In context, of course, these declarations do make a point (based on the fact that critical reading is re-reading) ; one trembles, however, at the thought of the confusion they could cause in the mind of an unprepared reader hoping to learn which critics are structuralists and which are not. Derrida has since produced a further study entitled *La Dissémination* (Paris: Seuil, 1972) , in which he equates the couple writer/reader with the couple lover/loved. He also equates two modes of intercourse, the literary and the social ("chaque terme est bien un germe") , and fuses two modes of discourse, the critical and the philosophical: "Le terme, l'élément atomique, engendre en se divisant, en se greffant, en proliférant . . . Toutes les théories atomistes . . . furent aussi des théories du sperme." What, then, is *la dissémination?* It is essentially a perspective on the act of writing. The conception of the latter as alienating and therefore suspect (Derrida, Lévi-Strauss, Rousseau) recurs here ("ce poison de l'écriture") , motivated by the observation that, in the novel under consideration (*Nombres* by Philippe Sollers), there is a "réciproque contamination de l'oeuvre et des moyens" which poisons the work: "L'écran, sans lequel il n'y aurait pas d'écriture, est aussi un procédé décrit dans l'écriture. Le procédé d'écriture est réfléchi dans l'écrit." Derrida (in the course of presenting, espousing, or extrapolating from a passage in Plato) appears to compare *écriture* with masturbation, because of the absence of the Other. This view, however, is somewhat superficial, since the absence of the Other is only apparent: according to modern psychoanalysis, just as all apparent dyads are really triads, so all apparent monads are really dyads—we are never alone. Furthermore, while the pen, like the penis, may be seen as similarly instrumental, this assimilation scarcely supports the down-grading of *écriture*, for it emphasises the pen's need for a partner (paper): if pen without paper is like penis without vagina, that may surely be interpreted as throwing a more favourable light (in Derrida's own terms) on *écriture* than on mere *parole*. If such biological analogies are desirable, surely more appropriate ones can be found; one is tempted, indeed, to propose a revalorizing conception of *écriture*, which unlike *parole* produces an externalized object that is concrete and visible, thus creating a satisfying feeling of Otherness relating to the creation of the universe by the Self. (This tames the feeling of menace normally associated with the Otherness of the universe around us.) This production of a visible object relates *écriture* to certain biological functions of prime significance to the organism, namely excretion and female reproduction; on the social level, the corresponding function is the expulsion of the scapegoat. There are two categories of function in which the process of expulsion is preceded by congestion of the organism involved, and followed by relief and satisfaction. (Girard speaks in connection with scapegoating of unanimity of violence followed by unification of the community.) These two categories may be termed the category of the potential and ephemeral (ejaculation, menstruation, *parole*) and the category of the actual and permanent (excretion, childbirth, *écriture*). The second category, then, would include all artistic creation productive of *permanent* "residue": however lucid and rational the actual process of creation, the drive to create (externalize, expel) art works is rationally inexplicable, except as an analogue of the drive to expel excreta, progeny, scapegoat. This perspective, of course, distinguishes the *écriture* of creative writing from other modes of *écriture* (which have a rational and usually even a utilitarian basis), and thus may provide a clue to the elusive criterion of *littérarité*. The arts, then, are related by this common drive to imitate the various movements of expulsion and to tame the irreparable Otherness of the Universe by producing that universe oneself.

If the Derrida stage, launched primarily in 1967 (although so many of these volumes are in part collections of articles published earlier), marked the first veering away from a certain central development of the structuralist movement, a second such stage was in preparation, and followed swiftly upon the first. This was the Deleuze stage. Gilles Deleuze first achieved critical acclaim with a brief but dense essay entitled *Proust et les signes* (Paris: Presses Univ. de France, 1964), to which he added a supplementary chapter in a new edition in 1970. Reviewers declared that Proust criticism, and indeed literary criticism in general, had been changed radically and permanently; however, Deleuze's work is not without serious defects. First, that immanence which is the most characteristic mark of modern criticism is totally lost sight of: the fictional narrator of the *Recherche* is simply assimilated to Proust himself. Second, all that this entity says is taken as truth and merely presented and described, instead of being weighed and evaluated as should be done even in the case of an author, let alone in the case of a character in a work of fiction (and the fictional narrator is of course such a character). The result is distressingly naïve: the hidden meaning of the bell-towers of Martinville is simply equated with the girls from some legend evoked by the narrator as a boy just after he has seen them. In the present writer's opinion, the real key to the narrator's fascination with triads such as the three bell-towers, the three farms, or the three trees stems from the fact that they symbolize the triangle, which constitutes the smallest stable "molecule" or building-block of inter-subjective relationships. Proust's fictional narrator is subject to a schizophrenia produced not by the dehumanizing pressures of modern capitalist society (as Deleuze will suggest in a later work) but by that most common cause of schizophrenia,[2] an excessively symbiotic relationship with one of his parents,[3] a constricting symbiosis represented on further levels by the undifferentiated ego mass of his family, whose delegated mouthpiece is Françoise, and by that of the *clan Verdurin*, which absorbs his alter ego, Swann. Autonomy is inhibited to a critical degree. The Proustian narrator does not want to give up those pleasures of intimacy which he associates with the symbiosis

---

[2] See J. Framo, ed., *Family Interaction: A Dialogue Between Family Researchers and Family Therapists* (New York: Springer, 1972), especially the anonymous paper (by Murray Bowen) entitled "Toward the Differentiation of a Self in One's Own Family."

[3] Furthermore, in the present case, the mother's undifferentiation from the father is projected onto the child.

that perpetuates his condition. When he is faced with triads, especially of vertical objects like bell-towers and trees, his manner of relating to reality leads him naturally to anthropomorphise them. This gives him pleasure in various ways: first, it reminds him of his intimate, pleasure-giving relationship with his mother; second, it enables him to see in them an image of the "triangling-in" of a third party which can provide relief, if temporarily desired, from the symbiotic two-person relationship, which is necessarily unstable.[4] The third source of pleasure is provided by the literary transposition of the triads: this enables him to trade a partial avowal of the truth (through anthropomorphous comparisons) for the right to claim that all the truth has been disclosed.[5] "Writing-up" thus becomes a sort of alibi for the schizophrenic, who does not want to face the unpalatable truth that he really ought to free himself from the symbiosis, from the undifferentiated ego masses, which maintain him in his schizophrenic state. Critics like Deleuze, who neglect the principle of immanence, naïvely accept the narrator's alibi without question: they rush headlong into the cunning web of his *parole*. Subsequently Deleuze published two theoretical essays entitled *Différence et répétition* (Paris: Presses Univ. de France, 1968) and *Logique du sens* (Paris: Edit. du Minuit, 1969) which so impressed Michel Foucault that he declared in a review published in *Critique* that in future times people may well look back on our century and term it "the century of Deleuze." Deleuze's most recent work, written in collaboration with Félix Guattari, is *Capitalisme et schizophrenie: L'anti-Oedipe* (Paris: Edit. du Minuit, 1972). Here schizophrenia is located not on the level of the nuclear family but on two other levels, the one below and the other above, namely the microcosmic and macrocosmic (or what they term the "molecular" and "molar") levels, the family being merely an agent for the displacement of these more authentic but repressed pressures. The difference between these two levels is illustrated by reference to the *Recherche,* in which the narrator passes from a "molar" or collective view of Albertine (indistinguishable from the rest of the group of girls) to a "molecular" or fragmentary view (the first kiss brings her face so close that only parts of

---

[4] See Framo, pp. 123–25, 167, 172.

[5] The pleasure experienced at the end of the "writing-up" comes not from the "discovery" of three girls in the bell-towers but from the fact that this image, being anthropomorphous, comes close to revealing the real characters represented by the triad, namely Self, Mother, Father.

it can be perceived separately). More generally, the hypothesis developed is that, in the modern political state, the castrating Father-figure of the Freudian Oedipus complex is replaced by the State itself (the *archi-Etat*, or *Urstaat*). In the capitalist system, all is production and process. Within this system, Eros takes the form of *machines désirantes* (means of production), Thanatos that of *corps sans organes* (capital). The Marxist notion of a historical dialectic, the next phase of which will see the capitalist system reach its limits and self-destruct, is replaced by a perspective in which capitalism may progress indefinitely from one insane crisis to another, ever more severe and more alienating: the dialectic is replaced by growing schizophrenia. Now this theory inevitably has an attraction for those of us who, while accepting the enormous significance of the thought of Marx, recognise that his analysis of the development of capitalist society has not been confirmed by subsequent history. However, I am inclined to think that, contrary to the predictions of Deleuze and Guattari, capitalist society will probably veer more and more toward socialism (as communism, which provides an excellent therapy against poverty and exploitation in undeveloped countries but probably should never be more than a passing phase, will veer toward "revisionism").

It was in the same year that René Girard, author of a work on the psychology of imitation (developing the concept of *amour triangulaire*) entitled *Mensonge romantique et vérité romanesque* (Paris: Grasset, 1961) and a study of Dostoievsky entitled *Du double à l'unité* (Paris: Plon, 1963), produced a major work entitled *La Violence et le sacré* (Paris: Grasset, 1972). The bases of his thesis are the mechanism of the scapegoat and the unanimity of violence. Initially, one must posit the existence of a primordial impulse or drive to imitate, including the imitation of the Other in his desires. But the Other is both model of desire and rival in desire (and therefore obstacle to fulfillment), a situation which causes frustration and repression productive of interior conflict, and ultimately of schizophrenia. This impulse is the most general form of the double binds in which Gregory Bateson sees the source of psychosis. The mimetic definition of desire makes it possible to derive rivalry without recourse to the Oedipus complex, and it engenders an unlimited number of doubles without reference either to myth or to the nuclear family. The notion of mimesis is often expressed in myths of origin which tell of a primordial conflict between two brothers, one of whom is killed or expelled in a form of scapegoating—a violence which unifies the community. (The doubling masks the conflict between the Self and Alter Ego, the rival-obstacle.) This violent event is then imitated in ritual form: Oedipus is the classical scapegoat who carries away from the community into his lonely exile all guilt, in the form of patricide and incest. For Girard, the mimetic rivalry between son and father threatens to destroy all family life and law, and this intrinsic problem leads to conflict, crisis, and schizophrenia. Girard explicitly condemns the current scepticism as to the capacity of language to attain truth (this presumably includes theorists like Derrida). Like Genette, he differs from Riffaterre in affirming the validity of using one and the same structuralist model (that of the scapegoat) to explain an unlimited number of texts. As for Deleuze and Guattari, he agrees with them in rejecting the Freudian reduction of social malaise to the frustration of early childhood drives, but he opposes them in insisting that schizophrenia be approached on the level of the individual. The importance of this work certainly rivals that of Deleuze; it may well prove in the long run to be more significant and far-reaching.

Julia Kristeva is a prominent theorist of the latest phase of structuralism or rather of its successor, semiotics. Since her theoretical volume entitled *Semiotikè. Recherches pour une sémanalyse* (Paris: Seuil, 1969), and pursuing the same preoccupations (and studying essentially the same literary texts), she has produced two studies which are devoted more explicitly to practical analysis. *Le Texte du roman* (The Hague: Mouton, 1970) begins by criticising structuralism for its application to the novel of methods of analysis developed for folk-tales (Propp) and myths (Lévi-Strauss): it proposes a semiology based, on the contrary, on the differentiation, drawn from Lukàcs, between epic and novel. The texts studied are those of Antoine de La Sale (c. 1385–c. 1460), and notably the novel *Jehan de Saintré* (1456), the "first French novel," in which the medieval community based on the symbol is replaced by the Renaissance art of the sign, a development of which Kristeva finds *Jehan* to be not only the illustration but the metaphor. In *La Révolution du langage poétique* (Paris: Seuil, 1974), Kristeva studies the contributions of Mallarmé and Lautréamont to the modern conception of language. Her method is extremely psychoanalytical (Freudian) and sociological (Marxist). Unlike Riffaterre (but without adverting to his objections or to those of at least a dozen later commentators), she accepts the Lévi-Strauss thesis that Baudelaire's *Les Chats* is centered thematically on sexual ambiguity, which she declares proved "à partir de la structure linguistique même"—a much disputed view. She disagrees with Girard's refusal to attribute to man's tendency to violence, to which religious thinking is blind, the sexual character given it by Freud; and whereas Girard sees sacrifice as an outburst and a commemoration of prehuman bestiality, Kristeva, more traditional, sees it as symbolisation, localisation, and regulation.

More centrally characteristic, perhaps, is her use of terms such as "geno-text" and "pheno-text" and her narrow definition of *le sémiotique*. The term *semiotics* was introduced into philosophy (from the medical theory of symptoms) some three hundred years ago by John Locke, and more recently disseminated by the work of Charles Peirce in the field of logic. Semiotics, which may be defined as the general science of signs, was divided by Charles Morris in 1938 into three branches of natural language: syntax, semantics, and pragmatics. These categories may be used in many ways. They may, for example, be applied to the development of criticism in this century, in that we may be said to have moved gradually from the pragmatic (history-biography) through the syntaxic (New Criticism) to the semantic (Nouvelle Critique)—that is, from the social-rhetorical through the contextual to the ideological. Whereas such Russian semioticians as Lotman and Uspensky (*vide infra*) have been criticised by scholars like Zolkiewski for neglecting pragmatics, Kristeva gives that dimension particular attention. This is reflected in her use of the concepts of "geno-text" and "pheno-text," presumably extrapolated from those of "geno-type" and "pheno-type" imported into psychology from biology by Kurt Lewin some forty years ago. (Actually, there is nothing "textual" about the phenomena grouped by Kristeva under the concept "geno-text," which is merely a broader version of the familiar notion of the *élan structurant*.) What is strange is her limiting of *le sémiotique* to merely one aspect of the "geno-text" (that is, of the pragmatic dimension, which is itself one of the three subcategories of the broader science of semiotics). As for her discussion of Mallarmé's *Un coup de dés* and Lautréamont's *Chants de Maldoror,* it would have benefited from a broader perspective including the nonliterary arts of the period in the total system of intelligibility. When such a perspective is adopted, it becomes apparent that the dilution of the chief metaphorical signifiers of literature (verse and rhyme) in these two poems, which in fact represents a belated fulfillment of the programme adumbrated in Verlaine's *Art poétique,* is merely the literary expression of a movement toward the metonymic which affects all the arts in the late nineteenth century, including painting (Monet) and music (Debussy).

Kristeva has followed Todorov in helping to disseminate Russian formalist and structuralist theory. Whereas in the work of a Rousset, for example, we have witnessed a gradual movement from cultural typology (*La Littérature de l'âge baroque* [Paris: Corti, 1954]) to textual analysis (*Narcisse romancier*), the Russian semioticians who are beginning to influence French structuralism appear to be moving in the opposite direction, from textual analysis (Iuri Lotman, *La Structure du texte artistique* [Paris: Gallimard, 1973]; Boris Uspensky, *Poetics of Composition* [Berkeley: Univ. of California Press, 1974]) to cultural typology (as reported in *Semiotica* through such vehicles as review-articles by Stefan Zolkiewski). It is in this and the allied field of the relationship between verbal "constructs" and visual "texts" that we may expect to see the most exciting speculations in the decade to come.

The articles included in the present volume reflect the preoccupations of the past decade. The investigation of the relationships among anthropology, psychoanalysis, and myth (Caldwell), religion and sociology (Filstead) was intensified by interest in the work of scholars like Dumézil (Stewart), Lévi-Strauss (Bernstein and Schwimmer), and has been revived and again reoriented by the latest work of René Girard—as yet too recent to be reflected here. Modern criticism is highly conscious of its philosophical dimensions, among the most significant of which has been the movement from empiricism to phenomenology to formalism to structuralism to semiotics (partly a continuous swing of the pendulum, partly an almost circular trajectory), the first two phases of which are examined here (Gillis). The essay by the late Ludwig von Bertalanffy, the eminent theoretician, gives us a larger perspective through which we may consider these theories. The critical scene has been full of theoretical agitation and polemics ever since the Second World War, dominance passing from Sartrean existentialism to Kristevan semiotics (Girard and Wittig), via earnest attempts at systematising the discipline of criticism on the part of thinkers like Todorov (Bennett). However, the proof of the pudding is still in the eating, and no amount of theorising can replace practical critical analysis, of which we present three demonstrations that reflect the influence of these recent theoretical preoccupations: studies on Donne (Welch), Keats (Pison), and Sarraute (Wright).

Phenomenology

A. The Humanities

B. The Social Sciences

Nathalie Sarraute:
Alienated or Alienator?

Madeleine Wright

University of Wisconsin Center System

THE premise on which this paper rests is that narrative fictions which reject characters, plot, stylistic effects and art for art's sake point to a literature which also rejects society: in works of literature, stylistic research, psychology and plot all postulate that the elaboration of a single work involves more than a single consciousness.

If by "character" we mean that element of the narrative to which actions and attributes refer, the syntactic subject of a narrative clause somehow constitutes the "character" of that clause. The subject or subjects of Nathalie Sarraute's narratives are mainly personal pronouns; and, since personal pronouns are deictic terms, since, furthermore, the referent of a deictic term can be identified only in relationship to the other participants, a discourse in which all the participants are deictic terms has no distinct and precise referents. As a result, the function of these subject pronouns in Sarraute's narrative is not, cannot be that assumed by proper names in the traditional novel, in which proper names stand for individualized persons.

Thus, the "he" of *Entre la vie et la mort*, for instance, continually changes identity; his multiple aspects cast him in a wide variety of roles, but these roles are nevertheless linked through the very lack of stable referents: a new syntactic approach creates a new meaning. Sarraute's characters no longer exist in relationship to other characters; but they exist in relationship to the different levels which they may observe within their own consciousness. They are their own referents.

29

So a Sarraute text presents, on the one hand, as many predicates as the number of roles a single consciousness can assume, and on the other, a variety of syntactic subjects completely devoid of semantic content: between these two parts of speech, nothing suggests the relationships of coincidence and continuity without which the "individual person" cannot emerge. Consequently, Sarraute's vast but undifferentiated human cosmos includes none of the psychological "laws" which seem to have guided the development of the character in the traditional novel: nothing between predicates and subjects permits the balance of similitudes and opposites through which characterial edifices can be built; consciousness, in Sarraute's novels, remains global because no paradigmatic process of association through resemblances or contrasts divides it into distinct characters. Instead of "psychology," Sarraute therefore evolves a "psychologism" in which an infinity of possibles replaces selective characterial constructs. By upsetting syntactic interpropositional relationships, she upsets the reader's traditional vision of the world. Indeed, Sarraute contends that each of us contains the seeds—possibly even more than the seeds—of all possible behavioral patterns; according to her, there is, for instance, a murderer in each of us.

The traditional plot brings into the novel a world which is alien to the novel and to the novelist but which enables the novel to transcend its boundaries and reach into the world of the reader. In Sarraute's novels, the action is centered upon what she calls "tropisms" (movements which, in her own terms, "glide quickly round the border of our consciousness and compose the small, rapid, and sometimes very complex dramas concealed beneath our actions, our gestures, the words we speak, our avowed and clear feelings.") [1] Tropisms are inner manifestations that precede the classifications to which characters and organized plots must sacrifice; these classifications are selective and exclusive; they breed the unity of action which remains one of the criteria of success of the traditional novel. Tropisms, however, are irreducible to such classifications; in a world in which all actions are possible, no specific pattern has priority over any other. In addition, an action which takes place at the level of inarticulate tropisms within a single consciousness automatically eliminates the possibility of that consciousness communicating

---

[1] Nathalie Sarraute, "New Movements in French Literature: Nathalie Sarraute Explains Tropisms," *The Listener,* 9 March 1961, p. 428.

with another: it takes words to communicate; Sarraute's novels being in the main the translation of the preverbal into language, any interaction between two or more "persons" would have to take place *after* the writing of the work! In other words, our traditional concept of a "plot" is bound to disappear because there can be no conflict between the tropisms of one consciousness and those of another consciousness. This does not mean that Sarraute's novels offer no action; but their action is movement; the movement of tropisms which continually try to exteriorize themselves; and the elements of these conflicts result from the attempts of the preverbal to permeate linguistic, conscious forms.

Stylistic effects are dictated by a set of conventions which constitute a repertory of universal—or quasi-universal—prescriptions. These prescriptions reflect a social, or collective, consciousness. The collective consciousness delegates to words the function of expressing its full scope and weight. Words are communicable symbols, interchangeable commodities. Tropisms, on the other hand, are preverbal and do not yield easily to naming: "Cela ne porte aucun nom."[2] Their animal or vegetal characteristics are more easily perceived through the senses. Collective consciousness rejects the senses as a mode of communication, possibly because they are inner, subjective and therefore exclusive realities. Tropisms are irreducible to the decrees of collective consciousness, and, therefore, of stylistic conventions. Tropisms are as crude, as disorganized, as jarring and as unbalanced as the psyche of the individual in whom they form. Stylistic purists, however, cannot tolerate the vague reporting of a vague feeling, nor the realistic rendering of a distasteful reality, nor the jerky progression of dislocated emotional states. Nathalie Sarraute does not belong to that school of thought which claims that styles are imbedded in the language, built-in consequences of its structure.[3] Rather, she evolves a style in order to reproduce as closely as possible the circumvolutions, nuances and depths of her own psyche. All her efforts tend to subordinate language to those inner states which she proposes to transcribe on paper as accurately and as realistically albeit incoherently as

---

2 Nathalie Sarraute, *Entre la vie et la mort* (Paris: Gallimard, 1968), p. 102.

3 See, e.g., Oswald Ducrot and Tzvetan Todorov, "Les styles sont dans la langue, et non dans la psyché des utilisateurs, le style reste une propriété structurale, non fonctionnelle," in *Dictionnaire encyclopédique des sciences du langage* (Paris: Editions du Seuil, 1972), p. 384.

she possibly can, and without the slightest regard for the ultimate refinements of an elegant prose.

Stylistic effects, when they are merely structural properties, belie the inner reality which is the object of Sarraute's investigation; they tend to separate form from content, thereby actually proclaiming the supremacy of content over form: content no longer needs an appropriate, matching form to come through clearly; whatever the author's intentions, a preestablished form stands ready to receive his message, be it emotive or symbolic,[4] poetical or argumentative. These recognized stylistic effects help a text to meet the reader's preconceived criteria of literary excellence, independently from the kind of rhetoric specifically required by the particular work he is reading.

Paradoxically enough, art for art's sake, which proclaims the supremacy of form over content, would also belie the particular inner reality of concern to Sarraute. Art for art's sake suggests a form of Beauty accessible to all; but the highly subjective and therefore unique type of phenomenon represented by the tropism is, by definition, the very opposite of uniformity. Tropisms are movement, eternal Beauty is static; and the capture of Beauty (with a capital B) is not the object of Sarraute's quest: what she pursues, rather, is a certain form of authenticity—an authenticity that relies on integrity, on the exact reproduction of realities experienced, witnessed by the author herself. Viewed from this angle, Sarraute belongs to the school of realism; one might even suggest that she spearheads a new naturalistic movement. By rejecting content as nonessential, art for art's sake delegates inspiration to what should remain, for Sarraute, a mere vehicle: language and its components, words; and language is never the object of Sarraute's narrative. Her intention, therefore, seems to be to rule out—not arbitrarily but necessarily—most of the technical props which traditionally helped bridge the gap between the world of the writer and the world of the reader. The goal she has set herself not only is extraneous to those props, but is contrary to them. In two cases, nevertheless, modified versions of the traditional props reappear in Sarraute's novels. Her quest for reality leads her to demystify those fictions which conceal

---

4 In a study of the influence of language upon thought, C. K. Ogden and I. A. Richards oppose emotive words to symbolic ones as follows: "The symbolic use of words is *statement;* the recording, the support, the organization and the communication of references. The emotive use of words is a more simple matter; it is the use of words to express or excite feelings and attitudes. It is probably more primitive." (*The Meaning of Meaning* [New York: Harcourt, Brace & World, 1946], p. 149.)

the real. The plot is no longer for her the indispensable ingredient of a fictive work; and the adventures of the tropisms she projects constitute an action that takes place within a single consciousness, but on two distinct levels: the tropisms either confront one another; or, when they are caught in the nets of verbal consciousness, they confront the external, social, and collective world.

Sarraute's modified versions of fiction and action, however, exclude all concern other than what is required by her initial goal: to intercept inner reality. The game is therefore played between the writer and his double, not between the writer and his public. She is engaged in a creative act that goes far beyond the definition of literature as a universally recognizable art form. Literature for Nathalie Sarraute becomes a strictly personal pursuit, a quest for identity which revolves entirely around the subject's psyche. From inspiration through form to the author's ultimate reincarnation, a loop is looped.

Nathalie Sarraute sets up for herself two very stringent criteria of success: the work must come alive, and some kind of contact must be made.[5] But two questions immediately arise: for whom should the work come alive? and with whom is the contact made? The life of the work is subordinated to tropisms which must remain intact throughout their verbal translation. Tropisms are transferred from the subconscious to the conscious with the help of language. This means that any man for whom an articulate awareness of his deeper self is vital engages in a literary quest of his own. This literary pursuit then becomes a matter of "life or death" for the writer, the life or death of the work being equivalent to the life or death of his own psyche. But in itself the content of a psyche has no meaning for another psyche. It is too shapeless and too erratic; it offers no essential point of reference, no basis for analysis and interpretation. As a result, the more accurate, the more faithful, the more literal even its verbal, or literary translation happens to be, the more opaque that translation becomes to a consciousness other than the subject's. The very qualities of a literary technique aiming at the linguistic expression of a preverbal state consequently become directly responsible for the probable hermetism of the

<hr>

[5] The first of these criteria is clearly stated by the narrator of *Entre la vie et la mort:* "Mais entre nous deux mots suffisent. Aussi grossiers que ceux-là: c'est mort. C'est vivant" (p. 99). The second criterion was voiced by Nathalie Sarraute herself in the course of an interview granted to me on June 13, 1972.

finished product. A second argument reinforces the first: only the author can evaluate the life of a work that sets out to reproduce an experience known to the author alone. Only Sarraute possesses the frame of reference against which the life of her novels can be measured: the initial tropisms that are her models and her inspiration, the personal impulse that gave birth to the literary form. As a result, no one but Nathalie Sarraute can fully evaluate the life or death status of her production.

Contact is established mainly between the writer and her work for very similar reasons. Such contact can come about only within a very closed circuit. The literary form best capable of capturing tropisms does not include universal frames of reference and does not yield to universal recognition and understanding. For Sarraute, tropisms are privileged means of communication, not with the outside world, but with her double, with her many doubles. The consciousness at work in Sarraute's novels is that of a character looking for an author. The contact takes place and the work comes alive when there is a fusion between both.

This does not necessarily mean that contact between work and reader is totally out of the question. But the nature of tropisms makes any subjective form of interpretation hazardous, if not preposterous. A look at Sarraute's imagery will help us verify the accuracy of this statement. Like Gaston Bachelard, she seems to differentiate sharply between metaphors that offer rational frames of reference accessible to all, and images that function like Proust's involuntary memory, skipping a number of echelons in the associative process. Such images can only be apprehended through personal efforts of interpretation and recreation; they do not yield to the intellectual process; they cannot be discussed. Sarraute entrusts the translation of tropisms into words almost exclusively to images; but Bachelard's intense faith in the communicative power of images[6] is of no avail in Sarraute's case: her brand of "rêverie" does not purport to transcend reality, but rather to grasp and possess it in its entirety. In other words, the deeper the reality which she tries to express, the more subjective the form she adopts in order to do so. The decoding of such images may be rich in possibilities for the outsider; but there can be no guarantee whatsoever that the result

6 Gaston Bachelard in his *Poétique de la rêverie* (Paris: Presses Univ. de France, 1960) strongly suggests that images can indeed be transmitted: the writer who indulges in his "rêverie" communicates with an ego on a higher level than his original self; and the reader who recognizes the increased value of the writer's new ego is eager to improve his own self through the intermediary of the writer's image.

will coincide with the reality behind the image itself. The opacity of Sarraute's images is the by-product of a self-contained psyche which must block out all outside interferences in order to communicate with itself.

For the critic, therefore, only one avenue of investigation perhaps remains open: the linguistic, semantic and formal analysis of the work. The reader confronts what is, in fact, an individual language within a code language. The code language consists of very common words, about which Sarraute herself wrote: "I had to create . . . an unreal dialogue made up of usual words to express what is not ordinarily spoken about. The most ordinary words are used, but what is said is not what is being talked about. . . ."[7] This code language, which is immediately accessible to the reader, does not reveal the writer's inner truth; to the contrary, it constitutes the fictive portion of the work. It relies largely on humor, which Sarraute manipulates in order to denounce the collective myths—mostly verbal—which blur our vision of reality. The techniques that preside over the writing at this level can be analyzed systematically, but such an elucidation leads only to the negative aspect of the work: a void is created, which tropisms will fill once the clichés have been swept away. In contrast, Sarraute's individual language, which is immediately accessible to her, is not immediately accessible to the reader; and its deciphering is an exercise in hermeneutics. Sarraute's literary techniques seem to rest on the double postulate that the usual semantic content of words is deeply misleading, and that reality is best expressed through whatever escapes the linguistic conventions of symbolic meaning.

In conclusion, I should like to suggest that Nathalie Sarraute, as a writer, is not alienated from herself, since the very theme of her work is the pursuit and capture of those inner realities which constitute her true, authentic self. She is a writer very largely reconciled with herself. True, her quest for identity is not a continuous success; she admits willingly the perilous moments of her literary journey, the fragile, evanescent quality of the matter she pursues, the frequent failures, the occasional discouragement. But the creative act, for her, is at the polar opposite of self-alienation: she starts from a reality within herself, expresses it through the media of her choice, and considers the endeavor a success if and when her writings bring her back to the reality she started from. The reader, however, is forced to accomplish the itinerary backwards. He must start

[7] *Le Monde*, 18 Jan. 1967.

from the text in the hope of capturing a reality which is not his, and the narrative techniques at work make no attempt at bridging the gap between his world and the author's. The traditional novel goes at least half-way in presenting the public with an assortment of common denominators, apparently bridging the gap between the real and the fictional; the new novel does not. Paradoxically enough, the more of these common denominators a novel can boast, the more fictive the result. Sarraute's novels come the closer to the truths she wishes to express as their form breaks more sharply away from accepted formal codes. There is a definite progression in her literary production, a progression that goes from her relatively accessible works like *Tropismes* and *Le Planetarium* to her latest (and more obscure) novels, *Entre la vie et la mort* and *Vous les entendez?* The earlier works include, if not characters, at least occasional proper names and the embryo of a story; but the expression of tropisms in these novels remains somewhat ambiguous; it owes too much to psychology, to introspection, to the form of introspection which reasons, argues, discusses—i.e., analyzes. It stems from the writer's intellect. The role of the intellect, in her latest works, is much more strictly delineated: as a professional writer, she uses it to choose her techniques and control the structure of her works; she is definitely highly conscious of her goals, of her efforts and of the results obtained. But she no longer allows her intellect to tamper with the raw material she starts from. It is quite possible that the closer she gets to her goal, the greater will be the distance between novel and reader. The reader approaches the novel through the formal deciphering of a work that rejects formalism: a certain discrepancy seems unavoidable. Yet, formalism may well be the most valid approach for the reader or critic anxious to break through the deceptive layer of her code language in order to reach the inner core of her private world. Her work, which sets itself over and beyond style, is nevertheless at the mercy of stylistic analyses. The public is likely to feel somewhat alienated from novels written not only *by* but mostly *for* the author herself.

A Phenomenological Approach to Keats's "To Autumn"

Thomas Pison

J AMES DICKEY'S apparently casual remark that "poetry is
the only nonmanipulative enterprise around" is actually a
trenchant formulation of a posture basic not only to the creation
of poetry but, currently, to some of the best criticism of poetry.
That the creative moment is one of alert passivity is at least as
old as Keats's "negative capability," but that the critical experience should exhibit a similar unassertive receptivity is as new as
twentieth-century phenomenology. Just as the phenomenological
philosophers have obliterated the Cartesian dichotomy of subject and object, so the phenomenological critic abjures the
poem-as-object for the poem as an event that is essentially a
dialogue between two subjects, the poet and his reader. In order to perceive truly "how it is" with the poet and thus participate in the Being in which the poem is grounded, the critic must divest himself of his will-to-power, which would master
the poem through the perfected use of the intellect and its sophisticated tools. This is to say, in terms of recent critical history, that the phenomenological critic preserves from the New
Critics the primacy of the literary text, but discards the New
Critical analysis of the poem as structure and texture. Instead,
the poem becomes an occasion for a human encounter between
critic and poet. Assuming the impersonality of the artist, the
New Critic countered it with the assumed objectivity of the
critic, and the two never met over the body of the poem. The
phenomenological critic, to the contrary, does not wish to learn
that the poem *is* or how it *means,* but through the poem, what
it means to *be.* John Crowe Ransom's ontology must give way

to Martin Heidegger's, as the being of the poem is subordinated
to the being of things.[1]

The phenomenological approach to literature, however, does
not go "beyond formalism" in the same sense as do sociological
or psychoanalytical criticism, both of which tend to read the
literary work as a confirmation or rejection of theories formulated within their own disciplines. It would be more to the
point to say that phenomenology seeks to go *beneath* formalism,
to the meaning below the text and perhaps below consciousness
which can be only imperfectly encompassed by the written language. The phenomenological critic works through the language
in order to establish himself beyond it, in the position of the
poet, to whom the essences of existent things are revealed in an
experience which is preverbal. The phenomenological critic's
method is that of Husserl: "To the things themselves!" And his
critical question is that of Heidegger: "How goes Being?" All
answers are as relevant for art as for life, because they have
simultaneous reference to the life lived by the poet in common
with all humanity and to the unique creative moment at which
the poem is engendered. In other words, the point at which the
poem clears for the critic will be the identical point where the
poet, expressing his own being, is most expressive of all human
being. The phenomenologist, therefore, concerns himself with
the broadest and most basic horizons within which Being discloses itself; and searching for the constitutive factors of human
existence—the ontological "within which" everything must happen—the phenomenologist uncovers the essential significance of
time and space. A summary view of two diversive phenomenological descriptions of time and space will ease the way for their
ontological disclosure within Keats's poem.

Martin Heidegger is preeminently the philosopher of time.
Since the 1927 publication of *Sein und Zeit,* Heidegger has giv-
en his constant attention to refining his initial formulation, that
to be in the world is to be in time. *Dasein,* or human being, finds
himself thrown into a world that is already an ongoing process;
thus, without consultation, *Dasein* is given a past which has

---

[1] In according poetry a privileged place as "the founding of truth," phenomenological criticism is distinguished also from the structuralist enterprise, which
places language-as-object at its center, with the result—as Gérard Genette has observed—that "literature is now defined as a dialect and its study becomes an annex
of dialectology." Quoted in B. Jean and T. J . Lewis, "Structural Linguistics and
Literature in France," *Journal of the British Society for Phenomenology,* 2, No. 3
(October 1971) , 27–36. See also Martin Heidegger, "The Thinker as Poet," in
Poetry, Language, and Thought, trans. Albert Hofstadter (New York: Harper, 1971) .

shaped and defined him. His existence discloses itself to him as a project, which offers him the possibility of redefining himself and transforming his world by projecting himself forward into a uniquely personal future. *Dasein* must always resist the universal tendency to exist as mere presence in a meaningless present, for that would be to alienate himself from the powerful pull of the future, which is that aspect of time that enables existential man to achieve self-definition. His present must therefore be the field of active intentionality wherein the factuality of the past is continually being transformed into an existentiality for the future.

While the German phenomenologist argues that man is constituted in time, a French phenomenologist reveals that man dreams of space. Gaston Bachelard, in *The Poetics of Space* (*La Poétique de l'espace,* 1957), tenderly records the various images of valorized space which the human imagination has created. To the oneiric imagination Bachelard attributes the cosmic power of origination; far beyond a mere reproduction of reality; and to its images, an absolute newness and fidelity to Being, far beyond the employment of metaphor as a literary convention. The freshness and authenticity of the image is directly dependent upon the poet's receptivity to his childhood experiences, for childhood, by virtue of its being the place of human origins, preserves the most suggestive shaping powers for the imagination. And what the child knows is that space is protective: he is not "cast into the world" (as Heidegger's *Geworfenheit* insists), but he is "laid in the cradle of the house."[2] The child's first experiences are of the non-I enclosing and embracing the I. Cellars, attics, and corners all make daydreaming a safe activity; and a lifetime of daydreaming, the poet's occupation, will make of the universe a great cosmic house that is totally habitable. For Bachelard, the fulfillment of human being is achieved whenever the full intensity of the imagination within touches, and is touched by, the full immensity of space without. This interpenetration of interior and exterior space, of the concrete and the vast—this "transaction between two kinds of grandeur" receives its fullest ontological statement from Karl Jaspers: "Jedes Dasein scheint in sich rund." (Every being seems in itself

---

2 *The Poetics of Space,* trans. Maria Jolas (Boston: Beacon, 1971), p. 3. Hereafter cited in the text as *S.* Hereafter cited as *R* in the text will be *The Poetics of Reverie,* trans. Daniel Russell (Boston: Beacon, 1971).

round.) [3] Only the purest sort of phenomenological meditation can dream beyond the images of roundness of Being to the plumpness of spatial plenitude, to its globular abundance, and to the consequent generosity and reciprocity of all things within a space that is full; yet this illumination is basic to human being when it is being truest to its concrete origins.

Both Heidegger and Bachelard share the phenomenological quest for the subjective reality which is prior to all the objective systems created by the human power for abstraction; therefore, just as human time is more authentic for Heidegger than clock time, so for Bachelard, "Inhabited space transcends geometric space" (*S*, p. 7). The similarity of their aim and method aside, there are between them frank oppositions of reverie and reality, art and life, space and time as the mode and circumstance of the ontological revelation. Furthermore, it would appear that the glorification of space is accompanied by a detemporalization of time, that a sense of space as full carries with it a sense of time as retarded, compressed, or stopped. On the other hand, Heidegger's emphasis on time, especially in its future aspect, implies that being achieves its potential only by divorcing itself from protective space and thrusting itself into time.

It is not to our point to dispel these oppositions through a false reconciliation, nor to strengthen them in positions of mutual exclusion that would be contrary to all logic and common sense. As a human being lives and daydreams, he experiences both Heideggerean time and Bachelardian space. It is to our point to discover the nature of the transition which man makes between these two modes of response to human reality. Keats's great ode, "To Autumn," records such a movement from art to life and from space to time. It is as profound a temporal experience of life as it is an artistic evocation of praiseworthy space, for Keats both preserves and transcends the apparent polarities. Any sensitive reader of "To Autumn" knows that it speaks at once a filled space *and* a fulfilled time. The character of the transition—of this shift in consciousness which reconciles poetic space with lived time—is the ontological disclosure revealed through the poem.

---

[3] Quoted in *The Poetics of Space*, p. 232, from Jaspers, *Von der Wahrheit*. In quick succession, Bachelard quotes three other statements in his inquiry into "The Phenomenology of Roundness." Van Gogh: "Life is probably *round*." Joe Bousquet: "He had been told that life was beautiful. No! Life is round." La Fontaine: "A walnut makes me quite round."

A phenomenological description of this temporal transition is offered by Hans-Georg Gadamer in an essay first delivered at a colloquium honoring Martin Heidegger. In "Concerning Empty and Ful-Filled Time," Gadamer argues that the human experience of time is determined by the character of transition. Human time neither flows nor is a series of now-moments linked together; it is, instead, the recurring moment of leavetaking. For *Dasein* even to be able to have the Heideggerean future, he must have "the ability to bid farewell." Only he "who can leave what lies behind him or what is removed from him beyond his reach, who does not cling fast to what is past as something which he cannot relinquish" is enabled to move through time to his temporal destiny.[4] Within human experience, departure and dissolution are inseparably bound to beginning and to new creation. Although Heidegger's emphasis upon the power of the future may suggest that time is without content until *Dasein* fills it with his deeds, time is never empty. It is at its fullest in that moment when human being is ready to move on to the next moment, for that is when the human consciousness perceives most keenly all of the past in an intense present which will give way to a desired future.

In the imagery of Keats's poem, the poet experiences the transitive moment when Autumn's spatial fullness is emptied out and the deceptive timelessness of the season yields to temporal linearity. The poet's voice is as consoling as it is resolute. It is this voice which intrigues and delights the phenomenological critic, for it expresses so tenderly the consolation that human being needs to accompany the difficult resolution to depart. The poetic imagination permits human experience its sanity, but lovingly preserves for the strider-into-the-future all that ever was of space and time. A careful reading of each of the ode's three stanzas will disclose the poet's awareness of Bachelard's space, Heidegger's time, and Gadamer's moment of transition.

> Season of mists and mellow fruitfulness,
>   Close bosom-friend of the maturing sun;
> Conspiring with him how to load and bless
>   With fruit the vines that round the thatch-eves run;
> To bend with apples the moss'd cottage-trees,
>   And fill all fruit with ripeness to the core;
>   To swell the gourd, and plump the hazel shells

---

[4] "Concerning Empty and Ful-Filled Time," *Southern Journal of Philosophy*, 8 (1970), 351–52.

With a sweet kernel; to set budding more,
And still more, later flowers for the bees,
Until they think warm days will never cease,
　　For Summer has o'er-brimm'd their clammy cells.

A critical reading of "mists" as "cold, spectral, disembodied"?[5] Surely not, for they are too intimately co-present with "mellow fruitfulness." Although existing before and after and beneath sunlight, *with* the sun they have made possible this great bounty on earth. Blessings are both rained and sunned upon the earth by the heavens. "Mists" are benevolent moisture, a gift which Keats recalls elsewhere gratefully as "the feel of the clouds dropping fatness."[6] In this same sense, the heartfelt "close bosom" friendship of autumn and the sun speaks a vertical harmony within space, a conspiracy of generous receiving and giving between the low and the high, the base and the zenith. Just as the sky gives to the earth, so the earth's gift to the rest of the universe is its vegetative abundance. On earth itself, this embrace of loving reciprocity unites the things of man and the things of nature. The cottages, which human being builds for his protective comfort, are further protected and comforted by "the vines that round the thatch-eves run," and by the enfolding proximity of "moss'd cottage trees." It is as if the vines of nature were so fond of man that they would make a nest for him of their own greenery. The enclosure which expresses love is in the trees' sheltering of their apples, the hazel shells harboring the "sweet kernel," and the fruit, holding within its own ripeness, the flower's cup of nectar "for the bees." The care of the outside for the inside, expressed by enclosure, is met by the fondness of the within for the without, expressed through the filling of interior space which confers perfect roundness upon the formerly empty outer coverings. The conferring verbs indicate the force of love that produces globularity out of an interior void: *load, bless, bend, fill, swell, plump.* The apple trees are without identity until they are bent with apples, shells are hollow nothings until they are plumped, and the fruit is but its core until it is fulfilled with ripeness. Space is incomplete and merely profane, until it is blessed with a sacred destiny of fullness.

---

5 See B. C. Southam, "The 'Ode to Autumn,'" *Keats-Shelley Journal,* 9 (1960) , 93.
6 Letter to John Reynolds, April 9, 1818, in *Selected Letters of John Keats,* ed. Frederick Page (London: Oxford Univ. Press, 1968) , p. 103. Hereafter cited in the text as *L.*

We are not within time's processes so much as at their termination. There is only the slightest bit more time and space for surplusage, for an excess of love between earth and sun to squeeze forth an overabundance of "more / And still more, later flowers," and of oozing honey cells. The whole world is quiescent and laden, lulled in the curve of space in a satiety which is the end of time. A world dreamed in its roundness reveals being nested in cosmicity. Almost motionless (the bees in their easy circles and the vines that "run" only "round" really go nowhere), plumped space seems to sign a motionless time. But not quite. Somewhere beneath his full consciousness, the poet has cautioned himself that once summer was here and is here no longer, that the bees are mistaken in assuming warm days will never cease, and that after the maturing of the sun will come the decline of his warm strength.

> Who hath not seen thee oft amid thy store?
>   Sometimes whoever seeks abroad may find
> Thee sitting careless on a granary floor,
>   Thy hair soft-lifted by the winnowing wind;
> Or on a half-reap'd furrow sound asleep,
>   Drows'd with the fume of poppies, while thy hook
>   Spares the next swath and all its twined flowers:
> And sometimes like a gleaner thou dost keep
>   Steady thy laden head across the brook;
>   Or by a cyder-press, with patient look,
>   Thou watchest the last oozings hours by hours.

The critic who questioned parenthetically whether Autumn might be masculine[7] receives a firm negative from both Keats and Bachelard. A prose confession of the poet prefigures the delicate care which he tenders to the feminine personification of Autumn: "When I was a Schoolboy I thought a fair Woman a pure Goddess, *my mind was a soft nest in which some one of them slept,* though she knew it not" (*L,* July 18–22, 1818, p. 153, emphasis is mine). The poetic image is born out of the entirely feminine fecundity of silence and space in the state of reverie. Bachelard accepts Jung's picture of the human psyche as androgynous in its primary nature, containing *anima* and *animus;* and in discussing the time of the feminine *anima,* he closely approximates the sense of time which the poet—and his Autumn—

---

[7] See Leonard Unger, "Keats and the Music of Autumn," in *The Man in the Name: Essays on the Experience* (Minneapolis: Univ. of Minnesota Press, 1956), p. 21.

experience in this second stanza: "The clock of the feminine runs continuously in a duration which peacefully slips away. The masculine clock has the dynamism of jerks" (*R*, p. 60). In her incarnation as a girl of the countryside, Autumn is an extension of Keats's essential self.

In this stanza the earth is a full storage place, its plenitude a direct consequence of Autumn's friendship with the sun. Heaven confers possession upon Autumn with "thy store," as the natural world becomes the realm of a goddess or the home of a mother. "Amid" her store, she is bodily present at the place of man's work (the granary floor, the cyder-press), man's tools (the hook) in her hand. Yet her consciousness is muted in a reverie dreamed against the processes within time. Almost wholly nonparticipant in the labor of the season, she seems caught up in the infinity and eternity of the cosmos, her substance somewhere above the earth and caught by the element of air: "thy hair soft-*lifted* by the winnowing *wind*." "Sound asleep," she leaves the furrow only "half-reap'd," and "drows'd" in an opiate reverie, she "spares the next swath." Why this somnambulistic lack of concern? It arises from her feeling of being *already* done, finished, completed, full. Swollen with repletion and immense in her repose, she resists the fall into temporal linearity.

At most, the poet allows her a sense of a slow time which is almost no time at all, a time that is emptied of its urgency because space is so full. By the cyder-press, round with the wholeness of the pregnant and still, she is of the time that does not pass, or march, or consume, but oozes "hours by hours" like the sweet cider from the overripe apples. Still, while dreaming within the passivity of fecund space, Autumn is nevertheless the "gleaner" of purposeful labor, herself the means by which time empties out her realm, steadily and irreversibly: "like a gleaner thou dost keep / Steady thy laden head across a brook." And in that "steady" there is a thrust forward into future time or, perhaps better said, a resolute pull upon the present from its own future. This temporal movement receives its completion— and space, its final denudation—in the last stanza of the ode.

> Where are the songs of Spring? Ay, where are they?
> Think not of them, thou hast thy music too,—
> While barred clouds bloom the soft-dying day
> And touch the stubble-plains with rosy hue;
> Then in wailful choir the small gnats mourn
> Among the river sallows, borne aloft

Or sinking as the light wind lives or dies;
And full-grown lambs loud bleat from hilly bourn;
  Hedge-crickets sing; and now with treble soft
  The red-breast whistles from a garden-croft;
    And gathering swallows twitter in the skies.

Autumn—and with her, the reader and the poet—must be taught "the ability to bid farewell." We have all been lost in a dream of space that misplaced the reality of time, and for this beautiful error we are to be consoled. In giving Autumn her sounds, the poet jerks the sleeper awake to her temporal destiny, his images all declaring death, departure, and dissolution. Autumn's own sounds are bearing testimony to her death: her day is dying, the light wind dies, the insects "mourn," and the "croft" reverberates its archaic sense of "crypt." This is a scene of termination, after all; Autumn's great abundance has been devastated. The most striking image of the "stubble-plains," the fact of their leftover garbage-waste-refuse quality, the reduction of all that plumped space to these harsh remains—this is what shocks and grieves. We need to be consoled for the kind of temporal inattentiveness that permits us to ask, quite sincerely, "How could anything so perfectly full be so totally empty? How does abundant life contain death?"

Yet the poet uses all his art to ease the pain of leaving behind the beautiful, the qualification of the images of emptiness being his own generous gesture of consolation to us. How small is the threnody, really, how diminished the mourning. All that could produce irrevocable despair at its ending is lightened by what is preserved with it: The day dies "soft" and yet "blooms," the stubble-plains retain a "rosy hue," the small gnats not only sink but are "borne aloft." It is as if the poet's human care for Autumn caused him to share the tenderness of roundness and convey it back to her. By making time's process as gentle, hesitant, and unobtrusive as possible, the poet himself is bringing to consciousness the spirit of generosity and reciprocity within valorized space. At the moment of transition, when the season and the poet must be resolved to depart, time is at its fullest because the past dream of spatial cosmic care, which has governed the space of the poem, has been preserved with love. Unalarmed, we can now be reconciled. What evokes the poet's tenderness is the realization that time is as real as space, and that everything which happens within the one happens within the other.

What has emerged for us during this reading of the ode is a certain consciousness of time and space, which may belong to universal human being but which, we would like to insist, certainly belonged to John Keats. Since the argument, forward from the image to an ontological disclosure and back to the poet's consciousness, is new and may seem tenuous to some readers, two additional utterances of corroboration by the poet are here offered.

The first is a letter from Keats to Jane Reynolds, written in the autumn of 1817. In it, Keats shows himself well aware of the consolations of space and of the interpenetration of the vast and the concrete when the universe and man touch in "a transaction between two kinds of grandeur." He knows also of the ways in which space can be played against time, and how the antidote of spatial generosity may be applied to the "evil Spirit" of temporal anxiety. Keats writes:

> Believe me, my dear Jane, it is a great Happiness to me that you are in this finest part of the year, winning a little enjoyment from the hard World—in truth the great Elements we know of are no mean Comforters—the open Sky sits upon our senses like a Sapphire Crown—the Air is our Robe of State—the Earth is our throne and the Sea a mighty Minstrell playing before it—able like David's Harp to charm the evil Spirit from such Creatures as I am—able like Ariel's to make such a one as you forget almost the tempest-cares of life. (*L*, September 14, 1817, p. 25.)

Keats was also preoccupied with time in its two aspects of damnation and salvation: He refers to the time which ends all human possibilities as "cormorant devouring time," but he places it in close conjunction with the time which blesses all potentiality with fruition, which permits "that Honor . . . which shall make us heirs of all eternity" (*L*, May 10–11, 1817, p. 13). Much attention has been directed to Keats's fear of death as the ultimate temporal reality, but none, I think, to his imagery of death as the temporal depletion of interior space. This inverse relationship—of time beginning to move as space empties out—we have seen operating on the cosmic level in the last stanza of the ode. A similar temporal-spatial schema in the initial and closing lines of Keats's "Sonnet" suggests that it was a prevailing element of his consciousness:

> When I have fears that I may cease to be
> Before my pen has glean'd my teeming brain,

> Before high-piled books, in character,
>   Hold like rich garners the full ripen'd grain;
> . . . .
>   —then on the shore
> Of the wide world I stand alone, and think
> **Till love and fame to nothingness do sink.**

Like the exterior space of the ode, the human interior is imagined as a storage place. The expansion of the poet's powers is the providence of plenitude conferred upon the mental void, and the works of the poet will "plump" previously empty covers. Yet all his careful nurture will become "stubble-plains," for time threatens with a harvest that is the poet's own "cease to be." Even the thought of this temporal motion has the power to empty a whole world of its content, and it leaves the poet isolated "on the shore," beyond the protective curve of space.

The challenge, of course, is to leave one's space and have it too. "All really inhabited space bears the notion of home," says Bachelard (S, p. 5). In "To Autumn" John Keats has his home, for even at the moment of temporal transition, when he bids farewell to the space of the imagination in order to insert himself once again into the time of life, his great art insures that a cherished universe will endure, beyond the contingencies and caprices of time.

The Meaning of Nothingness
in Donne's
"Nocturnall upon S. Lucies Day"

Dennis M. Welch

Clarkson College

EVEN more enigmatic than the mystery of existence is that of nonexistence. In the history of Western philosophy, thinkers have grappled with the meaning of nothingness in two different ways. Ancient philosophers like Aristotle and medieval thinkers like Thomas Aquinas considered nonbeing a metaphysical conundrum. How can something come from something when it is already something; conversely, how can something come from nothing when nothing contributes nothing? Sartre and Heidegger do not consider nothingness an intellectual puzzle but a real phenomenon of our experience. According to them, it is *the* human "condition" which we must recognize, cope with, and transcend if we are to live authentically. John Donne's "Nocturnall upon S. Lucies Day," a poem that deals with the abyss of despair and death, expresses the metaphysical, existential, and phenomenological meanings of nonbeing. Donne confronted nothingness and transcended it through the poem's cautious sensualism, its creativity, and its Christian resolution as well as through his life as a clergyman. While not trying to make the Dean of St. Paul's an existentialist, this essay assumes that humanity possesses the common denominator of consciousness. With that assumption, I will show that modern phenomenological inquiries into the relationship between nonbeing and human awareness can be applied to "A Nocturnall" to reveal its profound philosophical significance.

Recent critics, at odds over the poem's conventions, have neglected to pursue its philosophical meaning. For example, N. J.

C. Andreasen says the poem is anti-Petrarchan, attacking idolatrous human love through a duped speaker.[1] Donald Guss, on the contrary, places it in the Petrarchan tradition, asserting that the speaker's despair over his lady's death is developed into "a sentimental hyperbole, like Petrarch's declaration that Laura's death killed him."[2] Prior to these critics, Herbert Grierson recognized the poem's gravity and suggested that its occasion may have been the death of Donne's wife.[3] Subsequent to Grierson's remarks in 1912, the evidence corroborating his suggestion about the poem's occasion has become convincing.[4] Given the intensity of the poem's emotion and the background behind it, we cannot consider "A Nocturnall" either a satire or a sentimental expression of inordinate human love. Although Donne was deeply aware of deceit and sentimentality in love, he did not think it truly damnable. In fact, his belief that human affection (particularly married love) is not only re-creative but also transcendent was a frequent topic of his sermons.[5] "A Nocturnall"

---

[1] N. J. C. Andreasen, *John Donne: Conservative Revolutionary* (Princeton: Princeton Univ. Press, 1967), pp. 152–60.

[2] Donald L. Guss, *John Donne, Petrarchist: Italianate Conceits and Love Theory in The Songs and Sonnets* (Detroit: Wayne State Univ. Press, 1966), p. 101.

[3] Herbert J. C. Grierson, ed., *The Poems of John Donne* (London: Oxford Univ. Press, 1912), II, xxii, 10.

[4] W. A. Murray, in "Donne and Paracelsus: An Essay in Interpretation," *Review of English Studies*, 25 (1949), 115–23, says that the conclusion of "A Nocturnall" looks ahead to the opening lines of Holy Sonnet 17 ("Since she whom I lov'd . . ."), which was clearly written in commemoration of Ann. Richard E. Hughes, in *The Progress of the Soul: The Interior Career of John Donne* (New York: Morrow, 1968), pp. 296–97, n.36, suggests that the sequence of poems was just the opposite— "the 'Nocturnall' [written in December] recalls the sonnet, which was probably written four months earlier." Hughes also says that, while "A Nocturnall" might have been written during Ann's illness in 1606, or during the Countess of Bedford's sickness in 1612, it actually deals with a woman already dead, not merely ill; and its intimacy is foreign to all of Donne's verses on the Countess (p. 215). Finally, Louis L. Martz, in *The Poetry of Meditation: A Study in English Religious Poetry of the Seventeenth Century* (New Haven: Yale Univ. Press, 1962), pp. 214–15, n.3, says that we must ignore Grierson's hesitant mention (II, xxii) that the poem may have been addressed to Lucy, Countess of Bedford; "for the imagery of the 'Saint Lucies night' . . . provides its own metaphorical occasion." Martz adds that if the poem is "fundamentally religious" we can disregard J. B. Leishman's difficulty in believing that Donne wrote it after Ann's death when he had been in orders two years (*The Monarch of Wit*, p. 176).

[5] The following passages from Donne's third and seventeenth sermons, published in *The Sermons of John Donne*, ed. George R. Potter and Evelyn M. Simpson (Berkeley: Univ. of California Press, 1953), reveal his conviction that human love is akin to divine love:

The highest degree of other [human] love, is the love of woman: Which love, when it is rightly placed upon one woman, it is dignified by the Apostle with the highest comparison, *Husbands love your wives, as Christ loved his Church*: And God himself forbad not that this love should be great enough to change natural affection, *Relinquet patrem*, (for this, a man shall leave his Father) yea, to change nature it selfe, *caro una*, two shall be one (I, 199). [Marriage is] *bonum Sacramenti*, a mysticall representation of that union of two natures in Christ, and of him to us, and to his Church (II, 340).

is a serious poem, not just in the sense of love lost which some critics have focused on,[6] but in the deeper sense of the poet's confrontation with the experience of nothingness in the death of his wife, Ann More, in August, 1617. We cannot ignore the philosophical significance of Ann's death when we recall the extent of Donne's love in secretly marrying her, neglecting both courtly favor and his own security.

Like Greek and Scholastic philosophers, Donne probed the metaphysical nature of nonbeing and being, distinguishing between them on the basis of potency and act. According to Aristotle and Thomas Aquinas, something that comes to *be* does not have before its becoming the perfection (the form, the act) it later acquires, but is only in potency to it. In the following passage from "A Nocturnall," Donne makes this and other metaphysical distinctions about being and nonbeing. He deals with both his beloved's death and the resulting emptiness within himself:

> All others, from all things, draw all that's good,   .
> Life, soule, forme, spirit, whence they beeing have;
>   I, by loves limbecke, am the grave
>   Of all, that's nothing. Oft a flood
>   Have wee two wept, and so
> Drownd the whole world, us two; oft did we grow
> To be two Chaosses, when we did show
> Care to ought else; and often absences
> Withdrew our soules, and made us carcasses.
>
> But I am by her death, (which word wrongs her)
> Of the first nothing, the Elixer grown;
>   Were I a man, that I were one,
>   I needs must know;[7]

    6 J. B. Leishman, in *The Monarch of Wit: An Analytical and Comparative Study of the Poetry of John Donne* (New York: Harper, 1966), p. 179, emphasizes the theme of lost love, mentioning that the poem was probably "at least partly inspired by Ann More [Donne]."

    7 *The Elegies and The Songs and Sonnets*, ed. Helen Gardiner (Oxford Univ. Press, 1965), p. 85, ll. 19–31. All other quotations from "A Nocturnall" will be from this edition, indicated with line numbers in parentheses.

In these lines Donne gives us various examples of nonbeing: the world drowned, chaos (a void), dead bodies, and primordial ("the first") nothingness.[8] He says that whatever possesses "soule, forme" (or act, in Aristotelian terms) exists. Conversely, the absence of act (or the soul, in Scholastic and traditional religious terms) is nonbeing; and, since death is the ultimate absence of the soul from the body and since Donne's beloved is his soul, her parting is also his death. To show the extent of their love, Donne pushes his metaphysical analysis further, saying that even mutual neglect and physical separation subjected them to a horrible emptiness, a kind of death. With the logic of a medieval Scholastic and the grammar of desperate argument, Donne proves he is nothing. Referring to the traditional distinction that makes man human, namely, self-awareness, he says, with emphatically repetitious subjunctives, that "were" he a man he should know that he is ("were") "one"; but, since he does not know, he is nothing. Aside from the metaphysical and logical ingenuity of these lines, there is also in their solemnity an existential import which critics have heretofore not considered.

In the first stanza of "A Nocturnall," the darkness and death of St. Lucy's Day (December 13, regarded as the shortest day of the year) signify not only a universal ("generall") condition but also a personal, interior one:

> 'Tis the yeares midnight, and it is the dayes,
> *Lucies,* who scarce seaven houres herself unmaskes,
>   The Sunne is spent, and now his flasks
>   Send forth light squibs, no constant rayes;
>   The world's whole sap is sunke:
> The generall balme th'hydroptique earth hath drunk,
> Whither, as to the beds-feet, life is shrunke,
> Dead and enterr'd; yet all these seeme to laugh,
> Compar'd with mee, who am their Epitaph. (ll. 1–9)

Like Donne, existentialists say that nothingness is a condition of the world. But nothingness ultimately abides, as Donne's last

---

8 Guss, p. 102.

two lines suggest, in the knowing subject, in human consciousness. The poet's implication indicates the very source of nothingness discovered by modern existential phenomenologists like Jean-Paul Sartre. According to Sartre, we encounter nonbeing in consciousness, in the confrontation between awareness and the world of objects. In Sartre's analysis, there are basically two kinds of reality: being-in-itself (*en soi*) and being-for-itself (*pour soi*). The former is the material thing, compact density full of itself, the only being which is justly called *being*.[9] The latter is consciousness; it is not self-contained but is the source of our experience of nothingness.[10] The source in two ways. First, when we are conscious of something, we nihilate it. In other words, we are conscious that we are not this or that something. Second, consciousness itself is non-material, nonbeing. According to Sartre, when we attempt to be aware of ourselves, we really nihilate our own identity.[11] Consciousness, in short, expresses only non-identity, nonbeing.

Thus, in addition to its rigid logic, Donne's couplet, "If I an ordinary nothing were, / As shadow, 'a light, and body must be here" (ll. 35–36), is a profound expression of the fundamental nonbeing of his despairing consciousness. The self-doubt in his lines, "Were I a man, that I were one, / I needs must know" (ll. 30–31), is as poignant as the identity-less murmurings of Ellison's Invisible Man. Indeed, if, as Sartre says, consciousness is the source of nothingness, then the comparisons between the world's loss of sunlight, of sap, of all life, to the poet's sense of vacuousness are certainly to the point. Donne's self is, as he admits, no ordinary nothingness ("But I am None," l. 37). His hyperboles, "For I am every dead thing" (l. 12) and "I, by loves limbecke, am the grave/ Of all, that's nothing" (ll. 21–22), are not just sentimental exaggerations but expressions of a despondent consciousness seeing everything as really nothing. Like the hero of *Nausea*, Roquentin, who feels threatened in his awareness of the fixity of objects (ashtrays, etc.), Donne feels himself ridiculed by the earth's *seasonal* deaths: "all these seeme to laugh,/ Compar'd with mee, who am their Epitaph" (ll. 8–9). If the poet was punning on "squibs" (mock-

---

9 William A. Luijpen, *Existential Phenomenology* (Pittsburgh: Duquesne Univ. Press, 1963), p. 104.
10 Luijpen, p. 105.
11 *Ibid.*

ing remarks),[12] then even the sun seems to ridicule him. Like Sartre's Roquentin and Bellow's Dangling Man, who listen to music (art, perfect *en soi*), longing for the security of "completely self-contained existence,"[13] Donne is so aware of being-in-itself (ll. 19–20) that he would enjoy participating in the order and integrity of *things*:

> I should preferre,
>   If I were any beast,
> Some ends, some means; Yea plants, yea stones detest,
> And love; All, all some properties invest . . . (ll. 31–34)

As noted above, Donne's experience of nothingness was precipitated by the death of his wife. According to Martin Heidegger, death brings man face to face with the negation of being; it is the "shrine of nonbeing."[14] Although Donne might have preferred (like Hamlet) to be a beast, he was able to confront the nothingness of death both as a spouse (a lover) and a poet, perfectly integrating emotion, thought, and language. As Heidegger says, "mortals are those who can experience death as death. The animal cannot do this. But neither can the animal speak."[15] Because of language's propensity for change (finitude) and also because of its capacity for adjusting to meaning, only man can articulate the experience of death as nonbeing. Thus, since Donne's beloved was his soul, he can honestly say: "I am by her death, (which word wrongs her) / Of the first nothing, the Elixer grown" (ll. 28–29). According to the poet's parenthetical clause and Heidegger's philosophy as well, death is not just the ontological end point of life. It is the culmination of man's self-disclosure of being; and, since Donne and his lady were so much a part of each other, her demise and self-revelation are paradoxically and existentially his too. In the last stanza of the poem, Donne strongly suggests his destiny with Ann when he says: "Since shee enjoyes her long nights festivall,/ Let mee prepare towards her . . ." (ll. 42–43). As James Demske says of Heidegger's philosophy, "it is in death that being leads man to recognize that his essence is constituted not by his re-

---

12 Andreasen, p. 156.
13 Richard Lehan, "Existentialism in Recent American Fiction: The Demonic Quest," in *Recent American Fiction: Some Critical Views*, ed. Joseph J. Waldmeir (Boston: Houghton, 1963), pp. 70–71.
14 *Vorträge und Aufsätze* (Tübingen: Neske. 1954), p. 177.
15 *Unterwegs zur Sprache* (Tübingen: Neske, 1959), p. 215.

lations to beings [things, etc.], but rather by his transcendental orientation to being."[16]

This understanding of death was manifest to Donne as Christian and lover, for, in Gabriel Marcel's words, love is "the essential ontological datum"[17]—*the* phenomenon revealing one's true destiny. In one of his sermons in 1617, Donne clearly defined the transforming ontological dimension of such love: "Love is a Possessory Affection, it delivers over him that loves into the possession of that that he loves; it is a transmutatory Affection, it changes him that loves, into the very nature of that that he loves, and he is nothing else."[18] Donne's words capture the essence of the modern phenomenology of love in which one's destiny is revealed as a destiny-for-the-other, freeing one from selfish preoccupation.[19]

The poet's recognition in "A Nocturnall" of the possibility of transcendence does not take us by surprise. His poem is based on paradoxes as equally resolvable as Heidegger's paradox that death is the shrine of both nonbeing and being. "A Nocturnall" begins with seasonal imagery, but Donne goes beyond the hope of nature's cycle of death and rebirth. In fact, he admits that with his lady's death he is no ordinary nóthing and that she will not come back to him as spring returns to winter ("nor will my Sunne renew," 1. 37). Nevertheless, the poem was written as a nocturnal, a midnight service, to the saint of light (Lucy— *luce*), with whom Donne identifies his beloved.[20] Anticipating St. Lucy's (and Ann's) commemoration, the nocturnal resolves in its conclusion the crucial paradoxes of darkness and light, of nothingness and being, and of the abyss and transcendence:

---

16 James M. Demske, *Being, Man, & Death: A Key to Heidegger* (Lexington: Univ. Press of Kentucky, 1970), p. 168. Because of his scrupulous adherence to phenomenological method, Heidegger does not concern himself with life after death (p. 174). Alluding to death as a transition but reluctant to go beyond that point in his philosophy (*Vorträge und Aufsätze*, p. 153), he says that man experiences death (and the fullness of being) on earth, under heaven, and before the godly.

17 Gabriel Marcel, *Being and Having: An Existentialist Diary*, trans. Katherine Ferrer (Westminster: Dacre, 1949), p. 167.

18 Potter and Simpson, I, 184–85.

19 Luijpen, pp. 217, 221. Donne's poem clearly transcends Sartre's notion that "Hell is other people" (*No Exit*).

20 Martz, p. 214. Obviously disagreeing with Professor Andreasen, who says the speaker's service is "a black vigil" (p. 154), I tend to accept Hughes's view that Donne "presents his wife as a manifestation of St. Lucy, identifies his own dejection with this anniversary of martyrdom, and forecasts a resurrection and reuniting" (p. 216).

> Since shee enjoyes her long nights festivall,
> Let mee prepare towards her, and let mee call
> This houre her Vigill, and her Eve, since this
> **Both the yeares, and the dayes deep midnight is.** (ll. 42–45)

"Festivall," "Vigill," "prepare," and "towards" indicate both the poet's exaltation of human love to the religious level and his own spiritual destiny.[21] He is not merely preparing "for" Ann's celebration but to go "towards her" in the recognition of his mortality and his transcendence.

With the imagery and resolve of its last lines, the poem's conclusion is certainly not sentimental.[22] But can we in contemporary terms accuse Donne of dishonesty, of "bad faith"? In light of both his poetry and his life, I think not. The quiet suggestion of renewal at the end of "A Nocturnall" was fully though subtly foreshadowed by the poem's alchemical metaphor. In the following lines, "wrought," "new," "Alchimie," "art," and "re-begot" indicate the creation from nothing of something new and, as the word "quintessence" implies, something more ideal:

> For I am every dead thing,
> In whom love wrought new Alchimie.
>   For his art did expresse
> A quintessence even from nothingnesse,
> From dull privations, and leane emptinesse:
> He ruin'd mee, and I am re-begot
> Of absence, darknesse, death; things which are not. (ll. 12–18)

The something new and more perfect that Donne comes to possess as a result of his wife's death is a penetrating awareness of both nonbeing and the capacity for transcending it. The poet implies the possibility of transcendence when he identifies himself with the quintessence ("the Elixer") of the first nothing out of which God created all things. The likelihood that Donne wrote "A Nocturnall" in December, four months after Ann's death, makes his reference to "dull privations, and leane emptiness" meaningful and poignant in terms of the duration of his dark night. The nocturnal on St. Lucy's day seems to have been the culmination (and liberation) from that night.

---

21 Hughes's discussion of Donne's use of breviary prayers for St. Lucy's nocturnal clearly reveals the spiritual nature of his "preparations" (p. 217).
22 According to Professor Guss, the poem "concludes with a sentimental extravagance, the poet's dedication of his life to a preparation for death" (p. 103).

But considering the poem's resolution, can we accuse Donne of dishonest otherworldliness? Again, I do not think so. His nocturnal is also a plea for cautious sensualism. Not only does he exhort other lovers to "Study" him but also to "Enjoy" their summer love. We cannot accuse Donne of unworldliness, for central to his spiritual development is the work of his own profane hands, his poetry. The persona of "The Canonization," speaking of his lady, talks about shaping his poem, like a well wrought urn, to be an everlasting monument to their love. "A Nocturnall" is Donne's "urn" for Ann.

In 1615, two years before Ann's death, the poet became an Anglican minister. But, for all his *contemptus mundi* as a clergyman, he never ignored, rejected or condemned the world. In fact, as a preacher, he attacked Puritanism for its excessive asceticism and for its doctrines of predestination and reprobation.[23] To withdraw from the world was against Donne's deepest beliefs. As he wrote in one of his sermons, "holy simplicity of the soule is not a darknesse, a dimnesse, a stupidity in the understanding, contracted by living in a corner, it is not an idle retiring into a Monastery, or into a Village, or a Country solitude."[24] Indeed, no truly *engaged* existentialist has ever made the case for the brotherhood of man more meaningful and convincing than the Dean of St. Paul's: "No man is an *Iland*, intire of it selfe; every man is a peece of the *Continent*, a part of the *maine*; if a *Clod* bee washed away by the *Sea*, *Europe* is the lesse, as well as if a *Promontorie* were, as well as if a *Mannor* of thy *friends* or of *thine owne* were; any mans *death* diminishes *me*, because I am involved in *Mankinde*."[25] Diminished by the death of his wife, Donne wrote "A Nocturnall" to confront the nothingness, the void, in his life and quietly to transcend it.

23 Potter and Simpson, II, 164–78; X, 162; II, 110.

24 Potter and Simpson, VI, 275. In 1624 Donne also wrote in one of his sermons that God left man "upon the Earth; and not only to tread upon it, as in contempt, or in meere Dominion, but to walke upon it, in the discharge of the duties of his calling; and so to be conversant with the earth, is not a falling" (VI, 69).

25 *Devotions Upon Emergent Occasions*, ed. John Sparrow (Cambridge: Cambridge Univ. Press, 1923), p. 98.

B. The Social Sciences

Sociological Paradigms of Reality

William J. Filstead

Northwestern University

A SUBSTANTIAL amount of literature has developed concerning itself with the scope, approach, and thrust of present-day sociology (see Gouldner, 1970; Friedricks, 1970; Glaser and Strauss, 1967; Berger and Luckmann, 1966; Denzin, 1970; Douglas, 1970; Filstead, 1970). These concerns in sociology and in other behavioral sciences (Tussman, 1960; Matson, 1966; Winch, 1958; Maslow, 1966) have centered on a number of interrelated issues: the theoretical, conceptual, and methodological schemes of the behavioral sciences; the behavioral sciences' interpretation of the social world; and, of greatest importance, the behavioral sciences' interpretations of reality and the manner in which the individual relates to it.

At the center of these issues is the nagging question of how similar or dissimilar are the behavioral sciences and the natural sciences; that is, is the approach of the natural sciences to its phenomena an appropriate model for the behavioral sciences to use in studying human behavior? This question has occupied the thinking of men for centuries and supporters can be lined up on either side of the question (Lundberg, 1955; Nagel, 1961; Kaplan, 1965; Natanson, 1963; Northrop, 1959; MacIver, 1931; Blumer, 1969). Rather than address this question directly, the intent of this discussion is to identify and describe two distinct approaches to the study of human behavior which play a crucial role in molding the substance of sociological theory. Sociological theories, schools of thought, frames of reference, etc., do not have an existence independent of the common-sense notions, assumptions, and ideologies that constitute their stance toward social life. In order better to understand sociological theories, it is important to be sensitive to the groundings on which these theories are based.

The aim of the following discussion is to describe two dominant sociological approaches to reality: the normative and phenomenological paradigms. These paradigms will be compared and contrasted along such dimensions as the nature of man, the nature of reality, the process of interaction, and the development of theoretical, conceptual, and methodological strategies to comprehend the social world. Finally, the implications of the phenomenological paradigm will be discussed with reference to current and future developments in sociology.

The Notion of Paradigms

The Structure of Scientific Revolutions by Thomas S. Kuhn (1962) has provided a framework for thinking about how science is done and how science changes. This work has stimulated a great deal of writing on how the ways in which a science conceives of its phenomena contributes to and shapes the kinds of problems that it considers for study, the types of and manner in which its theories are generated, the methodological principles, strategies, and tools for studying its phenomena, and finally, how the models of a science evolve, become modified, and change.

The thesis of Kuhn's work is that the life of science is dominated more by socio-cultural influences on the scientific community than the façade of formalized logic used by science to justify its methods of inquiry. Science is done by human beings, and scientists are subject to socio-cultural influences like those of any other professionals (Crane, 1972). In developing this thesis, Kuhn rejects the traditional image of science as the steady linear accumulation of knowledge. Instead, he substitutes a model which emphasizes sporadic and radical reformulations in ways of thinking about the world. Changes in science occur through a revolution and not an evolution in thinking.

Kuhn's original essay was limited to the process of scientific revolutions in the natural sciences. Subsequently, Kuhn (1970a, 1970b) has acknowledged the appropriateness of his formulation to the social sciences. Furthermore, Kuhn's argument has captured the imagination of social scientists and has generated discussions on such diversified topics as the sociology of sociology (Friedricks, 1970), the paradigms of political science (Effrat, 1972), the present state of sociological theory (Warshay, 1971; Lemert, 1973), the appropriateness of the Kuhnsian model in sociology (Lekowitz, 1971), and how methodological preoccupation has led to an insistence on deductive theorizing in sociology (Filstead, 1971).

According to Kuhn, the day-to-day work of science is organized around a paradigm[1] (Masterman, 1970). In its broadest sense, a paradigm represents a "disciplinary matrix" which encompasses the commonly shared generalizations, assumptions, values, beliefs, and exemplars of what constitutes a discipline's interests (Kuhn, 1970: pp 181–87). A paradigm serves to order the priorities of a discipline. The paradigm serves as a guide to the professionals in a discipline, for it indicates what are the important problems and issues confronting the discipline; goes about developing an explanatory scheme (i.e., models and theories) which can place these issues and problems in a framework which will allow practitioners to try to solve them; establishes the criteria for the appropriate "tools" (i.e., methodologies, instruments, type and form of data collection) to use in solving these disciplinary puzzles; and provides an epistemology in which the preceding items can be viewed as organizing principles for carrying out the "normal work" of the discipline. Paradigms not only allow a discipline to "make sense" of different kinds of phenomena, but provide a framework in which these phenomena can be identified as existing in the first place. In a very real sense, to understand a paradigm we must understand the processes by which it was "discovered."

Each paradigm explains a limited amount of reality. So to some extent, the areas of a discipline's concerns are to a greater or lesser degree adequately covered by any given paradigm. In Kuhn's words:

---

[1] Masterman offers a discussion of twenty-one different, but not mutually exclusive ways, in which Kuhn used the term *paradigm*. She points out that three general notions are implied when Kuhn used the term; "metaphysical paradigms" that provide organizing principles; "sociological paradigms" describing universally recognized achievements; "construct paradigms" that describe methodological tools and instruments. For the most part, it appears that Kuhn means "metaphysical paradigms" when he uses the word. Page 69.

> To be accepted as a paradigm, a theory must seem better than its competitors, but it need not, and in fact never does, explain all the facts with which it can be confronted . . . paradigms gain their status because they are more successful than their competitors in solving a few problems that the group of practitioners have come to recognize as acute (1962: pp. 18, 23).

Shifts in paradigms occur due to the ascendence of anomalies, i.e., findings that are not expected under the given paradigm. If a discipline tries to explain these anomalies within the existing paradigm and fails, the work of normal science changes from one of "puzzle solving" to self-reflection and self-examination. Kuhn states:

> The proliferation of competing articulations, the willingness to try anything, the expression of explicit discontent, the recourse to philosophy and the debate over fundamentals, all these are symptoms of a transition from normal to extraordinary research (Kuhn, 1962: p. 90).

The net result of this soul-searching is a revolution—a revolution in the basic ways in which the discipline thinks about its phenomena, the assumptions that it takes for granted, the logic of its theory development, and the methodological principles that underlie its approach to the subject matter. Again, Kuhn says it best:

> The transition from a paradigm in crisis to a new one from which a new tradition of normal science can emerge is far from a cumulative process, one achieved by an articulation or extension of the old paradigm. Rather, it is a reconstruction of the field from new fundamentals, a reconstruction that changes some of the field's most elementary theoretical generalizations as well as many of its paradigm methods and applications. During the transition period there will be a large but never complete overlap between the problems that can be solved by the old and by the new paradigm. But there will also be a decisive difference in the modes of solution. When the transition is complete, the profession will have changed its view of the field, its methods, and its goals (1970: pp. 84–85).

With this understanding of Kuhn's position in mind, and especially the notion of paradigms and what they entail, the discussion will now shift to a presentation of two dominant paradigmatic frameworks in sociology: the normative and the phenomenological.[2] Each paradigm will be analyzed in terms of how it conceives of the nature of man, the nature of reality, the process of interaction, and the development of theoretical, conceptual, and methodological strategies to comprehend the social world. But first, a look at the historical antecedents of each paradigm is necessary.

The Historical Background to the Paradigms

At the heart of the distinction between a normative and a phenomenological paradigm lies the classic argument in philosophy between the philosophical schools of realism and idealism, and their subsequent reformulations (see Aiken, 1957; Coser, 1971; Becker and Barnes, 1952). The writings of Hobbes, Locke, Bacon, Kant, Berkeley, Hume, and others focused on, among other things, the relation between the external world and the process of knowing. The essential question they concerned themselves with was: How do we know what we know? The continuing debate surrounding this question highlights the fact that there are sets of assumptions underlying our view of the world which to a great extent shape the world which we see.

The birth of science in the fifteenth and sixteenth centuries was made possible by the static conception of the world that dominated the thinking of men of ideas. There was faith in reason as the way of understanding the world and this reason eventually became based on a faith in science. The world was held to be capable of understanding through man's senses. As a result of this belief in science, science was proclaimed to be the way of understanding the world. The Baconian reality of "I see it because I experience it" sums up the thrust of thinking which became known as logical positivism.

Turmoil and rapid social change in the institutions of society during the eighteenth and nineteenth centuries caused scholars to question the logic and method of science as it applied to understanding human beings. This was particularly true of the German Idealists who acknowledged the existence of a physical reality but held that the mind was the source and creator of

---

[2] A number of writers have described similar dichotomies. Wilson (1970) describes a normative and interpretative paradigm; Douglas (1970, 1970a, 1970b, 1971) talks about an absolutist or objective stance and a natural or theoretic stance; Shearing and Petrunik (1971) describe a normative and phenomenological approach to the study of deviance. I have chosen to use their dichotomy and expand it to sociology in general. My discussion of these paradigms will rely heavily on these cited works.

knowledge. The world is not given; it is created by the individuals who live in it. This clash in philosophies is central to the differences between the normative and phenomenological paradigms. A discussion of these differences follows.

The Normative and Phenomenological Paradigms: Conceptualizing Basic Issues

The thrust of the normative paradigm conceives of man as reacting and responding to the situations in his world on the basis of a more or less structured set of situational responses. Social reality is thought to be objectively given, external to, and independent of man. This reality is said to impinge on all men, regardless of who or where they are in society, and, therefore, it is a force which makes for the development of clearly identifiable response-sets to situations.

Within this framework, all actors are said to know what is expected of them because they are introduced and socialized into a culturally specific, but generally shared system of symbols, meanings, and values. Thus the normative paradigm assumes that one can understand the situation and the actor in it by reference to the shared system of meanings in which the actor is located. In short, in the normative paradigm, the nature of reality is thought to be clear to all actors because of their socialization into a commonly shared meaning system (Homans, 1961; Parsons, 1937, 1951, 1961; Parsons and Shils, 1951; Merton, 1968).

By way of contrast, the phenomenological paradigm does not conceive of the world as an external force, objectively identifiable and independent of man. At the heart of the phenomenological paradigm is the assumption that there exist *multiple realities* which are constantly in flux. Actors in this paradigm are active agents in constructing and making sense of the realities they encounter rather than responding in puppet-like fashion to external stimuli. There exist no clearcut response-sets to situations, but instead, through a negotiated and interpretative process an agreed upon pattern of interaction emerges.

> Objects in the world are seen as having meanings constituted by human actors and not simply as entities with an independent existence. The meanings of objects arise from and are integrally a part of the uses made of them by humans (Psathas, 1973: p. 6).

The normative paradigm views the social actor as being disposed to engage in interaction due to a shared consensus among others as to the appropriate action to be engaged in vis-à-vis one another, with sanctions being the source of support for the system.

> Interaction in a given situation then, is explained by first identifying structures of role expectations and complexes of dispositions, and then showing that the relevant features of the observed interaction can be deduced from the expectations and dispositions along with the assumptions embodied in the model of the actor (Wilson, 1970: p. 699).

However, if the nature of reality and man's experience with it is thought to be an interpretative process as Blumer (1954, 1956, 1962, 1966), Turner (1962), and others (Mead, 1934; Thomas, 1923; Garfinkel, 1964, 1967) do, then basic issues which are unproblematic in the normative paradigm become problematic in the phenomenological paradigm. For example, Turner, in discussing ways of conceptualizing interaction, makes the point that:

> The idea of role-playing shifts emphasis away from the simple process of enacting a prescribed role to devising a performance in the basis of an imputed other role. The actor is not the occupant of a status for which there is a neat set of rules—a culture or set of norms—but a person who must act in the perspective supplied in part by his relationship to others whose actions reflect roles he must identify (1962: p. 23).

The explanation of interaction as an interpretative process is clearly spelled out by Blumer:

> The participants fit their acts together, first by identifying the social act in which they are about to engage and, secondly, by interpreting and defining each other's acts in forming the joint act . . . [the participants] have to ascertain what the others are doing and plan to do and make indications to one another of what to do (1966: p. 540).
> We can, and I think must, look upon human life as chiefly a vast interpretive process in which people, singly and collectively, guide themselves by defining the objects, events, and situations which they encounter . . . any scheme designed to analyze human group life in its general character has to fit this process of interpretation (1957: p. 686).

Within such a phenomenological paradigm, the nature of reality and man's strategies for interaction are viewed as problematic. Multiple options for action have to be assessed vis-à-vis the vibrations that are *imputed to* and *picked up from* the other actors and the contextual surroundings in the social milieu. The initial pattern of interaction an actor embarks on, as well as those which will follow, are viewed within the total context of what has transpired, what is transpiring, and what one can assume to transpire—all of course, subject to revision and redefinition.

Thinking about society, man, and interaction in these terms has led each paradigm to embark on distinctively different approaches to theory development, concept formation, and methodological strategies for studying social phenomena.

The normative paradigm starts with broad, general theories and moves in a logico-deductive fashion through propositions, hypotheses, and operational definitions. In the process, the scientist in the normative paradigm creates his own categories, builds scales, questionnaires, and instruments, runs experiments, manipulates independent/dependent variables in order to predict behavior. This logic, relying heavily on a natural science conception of science, atomizes reality into its component parts. Having done so, the scientist attempts to relate the parts to each other in a way that fits the preestablished theoretical framework.

Thinking about social phenomena in this way led scientists in the normative paradigm to concentrate on developing sophisticated methodological techniques. The twin issues of validity and reliability dominate the concerns underlying the development of research methodologies. In part, because of the assumption that a clearly identifiable, objective reality, independent and external to man existed, emphasis is placed on demonstrating the reliability of instruments to measure that world. Apparently, substantiation of a technique's reliability ipso facto stamps it as a valid assessment of the social world.

This conception of science has been seriously challenged by a number of writers (Blumer, 1969; Deutscher, 1966, 1969, 1973; Clinard, 1966; Matson, 1966; Filstead, 1970, 1971). Deutscher has remarked that:

> We concentrate on consistency without much concern with what it is we are being consistent about or whether we are consistently right or wrong. As a consequence we may have been learning a great deal about how to pursue an incorrect course with a maximum of precision (1966: p. 241).

The phenomenological paradigm approaches the social world from an entirely different point of view. First of all, an emphasis is placed on seeing the social world from the point of view of the actors who participate in it. Rather than impose a theoretical or conceptual framework on the phenomenon being studied, the scientist in the phenomenological paradigm insists that concepts and theory emerge from the data. A grounded, inductive approach to theory development utilizing sensitizing concepts that capture the subjective meanings of social actors are stressed (Glaser and Strauss, 1967).

> *Any scientific understanding of human action, at whatever level of ordering or generality, must begin with and be built upon an understanding of the everyday life of the members performing those actions.* To fail to see this and to act in accord with it is to commit what we might call the *fallacy of abstractionism,* that is, the fallacy of believing that you can know in a more abstract form what you do not know in the particular form (Douglas, 1970: p. 11).

Following from this insistence on maintaining the fidelity of the subject's social world, an emphasis is placed on understanding and describing how the actor "makes sense" of his world. This objective is embodied in Garfinkel's use of the "documentary method of interpretation" which refers to the "method that members use in discovering and portraying orderly and connected events" (1967, p. 78). According to the phenomenological paradigm, the actor is the principle source of information about his social world. Therefore, it is essential to learn how social actors construct explanations of their world. The social scientist in his direct examination of the subject's world has to comprehend and capture the experience of being involved in that everyday world. The social scientist has to see the world as the subjects see it. The meaning of events continually emerges from social interaction and it is important to understand the considerations the actor makes in assessing the meaning of events. These remarks highlight the primacy the phenomenological paradigm places on capturing and preserving the essence of the actor's world. Again, Blumer's remarks bear on this point:

> To try and catch the interpretative process by remaining aloof as a so-called "objective" observer and refusing to take the role of the acting unit is to risk the worst kind of subjectivism—the objective observer is likely to fill in the process of interpretation with

his own surmises in place of catching the process as it occurs in the experience of the acting unit which uses it (1962: p. 188).

It follows, then, that the primary way to accomplish this objective is to spend time in the natural environment of those being studied. There is no substitute for a *first-hand acquaintance* with the world of the social actors.

> No theorizing, however ingenuous, and no observances of scientific protocol, however meticulous, are substitutes for developing a familiarity with what is actually going on in the sphere of life under study (Blumer, 1969: p. 39).

Consequently, methods used in the phenomenological paradigm tend to be qualitative in nature, i.e., in depth interviewing, participant observation, field experience, etc., rather than the quantitative statistical procedures, mathematical models, and system analysis used in the normative paradigm.

Implications of the Phenomenological Paradigm

In contrasting the normative and phenomenological paradigm, I have attempted to highlight the salient issues that have a direct bearing on the conduct of the behavioral sciences. Each paradigm conceptualized the social world, the dynamics of human interaction, and the appropriate strategies for comprehending the world in markedly different ways. Neither paradigm is provable or disprovable. It is a simple matter of values, not facts, which determines the paradigm a science subscribes to. As Kuhn has noted, paradigms are never disproven; other paradigms simply become more believable.

Clearly, the phenomenological paradigm offers a framework for understanding which would force significant shifts to occur in the ways in which the social world is conceptualized and approached. At the core of the new criteria would be an insistence on understanding the subjectively experienced realities of social actors. This would necessitate radical changes in the logic underlying current theoretical, conceptual, and methodological approaches to the social world which are based on a natural science model of science. George Psathas has made this point in stressing the potential of the phenomenological paradigm.

> When social science recognizes that the objective reality of society, groups, community, and formal organizations is subjectively experienced by the individual and that these subjective experiences are intimately related to the subsequent externalization and objectification procedures in which humans engage as they think and act in the social world, then a more informed and reality-based social science will result (1973: p. 13).

Even more fundamental than an insistence on the primacy of subjective experiences is the challenge to the epistemological and ontological assumptions which underlie the natural science conceptualization of science. If the phenomenological paradigm is seriously considered, it would result in a major reformulation of the thinking about the nature of the behavioral sciences, especially the appropriateness of the natural science model for conceptualizing the social world. The impact of the natural science model on the behavioral sciences has been succinctly described by Deutscher.

> In attempting to assume the stance of a physical science, we have necessarily assumed its epistemology, its assumptions about the nature of knowing and the appropriate means of knowing, including the rules of scientific evidence . . . one of the consequences of using the natural science model was to break down human behavior in a way that was not only artificial but which did not jibe with the manner in which the behavior was observed (1966: p. 124).

The question which I place before you, the reader, is this: Which paradigm fits with what you believe human experience to be like? Too long have we tried to fit the social world into a paradigm which does not allow for sensitivity to the complexities of human behavior; perhaps it is time to change. To paraphrase a Blumer challenge to sociologists, we have to "respect the nature of the empirical world and develop a paradigmatic framework to reflect that respect."

The goal is to be faithful to and respectful of the everyday realities of the social worlds we study and the experiences of the people who live in those worlds. This is the spirit and the challenge of the phenomenological paradigm.

REFERENCES

Aiken, Henry D.
(1957)   *The Age of Ideology: The Nineteenth-Century Philosophers.* Vol. V
              of *The Great Ages of Western Philosophy.* New York: Braziller.
Becker, Howard P. and Harry E. Barnes

(1952)   *Social Thought from Lore to Science,* Vols. I, II. 2nd ed. Washington, D. C.: Harren Press.
Berger, Peter L. and Thomas Luckmann
(1966)   *The Social Construction of Reality.* Garden City, N. Y.: Doubleday.
Blumer, Herbert
(1954)   "What is Wrong with Social Theory?" *American Sociological Review* 19: 3–10.
(1956)   "Sociological Analysis and the 'Variable'." *American Sociological Review* 21: 683–90.
(1962)   "Society as Symbolic Interaction." Pp. 179–92 in Arnold M. Rose, ed., *Human Behavior and Social Processes: An Interactionist Approach.* Boston: Houghton Mifflin.
(1966)   "Sociological Implications of the Thought of George Herbert Mead." *American Journal of Sociology* 71: 535–44.
(1969)   *Symbolic Interactionism.* Englewood Cliffs, N. J.: Prentice-Hall.
Bruyn, Severyn
(1966)   *The Human Perspective in Sociology.* Englewood Cliffs, N. J.: Prentice-Hall.
Clinard, Marshall
(1966)   "The Sociologist's Quest for Respectability." *The Sociological Quarterly* 7: 399–412.
Coser, Lewis A.
(1971)   *Masters of Social Thought: Ideas in Historical and Social Context.* New York: Harcourt, Brace, Jovanovich.
Crane, Diana
(1972)   *Invisible Colleges: Diffusion of Knowledge in Scientific Communities.* Chicago: Univ. of Chicago Press.
Denzin, Norman K.
(1970)   *The Research Act.* Chicago: Aldine.
Deutscher, Irwin
(1966)   "Words and Deeds: Social Science and Social Policy." *Social Problems* 13: 233–54.
(1969)   "Looking Backwards: Case Studies on the Progress of Methodology in Sociological Research." *The American Sociologist* 4:34–42.
(1973)   *What we Say/What we Do.* Glenview, Ill.: Scott, Foresman.
Douglas, Jack D.
(1970)   (ed.) *Understanding Everyday Life.* Chicago: Aldine.
(1970a)   "Deviance and Order in a Pluralistic Society." Pp. 367–401 in John C. McKinney and Edward A. Tiryakian, eds., *Theoretical Sociology: Perspectives and Developments.* New York: Appleton-Century-Crofts.
(1970b) (ed.) *Deviance and Respectability: The Social Construction of Moral Meanings.* New York: Basic Books.
(1971)   *American Social Order: Social Rules in a Pluralistic Society.* New York: Free Press.
Effrat, Andrew
(1972)   "Power to the Paradigms: An Editorial Introduction." *Sociological Inquiry* 42: 3–33.
Filstead, William J.
(1970)   (ed.) *Qualitative Methodology.* Chicago: Markham.
(1971)   "The Sociology of Methodology." Paper presented at the American Sociological Association Meetings, 1971.
Friedricks, Robert A.
(1970)   *A Sociology of Sociology.* New York: Free Press.
Garfinkel, Harold
(1964)   "Studies of the Routine Ground of Everyday Activities." *Social Problems* 11: 225–50.
(1967)   *Studies in Ethnomethodology.* Englewood Cliffs, N. J.: Prentice-Hall.
Glaser, Barney and Anselm Strauss
(1967)   *The Discovery of Grounded Theory.* Chicago: Aldine.
Gouldner, Alvin W.
(1970)   *The Coming Crisis of Western Sociology.* New York: Basic Books.
Homans, George C.

(1961)   *Social Behavior: Its Elementary Forms.* New York: Harcourt, Brace & World.

Kaplan, Abraham
(1964)   *The Conduct of Inquiry.* San Francisco: Chandler.

Kuhn, Thomas
(1962)   *The Structure of Scientific Revolution.* Chicago: Phoenix.
(1970a)   *The Structure of Scientific Revolutions.* 2nd ed. Chicago: Univ. of Chicago Press.
(1970b)   "Reflections on My Critics." In Imre Lakatos and Alan Musgrave, eds., *Criticism and Growth of Knowledge.* Cambridge: Cambridge Univ. Press.

Lakatos, Imre and Alan Musgrave, eds.
(1970)   *Criticism and the Growth of Knowledge.* Cambridge: Cambridge Univ. Press.

Lekowitz, Barry
(1971)   "Paradigms in Sociology: Some Thoughts on an Undebated Issue." Paper presented at the American Sociological Association Meetings, 1971.

Lemert, Charles
(1973)   "Social Theory and the Relativistic Paradigm." Paper presented at the American Sociological Association Meetings, 1973.

Lundberg, George A.
(1926)   "The Natural Science Trend in Sociology." *American Journal of Sociology* 61: 191–202.

Maslow, Abraham
(1966)   *The Psychology of Science.* New York: Harper & Row.

Masterman, Margaret
(1970)   "The Nature of a Paradigm." Pp. 59–60 in Imre Lakatos and Alan Musgrave, eds., *Criticism and the Growth of Knowledge.* Cambridge: Cambridge Univ. Press.

Matson, Floyd W.
(1966)   *The Broken Image.* Garden City, N. Y.: Anchor Books.

Mead, George Herbert
(1934)   *Mind, Self and Society from the Standpoint of a Social Behaviorist,* ed. Charles W. Morris. Chicago: Univ. of Chicago Press.

Merton, Robert K.
(1968)   *Social Theory and Social Structure.* New York: Free Press.

MacIver, Robert
(1931)   "Is Sociology a Natural Science?" *American Journal of Sociology* 25: 25–35.

Nagel, Ernest
(1961)   *The Structure of Science: Problems in the Logic of Scientific Explanation.* New York: Harcourt, Brace & World.

Natanson, Maurice, ed.
(1963)   *Philosophy and the Social Sciences.* New York: Random House.

Northrop, F. S. C.
(1959)   *The Logic of Sciences and Humanities.* New York: Meridian.

Parsons, Talcott
(1937)   *The Structure of Social Action.* New York: McGraw-Hill.
(1951)   *The Social System.* New York: Free Press.
(1961)   "An Outline of the Social System." Pp. 30–79 in Talcott Parsons, Edward Shils, Kaspar D. Naegele, and Jesse R. Pitts, eds., *Theories of Society.* New York: Free Press.

Parsons, Talcott and Edward Shils, eds.
(1951)   *Toward a General Theory of Action.* Cambridge: Harvard Univ. Press.

Psathas, George, ed.
(1973)   *Phenomenological Sociology.* New York: Wiley.

Shearing, C. D. and M. G. Petrunik
(1971)   "Normative and Phenomenological Approaches to the Study of Deviance." Paper presented at the American Sociological Association Meetings, 1971.

Thomas, William I.
(1923)   *The Unadjusted Girl.* Boston: Ginn.
Turner, Ralph
(1962)   "Role-taking: Process Versus Conformity." Pp. 20–40 in Arnold M.
                Rose, ed., *Human Behavior and Social Process: An Interactionist
                Approach.* Boston: Houghton Mifflin.
Tussman, Joseph
(1960)   *Obligation and the Body Politic.* New York: Oxford Univ. Press.
Warshay, Leon
(1971)   "The Current State of Sociological Theory: Diversity, Polarity,
                Empiricism, and Small Theories." *Sociological Quarterly* 12: 23–45.
Wilson, Thomas P.
(1970)   "Conceptions of Interaction and Forms of Sociological Explanation."
                American Sociological Review 35: 697–710.
Winch, Peter
(1958)   *The Idea of a Social Science.* London: Routledge & Kegan Paul.

Phenomenology:
a Non-Alternative to Empiricism

Richard Gillis

Kingsborough Community College

THIS paper is based primarily on two assumptions: the first is that the cleavage within the social sciences between the subjective or normative approach and the objective or empiricist approach is genuine, unresolved and of the most fundamental importance. Questions concerning the status of value statements, the nature of subjective understanding and the role of the social sciences are vital to the social scientist both professionally and humanly. The relative absence in the past few years of journal articles on these questions is not evidence of any underlying agreement. Instead, the prevailing methodological tolerance is perhaps only a kind of exhaustion which reflects the complexity of the problems and the conviction that our intellectual opponents have learned their lessons too well and will be able to dispose of our best arguments without taking them seriously. Though the journals are predominantly empirical in orientation there have been clear signs recently of skepticism or, in some cases, outright disenchantment with the results achieved by empirical social science.[1] These doubts and dissatisfactions seem always to revolve around the same point, namely, the remoteness of empirical theory from the actual problems of social and political life.

The second assumption is that there is a tendency among those who are dissatisfied with empiricism to turn indiscriminately to twentieth-century European thought for a philosoph-

[1] See esp. Sheldon Wolin, "Political Theory as a Vocation," *American Political Science Review*, 63 (Dec. 1969) .

ically respectable alternative.[2] It seems to me this is a mistake. The terms "existentialism" and "phenomenology" have been applied loosely to styles of thought which are widely divergent. In addition, philosophers such as Sartre and Heidegger are discussed frequently in books under both headings. As a result, there is an inclination among non-professional philosophers to regard "existentialism" and "phenomenology" as more or less interchangeable words which refer to the same kind of basic philosophical position. This is not at all true. The phenomenological movement which was founded by Edmund Husserl has very little in common with the humanist existentialism popularly associated with Sartre's name. Husserl's major interests were not primarily in the philosophy of the social sciences and he wrote very little about these problems. Nevertheless, his philosophy had a significant influence on thinkers with a variety of interests. Among them was Alfred Schutz, a Vienna-born sociologist who emigrated to the United States in 1939 and taught for many years at the New School for Social Research in New York City. Schutz believed that he had discovered in Husserl's phenomenology a way of approaching the social sciences that is radically opposed to the methodology of empiricism.

The pages that follow will be devoted to two principal tasks: one, a description of phenomenology in terms of both its opposition to existentialism and its place in the tradition of Western philosophy. The failure to distinguish phenomenology from existentialism is a source of much confusion and is partly responsible for the erroneous impression that the former is fundamentally opposed to the idea of an objective science of society. The purpose of placing Husserl in the history of modern Western philosophy is not to penetrate deeply into the mysteries of phenomenological method but simply to convey a sense of the philosophical purpose of phenomenology. This is necessary in order to appraise Schutz's approach to the social sciences at all realistically. The second task will be an analysis of Schutz's attempt to apply phenomenological ideas to the problems of the social sciences. The main difficulty here involves the question of language. It is my impression that the idea of phenomenology as a significant alternative to empiricism results from the fact that phenomenologists regularly use certain words the mere

---

[2] Henry Kariel, "The Political Relevance of Behavioral and Existential Psychology," *American Political Science Review*, 61 (June 1969). Kariel's essay, though interesting, seems to me an example of how easy it is to mix different strains of thought.

appearance of which enheartens subjectivists and is more or less anathema to empiricists. However, as we shall see, these words are used in the vocabulary of phenomenology in special ways and their meanings have little to do with the substance of subjectivist arguments against empiricism. The purpose of the paper is to show that, despite the claims made by Schutz, a phenomenological approach to social science offers no meaningful alternative to empiricism and that Schutz himself says nothing that is clearly and seriously in conflict with the beliefs of empiricists about the aims of social science or the nature of social scientific inquiry.[3]

I

It is natural that students of the social sciences who have felt some doubt or disillusionment with empiricism should look to phenomenology for a wholly different approach to the problem of knowledge. To a certain extent this is perhaps justified since phenomenology, on a philosophical level, is opposed to empiricism. Moreover, in much of the literature of phenomenology words with strong emotive appeal such as "subjectivity," "intuition," "essence," *"Lebenswelt,"* "life-world," and *"Verstehen"* appear frequently. Thus the impression is created that phenomenology is made to order for those who are unable to find very much that is significant in the data collecting and conceptualizing of contemporary social science.

Phenomenology: Opposed to Existentialism

The idea that phenomenology and existentialism represent

---

[3] To anticipate an objection, I would argue that Schutz is not only the best known and most influential social scientist of the phenomenological school but also that his work follows more closely than that of other phenomenologists along the lines indicated by Husserl. For instance, see Berger and Luckmann, *The Social Construction of Reality* (Garden City, N. Y.: Doubleday, 1966), in which there is a suggestion that the social scientist is entitled to a certain latitude in his interpretation of social reality. I take this to be very much at odds with the avowed purpose of phenomenology. Husserl wanted to establish philosophy as a strict science. In line with this aim, Schutz's concern was to found the social sciences on a solid rational ground. For what in my judgment is an even more illegitimate interpretation of phenomenology, see Marvin Surkin's "Sense and Non-sense in Politics," in *An End to Political Science,* ed. Marvin Surkin and Alan Wolfe (New York: Basic Books, 1970), pp. 13-33; the claim here is that phenomenology can be used as a method to criticize existing social institutions. I find nothing in Husserlian phenomenology—nor in Schutz's approach to social science—which even remotely supports this claim. One can only conclude that theorists may often misunderstand what has influenced them.

the same philosophic position is sometimes fostered by phenomenologists themselves. Maurice Natanson, in his Introduction to
Philosophy of the Social Sciences, refers in dramatic fashion to
the "wars of the Weltanschauungen."[4] The antagonists in this
conflict are the "objectivists" and the "subjectivists" and Natanson goes on to say that he will take these "two distinctively opposed philosophic attitudes . . . as polar positions underlying
the social sciences." The objectivist position is identified with
behaviorism, naturalism, empiricism and positivism; in general,
with "an approach to the social sciences which strives for the location of hard data, which is concerned with exact measurement
of social phenomena, which considers intersubjectively verifiable
propositions as constituting the necessary core of any science. . . ." The subjectivists, on the other hand, are those "who
speak of interpretive understanding or verstehen, . . . [and who
may have been] influenced by phenomenology and existentialism." For the subjectivist, according to Natanson, the aim of
enquiry is to understand "the attitudes, feelings, and conceptual
awareness of the individual caught up in social reality and trying to come to terms with it."[5]

This dichotomy by Natanson is misleading insofar as it includes phenomenologists such as Husserl and Schutz among the
proponents of a subjective approach. It is misleading, too, in
the suggestion that existentialism and phenomenology have
identical or similar philosophic goals. According to Walter Kaufmann, who does recognize the inadequacy of the label, existentialism is not a philosophy at all but rather a name for several
different reactions to philosophy in the traditional sense. Kaufmann characterizes existentialism this way: "The refusal to belong to any school of thought, the repudiation of the adequacy
of any body of beliefs whatever, and a marked dissatisfaction
with traditional philosophy as superficial, academic, and remote
from life—that is the heart of existentialism."[6]

Whatever one may think of the various existentialist writers
and the familiar language of freedom, choice and commitment,
it is clear that Husserl was not an existentialist. Though it is
true that both Husserl and the existentialists speak often of sub-

---

[4] Maurice Natanson, ed., *Philosophy of the Social Sciences* (New York: Random
House, 1963), p. 16.
[5] *Ibid.,* pp. viii–ix. All the quotations in the footnoted paragraph appear in these
two pages.
[6] Walter Kaufmann, ed., *Existentialism from Dostoyevsky to Sartre* (New York:
Meridian Books, 1956), p. 11.

jectivity, they do so for different reasons. It is also true that phenomenology and existentialism are opposed to empirical or positivistic philosophy; however, again the reason is different. Finally, it is fair to say that Husserl and the major existentialist thinkers express dissatisfaction with traditional philosophy but the explanation of their objections must be understood in the context of fundamentally conflicting purposes.

For thinkers such as Sartre and Jaspers, subjectivity is but another way of talking about freedom. Their revolt against academic or traditional philosophy is meant as a recommendation of an attitude toward life. For Sartre, man's freedom is rooted in his nature as *pour-soi* or non-thingness, and since there is no objective or absolute value or meaning in the universe man has significance only when he acts out of his own freedom. Jaspers, though he is sometimes accused of a kind of irrationalism, would not agree with Sartre that the universe is purposeless but only that man cannot know in any final way what this purpose is. His revolt is not by any means against reason but against that conception of reason according to which man can attain perfect knowledge. Furthermore, Jasper's attitude toward some of the great thinkers in the history of philosophy is one of reverence. For instance, he says of Plato that as far as philosophy is concerned we in the twentieth century have scarcely regained his level.[7] Perhaps it would be more accurate to say that Jaspers was repelled mainly by "academic" philosophy, that is, either analytic philosophy or philosophizing that propounded or adopted a system of thought and claimed for it an unassailable validity as absolute truth or pure knowledge.

Husserl's idea of subjectivity, his anti-naturalism[8] and his criticism of traditional philosophy must be approached in an entirely different way. For him, the basic questions in philosophy were not existential but epistemological. He was not concerned about the problem of freedom but rather the problem of knowledge. Thus, in Husserlian language, "subjectivity" refers not to choice or commitment, or to the creation of meaning

---

[7] Karl Jaspers, *Way to Wisdom*, trans. Ralph Manheim (New Haven: Yale Univ. Press, 1954), p. 8.

[8] Neither Husserl nor Schutz makes a distinction between "naturalism" and "empiricism." In the context of Husserl's philosophy, this is of course understandable. Yet, with regard to problems within the social sciences, the failure to make a distinction is a cause of confusion. I would understand "empiricism" to have a stricter and narrower meaning than "naturalism." Thus many historians and social scientists who do not think of themselves as empiricists would nevertheless be regarded as naturalists in the sense of rejecting the idea of a priori knowledge.

through action but instead to the activity of consciousness itself in constituting knowledge. The well-known existentialist slogan "existence precedes essence" would have been meaningless to Husserl since the problem of existence was irrelevant to his philosophical purpose. Similarly, the anti-naturalism of phenomenology has nothing to do with the idea that a thoroughgoing empiricism is an obstacle to man's actual freedom; rather, it is an obstacle to philosophy itself in that it assumes or implies the impossibility of philosophy's supreme task, which is the establishment of the realm of pure knowledge. In this sense, Husserl was not at all a rebel. In his own mind, he was a true lover of philosophy and his work represented a sustained and intensive effort to provide a foundation for genuine philosophical inquiry. Husserl was critical of past philosophy not because it is remote from life but because he thought no previous philosopher had understood clearly the concepts and methods that made true philosophy possible. The result, according to Husserl, is that philosophy has never been able to realize itself as a strict science, that is, a science capable of producing non-contingent or pure knowledge.[9] It is philosophy in this sense of strict science that was Husserl's lifelong concern. His idea of the historic mission of philosophy is captured vividly in the following passage:

> From its earliest beginnings philosophy has claimed to be a strict science. What is more, it has claimed to be the science which satisfies the loftiest theoretical needs and which renders possible from an ethico-religious point of view a life regulated by pure rational norms. This claim has been pressed sometimes with more, sometimes with less energy, but it has never been completely abandoned; not even during those times when interest in and capacity for pure theory were in danger of atrophying, or when religious forces restricted freedom of theoretical investigation.[10]

When Husserl spoke of putting philosophy on a new basis, what he had in mind was not wholesale rejection but the clarification and resolution of the problems set by earlier philosophers. He regarded himself as squarely within the tradition from which, it is claimed, the existentialists have rebelled.

Phenomenology: The Philosophical Background

The three philosophers who seem to have contributed most to Husserl's conception of phenomenology are Descartes, Hume

---

[9] Edmund Husserl, "Philosophy as a Strict Science," trans. Quentin Lauer, *Cross Currents*, 6 (1956), 1–18.

[10] *Ibid.*, p. 1.

and Kant.[11] All three were concerned with the problem of whether absolute knowledge is possible and their answers can be regarded as the main part of the philosophical development which led to phenomenology. Descartes' dissatisfaction with the state of philosophy in the seventeenth century led him to look for a method that would guarantee a secure foundation for knowledge. His discovery was the technique of doubt with respect to everything that could conceivably be doubted. The rigorous application of this method forced Descartes to the conclusion that only the consciousness of his own doubt could withstand that doubt. In other words, the indubitable ground of knowledge is to be found nowhere but in consciousness, that is, in the knower himself. Husserl regarded this as the first major discovery in modern philosophy. However, he believed that Descartes failed to develop his fundamental insight consistently. Essentially Descartes' mistake was a reflection of his inability to free himself from the problem of the external world. He intended his philosophy, and the concept of clear and distinct ideas, to be the means by which certain knowledge about reality would be possible. Yet he was unable to provide a satisfactory explanation for his own metaphysical dualism. The need to supply a bridge between consciousness and the world forced him to fall back on the dubious assertion that God's truthfulness is the only but adequate guarantee of objective validity.

Considering Hume's skepticism it is perhaps surprising that he would have been so highly regarded by Husserl. His significance with respect to phenomenology is two-fold: first, his descriptions of the operations of consciousness and second, the profound effect of his thought on Kant. Hume, like Descartes, both deplored the situation of philosophy in his time and resolved to investigate the foundations of knowledge. His investigation took the form of a detailed analysis of the ways in which the mind functions in order to form ideas. In effect, Hume's philosophy was a kind of descriptive psychology and a foreshadowing of phenomenology. To Husserl, his importance consisted in the fact that he was "the first to treat seriously the Cartesian focusing purely on what lies inside."[12] Thus, in open-

---

[11] Edmund Husserl, *Ideas*, trans. W. R. Boyce Gibson (Norwich: Jarrold & Sons, 1933), p. 183. Here Husserl mentions Descartes, Hume and Kant specifically as forerunners of phenomenology. References to them individually are of course scattered throughout his writings.

[12] Quoted in Richard Zaner, *The Way of Phenomenology* (New York: Western Pub. Co., 1970), p. 97. Zaner is especially good in his discussion of the philosophical background of phenomenology.

ing the road to phenomenology, Descartes and Hume were important not because of their conclusions but because of their seeking to found knowledge in the mind, that is, in subjectivity. In a sense, though Hume's empiricism is obviously hostile to a satisfactory solution of the philosophical problem of knowledge whereas Descartes' rationalism is not, the former came closer than did the latter to an answer in phenomenological terms. Hume of course denied the possibility of certain knowledge about the external world. Instead, he explained the subjective feeling of certainty in terms of habits and beliefs which are produced by the effects of constant conjunction. Yet, despite the great importance he so obviously attributed to habit, Hume simply accepted the idea without analyzing it further. As Zaner says, "What is so crucial about Hume's study is that while he does see clearly that 'what lies in ourselves' is that which accounts for connection and regularity, he yet fails to push his inquiry into that region of belief and custom—and just that region is precisely what must be examined, . . . as essential to human nature."[13]

In other words, Hume had made a discovery the implications of which, in the mind of the phenomenologist, even he did not grasp. It is logical to conclude from his analysis that knowledge is constituted by the mind; the difficulty is that Hume did not see it that way. Thus both Descartes and Hume started in the right place, with consciousness itself, but came to the wrong conclusions because they conceived of knowledge exclusively in terms of true statements about external reality.

According to Husserl, it was Kant who had the first clear and explicit insight into phenomenological philosophy. The problem Kant set out to solve is well known: in the face of Hume's analysis how is knowledge of the external world possible? The solution to the problem in Kant's thought involves what phenomenologists regard as a genuine turn to the idea of the transcendental. Zaner quotes the following key passage from *The Critique of Pure Reason*: "Hitherto it has been assumed that all our knowledge must conform to objects. But all attempts to extend our knowledge of objects by establishing something in regard to them a priori, by means of concepts, have, on this assumption, ended in failure. We must therefore make trial whether we may not have more success in the tasks of meta-

---

13 *Ibid.*, p. 96.

physics, if we suppose that objects must conform to our knowledge."[14]

Kant's efforts were directed toward a demonstration that experience was not possible, that is, not intelligible, unless sensible intuitions such as space and time and synthetic a priori concepts such as causality were contributed to the matter of sensation by the mental apparatus of the knowing subject. In effect, Kant solved the problem of Descartes and Hume by eliminating it. The precise question, in Kantian terms, no longer involved the possibility of certain knowledge about reality itself. The transcendental turn made a divine bridge between subject and object unnecessary. Knowledge, according to Kant, arises directly out of experience but is made possible only by the constitutive faculty of consciousness. However, there is no question of knowledge about things-in-themselves but only of phenomena. Similarly, Kant answered Hume's skepticism not by claiming a knowledge of reality itself but rather a knowledge of appearances determined by the synthetic a priori concepts of the mind.

Phenomenology: Husserl's Solution to the Philosophical Problem of Knowledge

Husserl believed that a strict and complete science of philosophy is possible with Kant's transcendental subjectivity as a point of departure. As Quentin Lauer explains:

Kant has specified the ideal order as belonging exclusively to subjectivity and its necessity as attaching solely to the formalizing function of reason. Husserl sought to extend necessity from form to content, thus a priorizing the whole of knowledge. . . . Husserl was . . . not the first philosopher to identify being and intelligibility. Nor was he the first to seek in subjectivity an explanation of intelligibility. It is difficult, however, to find a philosopher who identifies being and intelligibility as deliberately as does Husserl in making both depend on constitutive intentionality. According to this theory not only is knowledge constituted in consciousness, but the very being of that which is known is so constituted; only absolute being is being in the full sense, and only being in con-

---

[14] *Ibid.*, p. 102.

sciousness is absolute being. Now, since being is in consciousness only as constituted, being is absolute only as constituted. Thus, intentional constitution has become a universal explanation or clarification of being.[15]

Thus, according to Husserl, Kant stopped short in limiting the a priori function of consciousness to the purely formal aspects of knowledge. As Lauer suggests, intentionality should be regarded as the central concept of phenomenology. In Husserl's mind, it was the key to the solution of all metaphysical problems. In *Ideas,* he says, "We understood under Intentionality the unique peculiarity of experiences 'to be the consciousness of something.' It was in the explicit cogito that we first came across this wonderful property to which all metaphysical enigmas and riddles of the theoretical reason lead us back."[16] The ground of Husserl's philosophical position depends on the validity of the concept of intentionality. This concept can be understood best in terms of a distinction between an object of thought as it is present in consciousness and an object, presumed to exist in the external world, about which we may think. It is the former to which Husserl refers as intentional objects or correlates of consciousness. Furthermore, intentional objects are not to be understood in a merely psychological sense. Just as the sum in an addition problem may be said to have a being of its own so too with the intentional objects of consciousness. Thus phenomenology may be understood as the analysis of intentional objects. Elsewhere in *Ideas* Husserl explains a bit more fully:

> It belongs as a general feature to the essence of every actual cogito to be a consciousness of something. . . . All experiences which have this essential property in common are also called "intentional experiences," insofar as they are a consciousness of something they are said to be intentionally related to this something. We must, however, be quite clear on this point that there is no question here of a relation between a psychological event—called experience—and some other real existent—called Object—or of a psychological connexion obtaining between the one and the other in objective reality. On the contrary, we are concerned with experiences in their essential purity, with pure essences, and with that which is involved in the essence "a priori," in unconditioned necessity.[17]

---

15 Quentin Lauer, *Phenomenology: Its Genesis and Prospect* (New York: Harper & Row, 1965) , p. 79.
16 *Ideas*, pp. 242–43.
17 *Ibid.*, pp. 119–20.

In capsule form, the quotation conveys vividly and succinctly a sense of the direction and concern of Husserl's philosophy. He envisioned a strict science of philosophy grounded securely in the immediate experiences of consciousness and culminating in the comprehension of the realm of pure experience or pure consciousness itself. One can understand the complex method of phenomenological reduction as a process of gradually refining the content of consciousness in order to purge any psychological elements and render possible a knowledge of the essence of the intentional object.[18]

Though one may doubt the attainability or even the comprehensibility of Husserl's goal, it is nevertheless possible to grasp the underlying motive of his thought. In effect, Husserl transferred or transformed the content of knowledge. In the context of phenomenology, knowledge does not consist in a relationship or connection of consciousness with the external world. In his own mind, Husserl solved the philosophical problem of knowledge by the ingenious and logically impeccable strategy of simply eliminating external reality from consideration. In this way, Husserl accomplished two objectives: first, in refusing to make any statements at all about reality, he avoided being caught in the agelong controversy between realism and idealism;[19] second, in seizing on the idea of intentional objects and attributing an independent existence to them, he laid a foundation for the claim that the objective of philosophy is pure knowledge. It is in this light that one must understand the antinaturalism of phenomenology. Specifically, Husserl was opposed to what he called "the naturalizing of consciousness," that is, any doctrine according to which consciousness and all of its "immanent data" are explainable completely in naturalistic terms.[20] In Husserl's mind, all such ideas can lead only to relativism and skepticism, but never to pure knowledge. Husserl most certainly did claim that his philosophy could make significant contributions toward the clarification of the presuppo-

---

[18] Phenomenological reduction seems to be a generic name for a process that involves several steps. Again, references to the method are scattered throughout Husserl's writing. A good discussion of it may be found in Lauer, *Phenomenology*, Chap. 3.

[19] This is a difficult point. For obvious reasons Husserl himself could certainly be regarded as an idealist. However, his precise point might be not that the mind constitutes reality but that it constitutes knowledge. Furthermore, Husserl did not like to be associated with the extravagant speculations of Hegelianism. He believed that in the concept of intentionality he had found solid ground for philosophy.

[20] *Philosophy as a Strict Science*, p. 5.

sitions of all the empirical sciences but his main purpose was
not to cast doubt on any of the particular findings of these sciences either physical or social. In the context of this paper,
what is most important is the idea that phenomenology must
be considered primarily as an approach to knowledge not in
the empirical or naturalistic sense but in the philosophical sense.
The phenomenological critique of empiricism should be regarded as originating from within a different level or area of concern.

II

Though Husserl believed in the applicability of phenomenology to all fields of inquiry he had little to say about the social sciences, and the specific character of social scientific theorizing was to him still problematic. In *Ideas* Husserl comments
on the mental or cultural sciences: "we provisionally leave it
an open question whether they are to be held similar to the natural sciences or placed in opposition to them, be themselves
accepted as natural sciences or as sciences of an essentially new
type."[21]

Thus it is clear that from the standpoint of phenomenology,
Schutz, in his work in the social sciences, was breaking new
ground. With phenomenologists there is always the question of
whether a particular approach is true to the principles of Husserlian phenomenology. This problem arises because Husserl's
concepts are difficult to understand and obviously open to different interpretations. Husserl himself frequently commented
that his ideas were often misunderstood even by his closest intellectual disciples. There is some disagreement among students
of phenomenology as to whether it is relevant to the problems
of the social sciences.[22] At any rate, there is no question but that
Schutz was profoundly influenced by Husserl and thought of
himself as a phenomenologist. He wrote articles specifically
about Husserl and phenomenology and kept in touch with him
for many years. Moreover, in his social scientific work, he acknowledges his greatest intellectual debt to Husserl. Schutz was
convinced that phenomenological concepts made possible an un-

---

21 *Ideas,* p. 52.
22 Hans Neisser, "The Phenomenological Approach in Social Science," *Philosophy
and Phenomenological Research*, 20 (1959), 198–212. Neisser argues that phenomenology is restricted in application to logic and mathematics.

derstanding of the social sciences in essentially new terms. The strength of this conviction is evident in the kind of question Schutz raised about society as presupposed, in his emphasis on the meanings intended by the actors in the common sense world, in his descriptive analysis of the structure of this world, and in his specific statements about the new possibilities opened up by phenomenology. In several places, Schutz echoed the sentiments of his teacher about the misinterpretations of phenomenology, and there is solid evidence that Husserl regarded Schutz as one of his most apt and faithful followers.

The Common Sense World as Presupposed

According to Schutz, the common sense world of ordinary life is presupposed or taken for granted. The fact of intersubjectivity which is the basis of all science, art, philosophy and society itself is merely assumed without question. But how are we to explain what makes mutual understanding and communication possible at all? Schutz asserts that this kind of question cannot be answered by the methods of the social sciences. Instead, it requires a philosophical analysis, specifically, a phenomenological one. As Schutz says, "a psychology from which a solution of the problems of the cultural sciences might be expected must become aware of the fact that it is not a science which deals with empirical facts. It has to be a science of essences, . . . [which deals with] the invariant, peculiar, and essential structures of the mind; but that is to say it examines their a priori structure. . . . such a true psychology of intentionality is, according to Husserl's words, nothing other than a constitutive phenomenology of the natural attitude."[23]

Obviously, it was Schutz's interest in phenomenology that led him to consider questions about the nature of intersubjectivity in an a priori sense. Husserl believed that a priori foundations were necessary to establish the validity of any empirical science. It was on this level, according to Schutz, that phenomenology could make its distinctive contribution to the social sciences. Undoubtedly, empiricists would argue with this position. However, there is serious doubt about the importance of the problem. The nature of Schutz's concern about the question of a priori foundations is far from clear, and it is difficult to un-

[23] Alfred Schutz, "Phenomenology and the Social Sciences," in *Collected Papers*, ed. Maurice Natanson (The Hague: Nijhoff, 1962), p. 132.

derstand his solution to the problem except in empirical or naturalistic terms.

There are different kinds of metaphysical problems, and apart from the general question of their usefulness or validity it is often possible to understand at least the sense of them. In other words, even if one has concluded that such questions are usually the result of logical or syntactical confusion one may nevertheless grasp the motive of a particular question and know in some specific way why it is being asked. This seems to me to be true of Kant's questions concerning the possibility of science and the possibility of freedom.

Kant of course was impressed by the achievements of the natural sciences in the seventeenth and eighteenth centuries. Nevertheless, he was at the same time convinced of the cogency of Hume's argument that reason could not establish the principle of causality and that therefore scientists could not legitimately speak about laws governing events in the external world. Hence, Kant was led to ask not whether science is possible but how it is possible. The point is that the sense of such a question can be grasped only if the impulse behind it is understood. In the absence of a solution to the problem of scientific knowledge in terms of synthetic a priori knowledge, one could fall back only on Hume's skepticism—to Kant an unsatisfactory alternative. Similarly, the specific character of Kant's interest in the problem of freedom is understandable in the context of his philosophical position. The idea of man as merely a thing in nature no different from other things in nature was repugnant to him. Yet the idea that reason could not know the truth about things-in-themselves dictated the course of his inquiry. Kant did not ask whether man was in fact free or if he could actually become free but rather the metaphysical question as to how it is possible to conceive of man as free. In the absence of a solution to the problem of freedom in terms of a will activated by duty alone, the only alternative is to think of man as essentially and absolutely determined; in other words, as merely a thing in nature. In Kant's mind, this alternative too was unsatisfactory.

As far as intersubjectivity is concerned, one may agree with Schutz that a great deal of the content of ordinary experience is taken for granted or presupposed. But what do these expressions mean? To say that we take an object or event or person or institution for granted clearly suggests a kind of blank acceptance of something which should or at least could be thought about in some productive way. Thus when I pick up the newspaper that is delivered to my house every day, it rarely occurs to me to reflect about what is involved in publishing and distributing a daily newspaper. Surely, if I understood this my appreciation of the accomplishment would be increased. The same is true of other activities, institutions, and events and even of society itself. But why is it not sufficient to investigate problems of this kind from a naturalistic point of view? In what sense is Schutz's question about communication a request for a priori knowledge?

A cardinal rule of phenomenology is to doubt whatever could conceivably be otherwise. The point presumably is to make possible clear intuitions about the inner nature of things. But perhaps the rule itself should be questioned—at least in relation to particular kinds of doubt. I believe the difficulty here has to do with the claim that phenomenology can contribute to the advancement of all natural sciences. Kant made no such claim and it is clear that his questions pertain only to the idea of man as a rational being. Therefore, his solutions are understandable strictly in metaphysical or transcendental terms. Aside from the vagueness of the philosophical problem of other minds, the entrance of phenomenology, with its a priori concerns, into substantively empirical areas of enquiry is a source of confusion. In other words, it seems that Schutz, though he would have denied it, is really asking an essentially naturalistic question. Again, the contrast with Kant is suggestive. For instance, animals do not construct scientific theories, and it makes no sense to ask how freedom is possible for them since they are wholly determined as are other things in nature. For Kant, the problem of society as the world of common sense meanings would have raised only empirical questions. Intersubjectivity is not at all peculiar to man as a rational being. Ants communicate with each other as do bees, fish and gorillas. Animals have complex social and political systems in which individual members understand each other, in which they cooperate in doing work, in which values are authoritatively allocated and so forth. It makes no sense to wonder how this animal intersubjectivity is "possible" in terms of some a prioristic meaning. By the same token, it may be as inapt to ask how human society is "possible" as it would be to ask how arms and legs are "possible."

An analysis of Schutz's solution to the problem he has posed strengthens the impression that he is not dealing with a non-naturalistic subject matter. In speaking of the constructs of the common sense world, Schutz refers to "stocks of knowledge," "the sedimentation of previous experience," the idea of "reciprocal perspectives," "because and in-order-to motives" and, in general, to the "social derivation and distribution of knowledge."[24] It is difficult to argue with Schutz's abstract descriptions. However, the reader is left to wonder why such concepts are anything more than simple, empirical generalizations or in what sense they are a priori or can lead to a priori knowledge. It seems to me that this point is crucial to the validity of Schutz's approach. The usefulness of a phenomenological analysis depends on the assumption that a meaning is a non-naturalistic entity which is not subject to understanding in terms of an empirical or naturalistic methodology. Some of the ambiguities involved in Schutz's treatment of this problem will be discussed in the next section.

The Common Sense World as Object of Knowledge

To avoid a potential misinterpretation, I should point out that Schutz's emphasis on the world of common sense is not intended as a recommendation of a way of thinking about practical social and political problems. For instance, Charles McClelland implies that common sense is not adequate as a method of understanding such complex problems and that scientific theories are therefore necessary.[25] On the other side, Leo Strauss argues in favor of the indispensability of common-sense understanding and tries to develop the argument that an empiricist approach to political matters leads more often to confusion than to clarity.[26] Schutz's treatment of the concept of common sense should not be interpreted as support for Strauss's anti-empiricist argument. Schutz does not contend that common sense is superior to science as a way of understanding social reality. His major concern is that the common sense world be understood by the social scientist; presumably, one attains a genuine knowledge of this world not through common sense itself, which merely takes what is given for granted, but scientifically.

---

24 Alfred Schutz, "Common Sense and Scientific Interpretation of Human Action," *Philosophy and Phenomenological Research,* 14 (Sept. 1953), 1–37.
25 Charles McClelland, *Theory and the International System* (New York: Macmillan, 1966), Chap. 1.
26 Leo Strauss, *Essays on the Scientific Study of Politics,* ed. Herbert Storing (New York: Holt, Rinehart & Winston, 1962), Epilogue.

According to Schutz, the basic problems of the social sciences revolve around the interpretation and analysis of the structure of common sense thinking. The task of the social scientist is to understand social reality in terms of the meanings that acts have for the actors involved in daily life. This task, he asserts, cannot be accomplished by a social science that patterns itself wholly on the methodological principles of the natural sciences. Here, Schutz makes his key distinction between the natural and social sciences:

> The facts, data, and events with which the natural scientist has to deal are just facts, data and events within his observational field but this field does not "mean" anything to the molecules, atoms, and electrons therein. Yet the facts, events and data before the social scientist are of an entirely different structure. His observational field, the social world, is not principally unstructurized. It has a particular meaning and relevance structure for the human beings living, thinking and acting therein. . . . The thought objects constructed by the social scientists refer to and are founded upon the thought objects constructed by the common sense thought of man living his every day life among his fellowmen. Thus, the constructs used by the social scientist are, so to speak, constructs of the second degree, namely constructs of the constructs made by the actors on the social scene whose behavior the scientist observes and tries to explain in accordance with the procedural rules of his science.[27]

This language is certainly suggestive and might sound promising to the proponent of some anti-empiricist point of view. Yet Schutz immediately asserts that this insight into the fundamental difference between the natural and social worlds should not lead to the "erroneous conclusion that the social sciences are *toto coelo* different from the natural sciences, a view which disregards the fact that certain procedural rules relating to correct thought organization are common to all empirical sciences."[28] Since Schutz does not discuss in detail the nature of these "procedural rules," it is difficult to know exactly what he is arguing with empiricists about and what he is conceding to them. In itself, the distinction he has drawn between the natural and social worlds does not have any necessarily significant implications. Elsewhere, Schutz clarifies his position. In reply to an argument by Ernest Nagel in support of the empirical approach,

---

27 Alfred Schutz, "Common Sense and Scientific Interpretation," p. 3.
28 *Ibid.*, p. 4.

Schutz, after agreeing with Nagel on several points, declares that Nagel is "prevented from grasping the point of vital concern to social scientists by his basic philosophy of sensationalistic empiricism or logical positivism which identifies experience wth sensory observation and which assumes that the only alternative to controllable and, therefore, objective sensory observation is that of subjective and, therefore, uncontrollable and unverifiable introspection."[29] In this, Schutz states what he regarded as of fundamental importance in the key distinction between the natural and social worlds. His argument can be understood in terms of four basic propositions: 1) the social world is constituted essentially by meanings; 2) the philosophy of sensationalistic empiricism, based as it is on the need for sensory observation, recognizes only overt behavior; 3) but meanings are different from overt behavior and as such are not susceptible to sensory observation; 4) therefore, since social reality consists of meanings, it cannot be understood by sensationalistic empiricism.

It seems to me that as a critique of contemporary empiricism Schutz's position is untenable in several respects. First, there is ambiguity involved in his use of the term "sensory observation." He agrees with Nagel that observation is necessary but not that it "has to be sensory in the precise meaning of this term."[30] Schutz never indicates exactly what he means by "observation." His argument that empiricism assumes a "face to face relationship"[31] suggests that he has identified empiricism in general with some form of rigid behaviorism. It has been pointed out often that such a view no longer describes the position of empiricists.[32] Schutz is at least imprecise in implying that Nagel identifies experience with sensory observation and therefore has eliminated the possibility of access to the realm of meanings. Second, to support his argument, Schutz cites examples of experiences which are not amenable to verification by means of

29 Alfred Schutz, "Concept and Theory Formation in the Social Sciences," *The Journal of Philosophy*, 51 (April 1954), 261.

30 *Ibid.*, p. 260.

31 *Ibid.*, p. 263.

32 See, for example, Arthur Kalleberg, "Concept Formation in Normative and Empirical Studies," *American Political Science Review*, 63 (March 1969). Kalleberg quite carefully points this out. However, it seems to me that his article is misleading in suggesting that Schutz is a normativist. Absent from the article is the note of surprise which is appropriate to the fact that Schutz apparently charges empiricism with not doing what empiricists usually do. Indeed, most empiricists would not know what to do instead.

sensory observation. For instance, we know that people called postmen will perform certain acts with respect to letters we have mailed so that we may usually look forward confidently to a particular result such as the delivery of a book we have ordered.[33] Probably no empiricist would deny the validity of this kind of knowledge. However, Schutz does not explain at all why he believes it is not the result of sensory observation. Every actor in the social world has had a great many sensory observations which are clearly related to mail distribution. Nagel did not outlaw inferences and he has never said that each and every step in a complex process such as mail distribution must be subject to direct sensory observation before we are entitled to make assertions about it. Third, though Schutz criticizes the empiricist requirement of sensory observation he explicitly acknowledges the need for "controlled verification," or "testable general hypotheses," or "empirically ascertainable regularities."[34] Again, we are faced with the problem of what Schutz has in mind. It is certain that he much preferred to approach the problem of verification in terms of "typical constructs" and "invariant behavior." But this merely raises again the question of why such concepts are any more than empirical generalizations. Fourth, Schutz has focused on the idea of common sense knowledge as though it could explain everything about social reality. Nobody will deny that there is a wide area of experience concerning which intersubjectivity may be taken as a fact. But the kinds of understandings involved in this area are trivial and unproblematic. It seems that Schutz, in concentrating on the idea of common sense knowledge, would have social science end precisely where it ought to begin.[35] The most important problems of the social sciences arise from the fact that genuine intersubjectivity does not exist with respect to the problematic and crucial areas of social experience.

The Postulate of Subjective Interpretation

The idea of subjective interpretation may well be the most fertile single source of controversy and misunderstanding among social scientists. There is perhaps no issue over which normativists and empiricists are apparently more decisively and

---

[33] Schutz, "Concept and Theory Formation," p. 263.
[34] *Ibid.*, pp. 270–72.
[35] This is a point on which many empiricists and normativists might agree.

hopelessly in disagreement. Natanson regards it as fundamental and justifies the description of Schutz as a subjectivist by referring to the latter's insistence on the need for subjective understanding.[36] Moreover, Schutz's repeated use of the word *Verstehen* is perhaps primarily responsible for the mistaken idea that his approach to social science offers a significant alternative to empiricism.[37]

At first glance, it appears evident that Schutz and the empiricists disagree sharply on this point. Here, as elsewhere, Schutz's language does suggest an approach that empiricists have taken great pains to discredit. However, a more careful reading of his work will reveal that there is no disagreement at all. As it often does, the issue centers around the ideas of Max Weber, who at one time or another seems to have been praised or blamed by practically everyone for almost everything. Schutz acknowledged an important intellectual debt to Weber and felt constrained to defend him against Nagel's critique of his concept of verstehen. The fact that Schutz does defend Weber on this point indeed strengthens the impression that he is defending an anti-empiricist position. Yet this impression is dispelled when we understand the exact nature of the defense.

Nagel's well-known critique of verstehen involves three related assertions: 1) there is no reason to believe that we can understand human motives better than we do events in the natural world; 2) in order to understand human behavior it is not necessary to identify with the human subjects under investigation; 3) empathy or identification does not entitle us to claim warranted assertibility for statements allegedly explaining human actions.[38] Nagel's position of course involves very complex questions and his argument goes to the heart of a subjective point of view. Schutz's defense of Weber is simplicity itself: "I merely submit that I do not know of any social scientist of stature who ever advocated such a concept of subjectivity as that criticized by Professor Nagel. Most certainly this was not the position of Max Weber."[39] Thus Schutz agrees with Nagel on all the substantive issues involved in the latter's critique of a concept of verstehen. His argument on Weber's behalf is to as-

---

36 Natanson, *Philosophy of the Social Sciences,* Introduction and pp. 186-87.
37 For example, Kalleberg, "Concept Formation."
38 Schutz, "Theory and Concept Formation," pp. 259–60.
39 *Ibid.,* p. 261.

sert only that Weber did not believe what Nagel thinks he believed.

This confusion can be unravelled without too much difficulty. Nagel understood Weber but did not agree with him. Schutz claimed to agree with Weber but did not understand him. According to Schutz, the discussion of the problem of verstehen is usually unsatisfactory because of a failure to distinguish three possible uses of the term: 1) as the experiential form of common-sense knowledge; 2) as an epistemological problem; 3) as a method peculiar to the social sciences.[40] To Schutz, verstehen is important in the first two senses but not in the third. In other words, it is understood by him to refer to the fact of common sense understanding itself and to the peculiar epistemological problem of how this understanding is possible. In regard to the third sense, Schutz claims that verstehen is "primarily not a method used by the social scientist, . . . It has nothing to do with introspection."[41] I would say that Schutz is clearly wrong in his reading of Weber. In his work on the methodology of the social sciences, Weber repeatedly uses expressions such as "empathy," "emotional understanding," "sympathetic participation," and refers to the investigator's capacity "to 'feel him-self' into a mode of thought which deviates from his own."[42] Thus in defending Weber, Schutz has explained away what is distinctively subjective in Weber's approach.

Perhaps it is possible to expose the root of this problem by mentioning the familiar empiricist distinction between the contexts of discovery and justification.[43] Nagel's argument is that though the method of verstehen may be useful within the context of discovery, it is not within the context of justification. In other words, verstehen, understood as empathy or sympathetic participation, cannot by itself serve to legitimize a knowledge claim. Schutz wholeheartedly agrees that private, uncontrollable and unverifiable intuitions do not make a scientific theory. He asserts that Weber, too, was in full accord. I would maintain, on the contrary, that Weber would probably have dissented

---

40 *Ibid.,* p. 265.
41 *Ibid.,* p. 264.
42 Max Weber, *The Methodology of the Social Sciences,* ed. Edward A. Shils and Henry A. Finch (Glencoe, Ill.: Free Press, 1949), pp. 40–41.
43 Hans Reichenbach, *Experience and Prediction* (Chicago: Univ. of Chicago Press, 1961), pp. 6–7.

from this position as stated by Nagel and Schutz.

This is of course an exceedingly difficult problem. I believe that the language used by empiricists on this point is usually not analyzed adequately. Furthermore, it is language which Schutz approves of and apparently accepts without question. But to what exactly do words such as "private," "uncontrollable," and "unverifiable" refer? What is meant by the statement that "knowledge must be statable in propositional form and capable of being verified by anyone who is prepared to make the effort to do so through observation."[44] I might be thoroughly prepared to make the effort to verify the propositions which are stated in mathematical form in quantum mechanics. Yet the chances are slim that I will ever do so because I have no idea what the propositions mean. In other words, in terms of this formulation, how can we tell in advance who is "prepared" to make what kinds of "efforts?" The formulation seems to imply that anybody is capable of understanding any kind of truth no matter how complex or profound. If the formulation is expanded to include a qualification about a requisite degree of intelligence the result is simply to beg more questions. No amount of careful phrasing can eliminate this difficulty. Anyone who takes his own views seriously would not think of describing them as private, uncontrollable or unverifiable. The most esoteric philosopher or mystic could easily and perhaps sensibly claim that his ideas are the result of controlled inference; that they are statable in propositional form and that they are most certainly verifiable by anyone who is able to make the effort.

The point is that the criteria agreed upon by Schutz and the empiricists as to what constitutes a valid scientific theory always seem reducible, under whatever formulation, to the likelihood of widespread agreement. As to the explanation of human motives and conduct there is little likelihood of significant agreement about significant problems. I think Max Weber might have argued along similar lines. The method of verstehen is a method peculiar to the social sciences and should be understood not only in the context of discovery but as an important element in the context of justification as well. Indeed, a strict separation between discovery and justification is unrealistic since empathetic understanding may itself be an important aspect of the evidence adduced to support an explanation of a particular

---

44 Schutz, "Concept and Theory Formation," p. 260.

situation or event. Where Schutz and Nagel appear to be talking about evidence, they are talking instead about agreement, and one does not necessarily have anything to do with the other. Furthermore, both seem to assume that verstehen, as I believe Weber understood it, is a passport to intellectual irresponsibility and that it implies an indifference to evidence. This is not at all true. The problem of care and integrity in research is one of which Weber was very acutely aware. Verstehen implies simply that social reality is complicated and that, as with any other subject, some people know more about it than others. The problem of subjective interpretation is crucial in its bearing on the issues that divide social scientists. I think it is evident that Schutz has misinterpreted Weber and has sided with empiricism on this fundamental question.

The Role of the Social Scientist

The essential compatibility of Schutz with empiricism is apparent also in his idea of the role of the social scientist. Here, too, I believe the point is best made by means of a contrast between Schutz and Weber. The specific problem involves the claim that the social scientist must be "objective" and "detached" in his scientific work. As with the problem of verstehen, there is some surface confusion here as well. This is the result primarily of two facts: 1) Weber, because of his advocacy of a "value free" social science, is generally regarded as a champion of scientific detachment; 2) Schutz's repeated acknowledgment of a profound intellectual debt to Weber.[45] Nevertheless, I think it can be shown that Schutz's misinterpretation of Weber was complete and that the two men had basically different ideas about the nature of social science.

Schutz explained clearly what he meant by "detachment." He states: "The attitude of the social scientist is that of a mere disinterested observer of the social world. He is not involved in the observed situation, which is to him not of practical but merely of cognitive interest."[46] Later in defining more completely the difference between common sense constructs and scientific ones, Schutz says that the latter have no "here"; that is, the

---

[45] Schutz, *Collected Papers*, p. 138. Here Schutz credits Weber with having "given the principles of a method which attempts to explain all social phenomena in the broadest sense."

[46] Schutz, "Common Sense and Scientific Interpretation," p. 28.

models of the actors which are created by the social scientist "are not human beings living within their biographical situation in the social world of every day life. Strictly speaking they do not have any biography or any history."[47] Schutz's idea of detachment involves the obligation of the social scientist to construct concepts that supersede those of common sense thinking. By "supersede" Schutz does not imply that the social scientist must understand more deeply than the average man the motivations or causes of particular events in the social world. He means that the social scientist must understand the subjective world of ordinary life "objectively" by devising models of invariant motives and constructs of typicality. Thus when Schutz speaks of detachment, he is referring to his own conception of the aim of social science: the acquisition of theoretical knowledge which is abstract and descriptive in the sense of being deliberately disconnected from any concrete event or problem. In effect, the object of Schutz's social science is a pure theory of the social world—in his own terms, a constitutive phenomenology of social reality.[48]

Weber seems to have had no such interest, and the fact that Schutz so frequently mentioned him as an intellectual progenitor is something of a mystery. Weber says: "The type of social science in which we are interested is an empirical science of concrete reality. Our aim is the understanding of the characteristic uniqueness of the reality in which we move."[49] And later, in a statement that almost seems to have been written in anticipation of Schutz's interpretation of him, Weber declares:

> For the knowledge of historical phenomena in their concreteness, the most general laws, because they are devoid of content are also the least valuable. The more comprehensive the validity—or scope— of a term, the more it leads us away from the richness of reality since in order to include the common elements of the largest possible number of phenomena, it must necessarily be as abstract as possible and hence devoid of content. In the cultural sciences, the knowledge of the universal or general is never valuable in itself.[50]

---

47 *Ibid.,* p. 32.
48 An empiricist might object that he is certainly not interested in something called a "pure" theory. My response would be in two parts: 1) there is certainly more than just a similarity between Schutz's theories and those of some of the more ambitious systems theorists; 2) apart from that question, my main purpose here is to indicate the agreement between Schutz and empiricists on the need for "detachment."
49 Weber, *Methodology of the Social Sciences,* p. 72.
50 *Ibid.,* p. 80.

In short, Schutz's reliance on Weber is a source only of confusion. Weber, it seems to me, has been widely misunderstood with respect to both his idea of value freedom and his concept of ideal types. What Weber said about values is simply that their ultimate validity cannot be established by empirical science and that therefore social scientists should not make extravagant claims on the basis of some alleged scientific knowledge. This is a recommendation of ordinary honesty which in no way implies the need for strict neutrality or detachment in the investigation of reality. Similarly, Weber's concept of ideal types was not meant to be understood in any technical sense or as some kind of pure essence. An ideal type is simply a generalization, made possible by verstehen and supported by evidence, about the motives or causes which allegedly explain some social or historical event. The purpose of the concept is not to establish "objectively valid" knowledge in some virtually unchallengeable scientific sense but to make understandable and subjectively meaningful a very complex order of reality. As Weber said, "Whoever accepts the proposition that the knowledge of historical reality can or should be a presuppositionless copy of 'objective' facts, will deny the value of the ideal type."[51]

Conclusion

Whether Schutz's emphasis on the primary importance of the world of common sense meaning is essentially new is a matter on which social scientists may disagree. There will be disagreement as well on the question of the nature of his approach to the social sciences. There can be no doubt that Schutz regarded himself as anti-empirical on the philosophical level. Yet his assertion of the need for a phenomenological analysis of the fact of intersubjectivity is not easy to understand or accept. The concepts he presents as apparently constituting the a priori foundations of a science of society seem to be no more than empty empirical generalizations. Indeed, in reading Schutz it is difficult to avoid the conclusion that his analyses of the common sense world consist of a series of complex and overdrawn truisms. In effect, his solution to the problem of a presupposed realm of intersubjectivity is simply to presuppose it again.

Furthermore, the argument that Schutz is an empiricist, his own statements to the contrary notwithstanding, is a strong one.

---

[51] *Ibid.*, p. 92.

His disagreement with empiricism on the need for verification by means of sensory observation is not at all clear. Generally, empiricists would not accept his apparently rigid interpretation of their position. Moreover, Schutz himself insists on the need for verification in some objective, scientific sense but never explains how it is to be accomplished. Since his opposition to empiricism centers on this point, the absence of any significant discussion of it is a serious weakness in the presentation of his ideas. His answer most likely would be that the common-sense constructs he deals with are given in experience as part of the structure of intersubjectivity. But, once again, if we cannot see how these concepts can be regarded as anything but empirical generalizations, then there is reason enough to suspect that phenomenology has nothing new to contribute to social science. In addition, Schutz seems to be in full agreement with empiricism on most other problems of fundamental importance.

Clearly Schutz believed that he had focused on a major problem of the social sciences. His emphasis on common-sense meanings was intended not only as a caution to those who might forget social reality itself in favor of a reified concept of government or nation or society but also as a way of illuminating the fact that people may often grasp truths without the need for proofs or demonstrations in a strict, empiricist sense. This is indeed a genuine problem. However, I think Schutz was led in the wrong direction by the influence of phenomenology. It seems that he could imagine only two alternatives: either a rigid empiricism or a search for a priori knowledge. The implication of his position is that within the natural attitude, sensory observation is the sole means of verification and that therefore no avenue to the thorough understanding of meanings is available except through phenomenology. At the same time, Schutz contended that phenomenological analysis is essential to clarification on the empirical level and he was certainly committed to objectivity in the sense of positive science. The result is a kind of theorizing which is as remote from the problems of social and political life as that of the most abstract systems theorist. Even if Schutz's objections to empiricism on the philosophical level are considered significant in themselves, it is nevertheless clear that his approach to the social sciences offers no alternative that would be acceptable to subjectivists.

Structuralism and Semiology

A. The Humanities
B. The Social Sciences

Structuralism
and Romantic Mythmaking

Gene Bernstein

University of Notre Dame

THE resurgence of interest in myth during the Romantic period has been well documented in recent years for it is of great importance to an understanding of Romantic thought.[1] As Thomas Ashton has pointed out: ."The romantic sense of distance lured antiquarians back to older days and primitive civilizations where *sublime* works that would inspire a fallen present might be found."[2] The significance of this revived interest has barely been examined however. Perhaps this is due to the fact that critics have passively accepted the pejorative connotation of mythology as a corpus of fantastic, irrelevant stories and legends, in which case their neglect is justifiable. But the recent work of Lévi-Strauss and other structurally oriented anthropologists indicates that primitive mythology is anything but fantastic and irrelevant.

On the contrary, their work reveals that primitive mythology is as sophisticated as modern technology and that the mythic consciousness which produced these myths represents a paradigm of the way in which the human mind is structured. It is

---

[1] Among the prominent works dealing with Romantic poetry and mythology consulted for this essay are the following: Douglas Bush, *Mythology and the Romantic Tradition in English Poetry* (1937; rpt. New York: Norton, 1963); Harold Bloom, *Shelley's Mythmaking* (1959; rpt. Ithaca: Cornell Univ. Press, 1969); Walter Evert, *Aesthetic and Myth in the Poetry of Keats* (Princeton: Princeton Univ. Press, 1965); Albert Kuhn, "English Deism and the Development of Romantic Mythological Syncretism," *PMLA*, 35 (Dec. 1956); and Alex Zwerdling, "The Mythographers and the Romantic Revival of Greek Myth," *PMLA*, 79 (Sept. 1964).

[2] Thomas Ashton, ed., *Byron's Hebrew Melodies* (Austin: Univ. of Texas Press, 1973), p. 3. Of course, Ashton's comment relates most directly to the Old Testament, but it is no less valid in relation to classical antiquity as well.

precisely this mythic state of mind which characterizes Romantic mythmaking and which lends itself to structural analysis. Both structuralism and Romantic mythmaking are concerned with self-consciousness, the relationship between man and nature, and the function of both language and poetry.

We can define mythology in the broadest sense as "a complex of stories—some no doubt fact, and some fantasy—which, for various reasons, human beings regard as demonstrations of the inner meaning of the universe and of human life,"[3] yet dealing with mythology is a genuine problem. No matter how seriously one approaches myth, as Lévi-Strauss informs us, "The notion of 'myth' is a category of our thought which we use arbitrarily in order to bring together under one word attempts to explain natural phenomena, products of oral literature, philosophical speculation, and cases where linguistic processes emerged to full consciousness."[4] Despite the arbitrariness of the notion however, the processes underlying the creation of myths are neither capricious nor imaginary; in fact, they represent real and significant structures of the mind which seek to order experience into a discernible pattern. Just as myths seek to demonstrate "the inner meaning of the universe and of human life," the Romantics attempted to explain the innermost recesses of the human mind and its relation to the world of experience. Thus, affinities between the mythic consciousness and Romantic esthetics are undeniable, as Alan Chaffee is quick to note: "In effect, they [the Romantics] desired to recover what stands as the object of every esthetic revolution; an understanding of the principles of mind which motivate poetic creation, which temper the mind of the responsive reader."[5] In attempting to understand these principles of mind through the structuralist method, we may hope to comprehend more clearly the Romantic revolution in esthetics, a revolution which asserted, in M. H. Abrams's words, that art was "for man's sake, and for life's sake."[6]

---

3 This definition by Alan Watts is cited in Philip Wheelright, "The Semantic Approach to Myth," *Myth: A Symposium*, ed. Thomas Sebeok (Bloomington: Indiana Univ. Press, 1971), p. 154.
4 Claude Lévi-Strauss, *Totemism*, trans. R. Needham (Boston: Beacon Press, 1963), p. 10.
5 Alan Chaffee, "The Rendezvous of Mind," *The Wordsworth Circle*, 3 (Autumn 1972), p. 203.
6 M. H. Abrams, *Natural Supernaturalism: Tradition and Revolution in Romantic Literature* (New York: Norton, 1971), p. 429.

I

The historical antecedents of the revival of interest in myth during the Romantic period have been definitively set forth in Douglas Bush's *Mythology and the Romantic Tradition in English Poetry*. As an encyclopedic work of abbreviated remarks about poems dealing with mythology over a 250-year period (1680–1930), with an occasional venture into explication, the book is primarily concerned with the letter of mythology rather than the spirit of mythmaking. Among the many valuable observations in the book is Bush's reminder that though mythology was used widely during the Renaissance, there was also a "steadily growing consciousness of disharmony between Christian and pagan ideals."[7]

Despite various attempts to rationalize this disharmony, a complete dissociation between Christian and pagan ideals occurred during the eighteenth century. Greek myths fell into disrepute and were considered solely in the context of "a poetic tradition which had become largely decorative," for though the Augustans had great respect for classical writers, they had "a general uneasiness about the danger of exposing the true Christian to the pagan idolater."[8] In spite of their adherence to classical norms of unity and decorum, the neoclassical poets had little of the genuine mythmaking consciousness of the Greeks.

The classical thinking of the Greeks "functions as a discourse, a fluid give and take with nature. By contrast modern literature intentionally congeals into stylistic blocks," according to Jack Burnham.[9] This interchange with nature, epitomized by Coleridge's lines "we receive but what we give, / And in our life alone does Nature live," suggests that Romantic poetry is, at least in spirit, more classical than the neoclassical poetry of the preceding age which congeals into stylistic blocks.

Tradition identifies the Romantic period as the source of modern thought and literature, and in many ways it is; yet I have just suggested that the Romantics were classical in at least one respect, and I will suggest shortly that they were even primitive in their mythmaking esthetic. By "primitive" I am referring

---

[7] Bush, *Mythology . . . in English Poetry*, p. xi. David Bidney offers an incredibly condensed survey of mythology through the ages in "Myth, Symbolism, and Truth," *Myth: A Symposium*.
[8] Zwerdling, "The Mythographers and . . . Greek Myth," p. 447.
[9] Jack Burnham, *The Structure of Art* (New York: Braziller, 1971), p. 19.

to the mentality characterized by ahistorical, cyclical, and mythopoeic thought, whereas by "modern" I am referring to a mentality primarily historical, linear, and non-mythopoeic in orientation. Needless to say, we cannot classify modes of thought in any absolute sense, for undoubtedly the two share common characteristics. Nor, as Lévi-Strauss reiterates throughout *The Savage Mind* and elsewhere, should we regard primitive or magical thought "as a beginning, a rudiment, a sketch, a part of a whole which has not yet materialized. It forms a well articulated system, and is in this respect independent of that other system which constitutes science, except for the purely formal analogy which brings them together and makes the former a sort of metaphorical expression of the latter."[10] It is, therefore, in no way demeaning to compare Romantic myth-making to classical and primitive thought, nor does the comparison in any way detract from the traditional view that the Romantic period is the predecessor of modern literature.

In my remarks about the eighteenth century I noted that the Augustans tended to demean mythology by relegating it to the function of poetic trope. Though there are poems in the Romantic period which do likewise, the major poems of the age are characterized by their mythopoeic impulse rather than their mythological allusions. Both English and Continental Romantics evidenced "a widespread interest in the origins, nature, and meaning of the myths of the ancient world," according to Albert Kuhn. Much of the credit for this revived interest belongs to Romantic syncretists such as Jacob Bryant, Charles Depuis, Edgar Davies, and Thomas Blackwell. The goal of these men and other syncretists was "to demonstrate the grand unity of all myths, to show that beneath the seemingly disparate and heterogeneous elements of ancient universal mythico-religious and historical tales there lay a harmonious tradition."[11]

Those of us familiar with the basic tenets of structuralism will recognize a limited similarity in the goals of these syncretists and those of modern structuralists. The former were interested in finding a "key myth" which would explain all others, while the latter are searching for the underlying mental processes which enable the mind to create myths. In addition, by insisting that classical and Christian myths "both proceeded

---

10 Claude Lévi-Strauss, *The Savage Mind* (Chicago: Univ. of Chicago Press, 1966), p. 17.
11 Kuhn, "English Deism," p. 1094.

originally from naturalistic, archetypal symbols in primitive thought and imagination,"[12] the syncretists implied that primitive thought is as sophisticated as modern thought. This point has since been emphasized by Lévi-Strauss, who claims that "the savage mind is logical in the same sense and the same fashion as ours."[13] We can summarize the distinction between the syncretists and the structuralists by saying that the former are more concerned with the ends—myths—while the latter are preoccupied with the means—mythopoeic thought.

Attempts at syncretization, in addition to reviving interest in myths, also made the age more conscious of language in terms of origins, properties, and communicability. This is reflected in the ubiquitous use of "concrete nature imagery" which reflects not only a classical give and take with nature but *a preoccupation with verbal image as a product of the mind in the act of ordering* as well. Chaffee remarks that nature imagery predominates in poetry about the mind and "exists, not as an end in itself, but essentially to illuminate the operations, perceptions and structure of that mind. Concrete imagery has no intrinsic interest; it acquires importance in so far as it signifies what craves signification, the mind. Furthermore, imagery of this kind exemplifies an element in human experience which is *most* traditional, namely, 'primitive thought.' "[14] Thus, the interchange with nature establishes a clear link between Romantic poetry and the classical thinking of the Greeks, and the heavy reliance upon nature imagery links Romantic mythmaking with primitive thought, the study of which gave rise to structuralism as we know it today.

As much as any twentieth-century scientific theory, totemism (the most essential characteristic of primitive thought) expresses the total relationship between man and culture. This primitive method of identifying a man's social position through homologies with nature represents a seminal esthetic choice, inasmuch as we consider the choice of metaphor in a poem an esthetic one. The use of such homologies implies an awareness of self, as we shall see shortly, and indeed totemism is the first intellectual operation clearly establishing that man, as the Romantics constantly reaffirmed, is self-conscious. The numerous isolated, alienated figures of Romantic poetry such as the

---

12 *Ibid.,* p. 1096.
13 Lévi-Strauss, *The Savage Mind,* p. 268.
14 Chaffee, "The Rendezvous of Mind," p. 199.

Ancient Mariner, Alastor, and Manfred radiate that chronic self-consciousness which Geoffrey Hartman considers as one of the most distinguishing characteristics of English Romanticism,[15] a view supported by Abrams's remark that

> Romantic thinkers regard philosophical reflections, the very act of taking thought . . . as in itself, in Schelling's words, "a spiritual sickness of mankind" resulting in the split "between ego and non-ego, subject and object, spirit and other, nature and mind."[16]

This excessive self-consciousness, or Romantic egoism, means that the self is the necessary starting point from which to explore man and the universe, as Albert Gérard argues so persuasively.[17]

The psychological manifestations of this insistence upon the integrity and value of the individual is our primary concern herein, and in this the Romantics precede the modernism of Freud, Jung, and Erikson. Rejecting Locke's proposition that the mind operates as a tabula rasa passively receiving and recording messages from the world, Coleridge and Wordsworth maintained that the mind is organic, vital and active, shaping and coloring perceptions as they are received. Coleridge affirmed that we "may not hope from outward forms to win / The passion and the life whose fountains are within." In a very real sense the goal of Romantic mythmaking is to locate and explain this source of poetic creativity, a search which establishes a clear and germane link between structuralism and Romantic mythmaking.

II

From Harold Bloom's study of *Shelley's Mythmaking* a paradigm of mythopoeic consciousness may be constructed and in turn serve as a point of departure into structuralist analysis.[18] Bloom employs Martin Buber's distinction between the two primary words, "I-Thou"—a subjective, intuitive, sympathetic

---

[15] Geoffrey Hartman, "Romanticism and Anti-Self-Consciousness," in *Romanticism and Consciousness*, ed. Harold Bloom (New York: Norton, 1970).

[16] Abrams, *Natural Supernaturalism*, pp. 181–82.

[17] See the Introduction to Albert S. Gérard, *English Romantic Poetry: Ethos, Structure, and Symbol in Coleridge, Wordsworth, Shelley, and Keats* (Berkeley: Univ. of California Press, 1968).

[18] I am referring here to Bloom's introductory chapter entitled "The Mythopoeic Mode."

experience defining the communion between two subjects— and "I-It"—an objective, rational, antipathetic relationship circumscribing the dominance of subject over object. The "I-Thou" experience engenders a mythic consciousness as attested to by the vital give and take between man and nature in primitive thought and Romantic mythmaking. It is similar to Coleridgean "imagination," Wordsworthian "joy" seeing "into the life of things," and Keatsian "negative capability" entering chameleon-like into everything and nothing.

Similar to Bloom's study of Shelley in terms of its reliance upon Buber's two primary words is Thomas McFarland's study of *Coleridge and the Pantheist Tradition,* wherein an analagous distinction is made between "I am" and "It is." The tension arising from these two alternative methods of verifying existence, the former arguing from subject to object and the latter reversing the process, "provides the ground for what Husserl calls 'primordial experience,' for the recognition of the untranslatability of consciousness."[19] We may consider Romantic mythmaking as an attempt to translate consciousness—an attempt which is self-defeating, as Bloom is quick to note,[20] and Wordsworth reluctant though willing to admit.[21] Perhaps it is this very enterprise which explains the tendency to think of the Romantics as poets who never quite managed to answer those very seminal questions, the mere posing of which so attracts us today.

Comprehending and conveying this state of mythic consciousness was a compelling task despite the inevitability of its defeat, for as indicated earlier, Judaeo-Christian thought is primarily non-mythic. The opening lines of Shelley's "Hymn to Intellectual Beauty" capture the remoteness of the "Thou" in modern thought: "The awful shadow of some unseen Power / Floats though unseen among us." Yet, not only does the "Thou" exist, but it demands that we search it out, as Shelley does in "Mont Blanc" by

---

19 Thomas McFarland, *Coleridge and the Pantheist Tradition* (Oxford: Clarendon Press, 1969), p. 236. On p. 239 McFarland distinguishes between Coleridge's "I-Thou" as "a deduction from the nature of consciousness" and Buber's as "an axiom of experience."

20 Bloom points out, quite correctly, that attempting to capture the communion between two subjects in the "I-Thou" experience necessarily results in a static circumscribing product, be it a poem or a set of religious tenets, and is therefore self-defeating despite the compulsion to do so.

21 Wordsworth bemoaned his inadequacy in measuring up to the epic task he placed before himself, particularly in Books I and II of *The Prelude.* (See 1:114–34; 220–42; 255–69; and II:228–30; 346–51.)

Seeking among the shadows that pass by
Ghosts of all things that are, some shade of thee,
Some phantom, some faint image; till the breast
From which they fled recalls them, thou art there!

Through the final imperative declaration Shelley insists upon our recognizing the presence of a "Thou" previously turned out from the breast of modern man. The fleeting vagueness of the vocabulary is not due to any weakness of Shelley's poetic powers, as Bloom correctly asserts throughout his study. Rather, it attests to the remoteness of historical man from the "Thou" of nature and thus demands such a groping vocabulary of Shelley.

Coleridge's distinction between "the finiteness of the Greek mind and the insatiable longing for the infinite characteristic of Christianity"[22] helps illuminate the problem faced by the mythmaking poet in an historical world. According to Mircea Eliade,

> The chief difference between the man of the archaic and traditional societies and the man of the modern societies with their strong imprint of Judaeo-Christianity lies in the fact that the former feels himself indissolubly connected with the Cosmos and the cosmic rhythms, whereas the latter insists that he is connected only with history.[23]

The Greek mind is finite, somewhat like the primitive mind though not to the same extent, because the cyclical pattern of myths is essentially repetitive. Paradoxically, then, a closed cyclical system which is finite is connected with the cosmic cycle (as in Ovid's *Metamorphoses*) and thus becomes infinite: there is neither a definite beginning of things nor a definite end. Primitive rituals, for example, *re-enact* or *reproduce* a paradigmatic act so that action "acquires meaning, reality, solely to the extent to which it repeats a primordial act."[24] Since everything is accounted for within these rituals, man can and does live in harmony with nature, and it is this harmony which, consciously or unconsciously, links him with infinity.

Conversely, modern man consciously accepts history and therefore, caught between a beginning and an end without repetitive possibilities, longs for the infinite. Caught between birth

---

22 Bush, *Mythology . . . in English Poetry*, p. 53.
23 Mircea Eliade, *Cosmos and History*, trans. Willard Trask (New York: Harper & Row, 1959), p. vii.
24 *Ibid.*, p. 4.

and death, he seeks somehow to become a part of the eternal cosmic cycle. But, he is a mere grain of sand in the cosmos unable to see the world within himself, the divinity within himself, as Blake puts it. Time and space limit the modern man's horizons in such a way that actions merely *commemorate,* never *repeat,* a primordial event.

> Nature recovers only itself, whereas archaic man recovers the possibility of definitively transcending time and living in eternity. Insofar as he fails to do so, insofar as he "sins," that is, falls into historical existence, into time, he each year thwarts the possibility [of transcending time and living in eternity] . . . Furthermore, archaic man certainly has the right to consider himself more creative than modern man, who sees himself as creative only in respect to history. Every year, that is, archaic man takes part in the repetition of the cosmogony, the creative act *par excellence.*[25]

Somewhat ironically, through his finite relationship with the "Thou" of nature, primitive man partakes of the infinite, while historical man deludes himself into believing he is free to earn immortality through actions which, lacking cosmic significance, are thus circumscribed and of limited value.

It is worth reiterating an important point, namely, that we cannot totally separate the mythic and the historical (or as Eliade calls them, the sacred and profane) consciousness in any absolute sense. On the contrary, *"By the very fact that it is a religion,* Christianity had to keep at least one mythical aspect —liturgical Time, that is, the periodical recovery of the *illud tempus."*[26] Vestiges of primitive religion survive in annual celebrations of the new year and the new harvest; in a relatively profane age, these rituals are among the most psychologically gratifying and socially solidifying that we have.

Earlier, I suggested that the use of primitive totems represented both a self-conscious and an intellectual-esthetic impulse. It was Rousseau, according to Lévi-Strauss, who first realized that such primitive discriminations represented the first act of intelligence. "Rousseau . . . sees the apprehension by man of the 'specific' character of the animal and vegetable world as the source of the first logical operation, and subsequently of a social differentiation which could be lived out only if it were con-

---

25 *Ibid.,* p. 158.
26 Mircea Eliade, *Myth and Reality,* trans. Willard Trask (New York: Harper & Row, 1963) , pp. 168–69.

ceptualized."[27] Whereas the primitive consciousness could conceptualize this logical operation through totemism, modern man has failed to do so and thus sinned by falling into history. In his most recent major work Abrams devotes three full chapters in an effort "to make it clear that it was indeed a cardinal concern of Wordsworth as bard, and of Coleridge as both metaphysician and bard, to help redeem man by fostering a reconciliation with nature, which because man has severed himself from his earlier unity with it has become alien and inimical to him."[28] It is, equally, a concern of Blake's: "Where man is not, nature is barren" he wrote in "The Marriage of Heaven and Hell," and because man's senses have self-imposed limitations, more often than not he finds himself "cavern'd." Nor is it any less of a concern in Shelley, particularly the Shelley of *Prometheus Unbound* wherein, to use a Blakean phrase, it is "the mind-forg'd manacles" that enslave Prometheus.

The conceptualization did take place in the primitive mind, however, through totemism. As the first instance of social differentiation, it has attracted the attention of Lévi-Strauss and other anthropologists. A logical operation, totemism marks the genesis of self-consciousness and is thus an invaluable testament to man's evolution from a predominantly natural animal into a predominantly cultural one. It is perhaps the supreme irony of evolution that this self-conscious act should eventually lead to the "fall of man," for inevitably man, in becoming human, was destined to willfully accept history in an effort to escape the Edenic innocence of which he was unaware. Such innocence is characterized by affective thought which is conscious of only the immediate present. Our experience after the fall is characterized by a consciousness of the past and the future as well as the present, or, intellectual thought.

Rousseau determined that the human mind is "indissociably both affective and intellectual"; as such the former allows man to identify with animals (and nature in general) while the latter enables man "to acquire the capacity to distinguish *himself* as he distinguished *them,* i.e., to use the diversity of species as conceptual support for social differentiation."[29] It is this differentiation taken to an extreme that leads to the alienation of man from nature to which Abrams alluded and to which Eliade ap-

27 Lévi-Strauss, *Totemism,* p. 99.
28 Abrams, *Natural Supernaturalism,* p. 145. See Chaps. 3, 4, 5.
29 Lévi-Strauss, *Totemism,* p. 101.

plied the term "sin" (i.e., fall into historical existence). It is also reflected in the Genesis account of the "fall of man," for the immediate effect of the original sin is to make both Adam and Eve conscious not only of themselves and their inherent differences, but of their differences from other animal species as well.

This seminal act of self-consciousness lies at the core of Lévi-Strauss's theory of the mind since it is based on a two-fold opposition: between self and mankind and between man and animal. The mind, says Lévi-Strauss,

> is based . . . on the emergence of a logic operating by means of binary oppositions and coinciding with the first manifestations of symbolism. The total apprehension of men and animals as sentient beings, in which identification consists, both governs and precedes the consciousness of oppositions between firstly, logical properties conceived as integral parts of the field, and then, within the field itself, between "human" and "non-human."[30]

In other words, man can become self-conscious only if and when he is capable of using symbols as instruments of comparison and contrast, which is precisely the function of totems. Totemic systems are basically metaphorical statements of the social structure and, of equal importance, represent an esthetic choice. The Coleridgean idea that "we receive but what we give" thus converges with Burnham's definition of classical thought as a fluid interchange between man and nature and Lévi-Strauss's conception of the mind as a receiver and transmitter of experiences in a coded form. It is myth that serves as the vehicle for such coded messages, incorporating what a given society thinks of itself, as a governing pattern, and what the mythmaking poet seeks to integrate into the field, as a re-creation or re-interpretation of the original mythic structure.

III

The coded messages which manifest themselves in myths reflect, as I have indicated, the structures of the mind. Coleridge may or may not have been aware of this modus operandi of the mind when he observed "that poetry, even that of the loftiest and, seemingly, that of the wildest odes, has a logic of its own as severe as that of science; and more difficult, because more subtle, more complex, and dependent on more and more

---

30 *Ibid.,* pp. 101–02.

fugitive causes." In all probability he had only an intimation of what we have now come to know about the mind. Nevertheless, he was preoccupied with difficult, subtle, complex, and fugitive causes motivating the mind, as the following observation in his notebooks indicates: "In looking at objects of Nature while I am thinking . . . I seem rather to be seeking, as it were *asking*, a symbolical language for something within me that already and forever exists, than observing something new."[31] I suggest that the "something within . . . that already exists" is equivalent to what Lévi-Strauss calls the "logic that . . . both governs and precedes" consciousness. A further gloss on Coleridge's observation is the following by Richard Haven: "Thoughts, images, things of which we are conscious are 'fixed' not because reality consists of fixed entities but because we 'fix' them by the act of thinking or seeing and at the same time 'fix' our individual selves."[32]

The parallel between the remarks of Coleridge and the explanation by Haven on one hand, and the following explanation of how the mind operates, by noted anthropologist Edmund Leach, on the other, establish affinities between structuralism and Romantic mythopoeic thought that cannot be overlooked. "The phenomena we perceive have the characteristics we attribute to them because of the way our senses operate and the way the human brain is designed to order and interpret stimuli which are fed into it."[33] We must now turn to the structuralist explanation of the mind in action.

The structure of the mind is based on three key ideas, according to the noted Swiss psychologist Jean Piaget in his excellent book *Structuralism*. The first of these ideas is "wholeness," which conveys "on the whole as such over-all properties distinct from the properties of its elements"; in other words, "the law of composition for perceptual wholes is non-additive."[34] The second key idea is "transformation," which Piaget explains as follows:

If the character of structured wholes depends on their laws of composition, these laws must of their very nature be *structuring;*

31 Kathleen Coburn, ed., *The Notebooks of Samuel Taylor Coleridge.* Vol. I (New York: Pantheon, 1957) No. 1387.

32 Richard Haven, *Patterns of Consciousness* (Amherst: Univ. of Massachusetts Press, 1969) , p. 16.

33 Edmund Leach, *Claude Lévi-Strauss* (New York: Viking Press, 1970) , p. 15.

34 Jean Piaget, *Structuralism*, trans. Chaninah Maschler (New York: Harper & Row, 1970) , pp. 7, 57.

it is the constant duality, or bipolarity, of always being simultaneously *structuring* and *structured* that accounts for the success of the notion of law or rule employed by structuralists.[35]

It is transformation which accounts for the integration of new stimuli into the perceptual whole without violating the first law of wholeness, thus allowing for, and even demanding, reinterpretation and re-creation of the old myth.

The duality of being simultaneously structuring and structured is of cardinal importance for it can be applied to many levels of intellectual activity. On the broadest literary level it accounts for what T. S. Eliot called tradition and the individual talent. From the student's point of view, notes Burnham,

Art is simultaneously connected to two systems: the first is based on a viewer's capacity to organize sense experiences, and the second is a learned system of plastic values. In a viewer's mind, both modify and supplement one another as complementary aspects of a single system of perception.[36]

Lévi-Strauss is primarily concerned with the dichotomy between nature and culture, a duality of a different sort. Because man partakes of both nature and culture, he is a mediator between the two, often relying on myths to conceptualize the bipolarity of his condition. Totemism is a nascent form of mythmaking which serves "to guarantee the convertibility of ideas between different levels of social reality."[37] Jack Burnham offers another way of summarizing the function served by the mythic poem: it "mediates between what is physically true and what is hoped for," particularly at the level of social reality, for "successful art serves the same mediating function as myth"—indeed, successful art is to a large extent myth.[38]

It is precisely this effort to convert an idea between two levels of social reality—from what is physically true to what is hoped for—that characterizes a group of Wordsworth's poems, among which are "Simon Lee, the Old Huntsman," "The Thorn," "The Idiot Boy," "Resolution and Independence," and "The Old Cumberland Beggar." In each of these poems the nature-culture dichotomy so important to Lévi-Strauss is resolved along totemic lines.

[35] *Ibid.*, p. 10.
[36] Burnham, *The Structure of Art*, pp. 8–9.
[37] Lévi-Strauss, *The Savage Mind*, p. 76.
[38] *The Structure of Art*, pp. 3, 48.

In considering the above poems as variations on a single mythic pattern we should keep in mind Lévi-Strauss's admonition that "if there is a meaning to be found in mythology, this cannot reside in the isolated elements which enter into the composition of a myth, but only in the way those elements are combined." From this he concludes that "the true constituent units of a myth are not the isolated relations but *bundles of such relations,* and it is only as bundles that these relationships can be put to use and combined so as to produce a meaning."[39]

In the poems under consideration the protagonists appear in a natural context (i.e., huntsman, deserted woman, leech gatherer, beggar, widow, idiot) which in a cultural context classifies them as totally useless. The basic binary opposition is between their physical or natural existence and their social or cultural non-existence. As a poet, a category of consciousness differentiated (according to Wordsworth) by degree rather than by kind, Wordsworth has to mediate this dichotomy. His mythopoeic consciousness enables him to rely on totem-like homologies (i.e., a leech, a hunter, a scavenger, a thorn, a crazy horse) and, in general, "concrete nature imagery," to awaken the reader's conscience. Wordsworth demands that we deem not these people useless.

Wordsworth's mythopoeic consciousness is more imaginative than ours, and as Thomas Ashton concludes in his reading of "The Thorn": "the imagination alone can free men from the dictates of false sympathy and so create spiritual compassion." He adds that "without human sound and imaginative light, nature cannot free Martha from the inner darkness that reigns at "The Thorn's" conclusion."[40] We are back to Blake's aphorism, "Where man is not, nature is barren."

Without imagination we cannot hope to free ourselves from the tyranny of custom either. Our excessive awareness of the distinction between the individual and mankind has led to an overvaluation of social differentiation at the expense of natural affinities between men as 1) elements of nature and 2) members of a common species. It is in this respect that Shelley considers imagination to be the great secret of morals, for, as he writes in "The Defence of Poetry," it allows

39 Claude Lévi-Strauss, "The Structural Study of Myth," in *Myth: A Symposium,* pp. 86, 87.

40 Thomas Ashton, " 'The Thorn': Wordsworth's Insensitive Plant," *The Huntington Library Quarterly,* 35 (Feb. 1972) , 186.

a going out of our own nature, and an identification of ourselves
with the beautiful which exists in thought, action or person not
our own. A man, to be greatly good, must imagine intensely and
comprehensively; he must put himself in the place of another and
of many others, the pains and pleasures of his species must become
his own.

The totemic homologies allow us to identify with persons not
our own, with the pains of our species, by reminding us of our
common humanity.

The way in which these homologies work is rather subtle,
however, for they usually serve to differentiate rather than to
unite people. In much the same way the title "Lyrical Ballads"
is ironic for it combines an essentially private genre with an
essentially public one in poems that are purposely non-dramatic
and non-heroic. Like Milton in *Paradise Lost,* Wordsworth is
relying on the reader's "learned system of plastic values," as
well as the accepted system of social values, to undercut the
traditional norm. Milton's poem asserts that the spiritual struggle against the temptations of Satan is "not less but more heroic"
than the conventional epic battles. Similarly, Wordsworth's ballads celebrate the instructive, humanizing lesson to be learned
from ordinary, not extraordinary people.

The common meaning of these mythic poems is thus derived
from the bundles of relations which serve to broaden our consciousness, which in turn enables us to redress the imbalance in
our social system.[41] Moreover, the repetitive appearance of these
bundles serves to reaffirm the mythic quality of these poems:

> There is a circularity to magical or mythical thinking which is
> matched in science by demonstrations of physical cause and effect
> relationships. Repetition is to magic what verification is to science;
> repetitions are timeless while verifications only exist in time.[42]

By repeatedly using similar structural bundles—namely, natural
signification, cultural signification, totemic homologies, and concrete nature imagery—Wordsworth is trying to transform a social reality which denies these people any utilitarian value into

---

41 See Abrams, *Natural Supernaturalism,* p. 144: "The individual . . . has become
radically split in three main aspects. He is divided within himself, he is divided
from other men, and he is divided from his environment; his only hope for
recovery . . . is to find the way to a reintegration which will restore his unity
with himself, his community with his fellow men, and his companionability with
an alien and hostile outer world."
42 Burnham, *The Structure of Art,* p. 10.

a new reality by stressing their spiritual worth as fellow beings of great strength and courage.

The structuralist analysis of these poems has been based on Lévi-Strauss's nature-culture dichotomy, but there are other binary oppositions of equal value in analyzing other types of poems. There is a bipolarity in the very nature of language itself which is "the most dynamic aspect of signs . . . the ambiguity of their fixed/unfixed and static/temporal nature. Not only do signs suggest opposition, but it is an essential part of their existence."[43] The "dynamic aspect of signs" is analogous to the dynamic aspect of the nature-culture dichotomy in that nature is fixed and unchanging in the sense that it is cyclical whereas culture is unfixed and temporal in that it is linear and historical. We may also think of this dichotomy in terms of the structuring-structured element operating within the perceptual whole.

These various levels of binary opposition must be synthesized in a manner that does not violate the wholeness of the structure. The third key idea to structuralism is "self-regulation" which, from a linguistic and a psychological point of view, is composed of the interplay between anticipation and correction. "From the cybernetic point of view," explains Piaget, "an operational system is one which excludes errors before they are made because every operation has its inverse in the system."[44] Because there is no automatic inverse in linguistics and psychology, self-regulation is performed by the individual acting as an equilibrating agent for the structure. Mythic art is the product of equilibration, as we saw in the Wordsworth poems.

In the "Ode on a Grecian Urn" Keats is equilibrating between both linguistic and psychological oppositions. The linguistic tension is found, as pointed out above, in the very nature of language and signs. The psychological tension arises from the acknowledged physical limitations of mortal man and his aspirations for immortality. At one extreme both the urn—through its cylindric shape—and the poem—through its stanzaic form—are cyclic and thus infinite. At the other extreme, the artist is linear and historial, thus finite. Mediating these two extremes are the events depicted on the urn, at once finite because cultural[45] and infinite because products of mythic art.

---

43 *Ibid.*, p. 17.

44 *Structuralism*, pp. 15–16.

45 Charles Patterson argues in "Passion and Permanence in Keats' 'Ode on a Grecian Urn,' " *Journal of English Literary History*, 21 (Sept. 1954), 208–20, that the urn depicts the most essential human activities—art, community life, religious sacrifice, and love—activities which in various ways can bestow a certain amount of immortality on the participants, I might add.

By intimating immortality the poem as well as the urn "teases us out of thought." Just as the mind is simultaneously structuring and structured so too is the urn-poem. Indeed, it is Keats's ability to enter into the moment of "arrested pre-ecstasy," as Kenneth Burke so aptly phrases it, that enables him to reach the zenith of happiness conveyed in stanza three. By identifying with the lovers about to kiss and the priest about to sacrifice, Keats approaches the immortality of these figures, only to exceed them by creating the poem itself.

The urn, with the figures on it, is warm and alive only if we can enter into it imaginatively, but to do so is no less difficult than locating the "Thou" of nature in Shelley. The real climax of the poem is reached in the words "Cold Pastoral." They enable Keats to transcend his mortality by reconciling the Christian yearning for the infinite and the Greek finiteness which, through repetition, insures its structural wholeness even as it transforms and regulates itself.

In using a Grecian urn, Keats has also invoked the mythopoeic consciousness associated with it, and it is this consciousness rather than any literal myth captured on the urn that is of cardinal significance. To understand such a consciousness we must turn to structuralism, bearing in mind that "structuralism is a method, not a doctrine."[46] Unfortunately, as Piaget notes, "the discovery of structure may, either immediately or at a much later stage, give rise to formalization. Such formalization is, however, always the creature of the theoreticians, whereas structure itself exists apart from him."[47] In other words, it is the desire to structure experience, rather than explicit patterns or forms which emerge from the process, that is of primary significance to structuralism.

Piaget's insistence upon the supremacy of "continual self-construction" is analogous to the concept of "process" underlying the Romantic theory of the organic mind. In discussing characteristic philosophies of the Romantic age, Abrams points out that the post-Kantian notion of

"system" differs essentially from the metaphysical structures of most of their [the Romantics] great predecessors; for these, whatever the nature of the world they described, had themselves, in theory, been composed of fixed concepts ordered by rational connections into a stable structure of enduring truths. The remarkable thing is that the system of Romantic philosophers . . . is itself

---

46 *Structuralism*, p. 142.
47 *Ibid.*, p. 5.

represented as a *moving* system, a dynamic process which is driven by an internal source of motion to its own completion.[48]

In this remark we find the very essence of modern psychological thought, and structuralism in particular, namely, the concept of mind as process, as a perpetual · becoming rather than a static entity.

The structural analysis of Romantic mythmaking reveals, then, that the "Romantic esthetic was of art for man's sake, and for life's sake," as Abrams concludes, adding:

> These writers, whatever their religious creed or lack of creed, were all, in Keats's term, humanists. They posited the central importance and essential dignity of man . . . they set as the aim of man an abundant life in this world, in which he may give play to all his creative powers; they estimated poetry by the extent to which it contributes toward this aim; and their poetic imagination was a moral imagination and their vision of the world was a moral vision.[49]

It was in an effort to establish the "essential dignity of man" that Romantic poets looked to primitive and classical civilizations for a mythopoeic consciousness which might "inspire a fallen present."

---

[48] *Natural Supernaturalism*, pp. 172–73. Cf. Herbert Lindenberger's explanation that ". . . what I meant when I spoke of Wordsworth's as a poetry of *process and movement,* was a poetry less interested in illuminating individual objects than in enacting the process of perception and the moment of the contemplatory mind." *On Wordsworth's* Prelude (Princeton: Princeton Univ. Press, 1963) p. 61, my italics.
[49] *Ibid.,* p. 429.

French Theories of Fiction: 1947-1974

René Girard

Stanford University

IN the Paris of 1947, the *existentialisme* of Jean-Paul Sartre reigned supreme; fiction was hailed as a means to celebrate the existential conception of freedom. The founder himself had severely rebuked such famous figures as François Mauriac for depriving their characters of that precious commodity. Some hardy souls tried to turn these strictures into a full-fledged theory of fiction, but we were never really told how a repentant novelist could make restitution and return this priceless freedom to dispossessed characters. Things looked almost as preposterous in 1947 as they look today, but in the opposite way; it is somewhat comforting to realize that fact. If Sartre meant anything, his meaning had to fall within the purview of a naturalistic aesthetics. He meant that the novelist should provide an imitation of freedom more true-to-life than his predecessors'. Instead of invoking heredity and determinism, like Zola, to justify naturalism, Sartre invoked freedom. The fusion or confusion between the literary text and *expérience vécue* was more extreme than ever. In retrospect, this *outré* kind of naturalism reads like a sign of impending doom. The pendulum had swung so far in one direction that it had to swing back in the other, ultimately to land at the other extreme and rest there for a while, which is just about where we find it today, at least insofar as the noisiest and most flamboyant element in French letters is concerned.

The great talent of Roland Barthes ushered in the new era, with a light touch and an irony all his followers should emulate. The *nouveau roman* played a mediating role. Robbe-Grillet had defined his own work in terms of a descriptive realism that sounded terribly old hat until Barthes came to the rescue and suggested that far from imprisoning the meaningfulness of external reality in the novel, the Robbe-Grillet technique was intended to exorcise all social and cultural connotations, perhaps to cast out meaning altogether. Then came Bruce Morissette, who showed that it was not so. Meaning was still there, in Robbe-Grillet, just a little more devious than before. Barthes agreed that Morissette had to be right but he was disappointed.[1] It may well be that the *nouveau roman* never truly recovered from that blow.

By that time the new formalism had been formally launched. The triumph of formalism in France came rather belatedly by American and especially Russian standards. That may be why foreign sources are rather well acknowledged, better perhaps than the French, notably Paul Valéry who, for a variety of reasons, does not make an acceptable patron saint. The distance perhaps is too small. It seems adequate in the case of the Russian formalists, probably because space is added to time. An anthology of these critics was published by Tzvetan Todorov to reasonable critical acclaim.[2] Even some Anglo-American critics have been translated—Northrop Frye is one of them—and also, lo and behold, that old standby of graduate English studies in the Fifties, Wellek and Warren's *Theory of Literature.*

In this country, formalism has been primarily a matter of self-discipline, an obligation to concentrate upon the text, not to take the easy way out into literary history, or some other nonliterary discourse. Critical practice came first. What was desired was an autonomous literary discipline with recognized academic standing. Philosophical implications were minimized if not denied outright. Not so in France, where the tendency to theoretical extremism is accelerated and magnified by the symbiosis that still exists, up to a point, between the critical and creative aspects of literary life.

Until recently it was creative literature that preceded and influenced criticism. But things have changed. As everywhere else, critical activities are on the rise but nowhere else could they inherit, as they did in France, at least at their rarefied summit, some of that Parisian glamour that was formerly reserved

1 Bruce Morissette, *Les Romans de Robbe-Grillet* (Paris: Ed. de Minuit, 1963) ; Preface by Roland Barthes.
2 T. Todorov, ed., *Théorie de la littérature* (Paris: Seuil, 1965) .

to the poetic avant-garde and the plastic arts. As a result, even the wildest critical trends may take on an air of pertinence, even of evidence, for one or two literary seasons. A theory that looks patently false the day it is born may become patently true three months later, simply because, in the meantime, a creative work has appeared that verifies it to the last comma, obligingly provided by some writer who, in some instances, may be none other than the critic who invented the theory in the first place.

No less characteristic than this extreme inbreeding is its very opposite, the compulsory marriage with extraliterary disciplines; this is the sort of thing Lévi-Strauss encounters in his own myths and he describes it as too little combined with too much exogamy. Lévi-Straussian categories are certainly appropriate here since, willing and unwilling, the great anthropologist has been very much at the center of everything. He comes under our jurisdiction here both indirectly, because of his influence on recent approaches to fiction, and also directly, because of his own work. His *Mythologiques* and associated works constitute, after all, a full-fledged theory of at least one fictional mode, and they really touch on several other modes, notably the folktale and the novel.

Structuralism recognizes no meaning in itself. All significance is differential. Thus, structuralism may claim that it transcends the form/content dichotomy. It may also be viewed as a more radical formalism.

The differential definition comes from linguistics, of course; it was first formulated by Saussure in his *Cours de linguistique générale*. A genuine application to *any field* requires a radical critique and rejection of those elements that have always appeared primary, fundamental, and irreducible. These are the false elementary particles which never really permit conventional analysis to decompose and recompose its subject matter. In his work on kinship, for instance, Lévi-Strauss asserts—and he is the first to do so—that the nuclear family is not the real building-block of primitive systems, whatever its relevance not only to our own system but to the biological facts of life. This is genius, of course, if the principle of organization you substitute for the one you discard proves more comprehensive and operates more simply and elegantly than the discarded one. Many people think that in the case of kinship Lévi-Strauss has proved his point.

It follows from this definition, however, that a successful

structuralist analysis in any one field cannot be carried over to another, simply because the false elementary particles which must be exploded are never the same; structuralist analysis is a new adventure each time, for which no guidelines exist.

Where are the false elementary particles discarded by literary structuralism? Where is the illusory evidence it has dispelled? The ruins left in the wake of its victory are nowhere to be found and the victory itself may well be illusory. Among those ruins, we should probably find these traditional categories of literary analysis, those genre distinctions, figures of speech, and principles of rhetoric which structuralism, on the contrary, has paradoxically revived.

There is a huge misunderstanding somewhere, and a too facile reference to linguistics may well be responsible for it. The literary critics heard that the emphasis on linguistic categories was turning anthropology into a science. If this emphasis could bring results in a subject matter not entirely made up of language, *a fortiori*—so did the reasoning go—should it pay off in the case of literature? If not at the level of the *signifié, alors* at the level of *signifiant*. Or vice versa. This reasoning simply disregarded the impossibility of carrying over genuine structural analysis from one field to another. Lévi-Strauss haughtily condemned the hasty application of his method so that structuralism is now unnecessarily turning into a dirty word; but he himself, both by word and deed, may have encouraged a loose conception of the method, both by presenting linguistics as some kind of panacea, which it is not, and by suggesting, at least implicitly, that his joint venture with Jakobson into poetic criticism is closely connected to his best work in anthropology.

The abuse of the term *structuralism* does not mean that the emphasis on language has been sterile. It has produced, among other things, much of the research that belongs in the category defined by the program of this meeting; it has produced, if not theories of fiction as a whole, at least theories of certain fictional modes. Besides those of Lévi-Strauss himself, to which I will return a little later, we have people like Todorov, who explored the *genre fantastique*.[3]

The Russian formalists and, more specifically, Vladimir Propp's *Morphology of the Russian Folktale,* have prompted a good deal of work on the structure of story-telling. The object

---

3 T. Todorov, *Introduction à la littérature fantastique* (Paris: Seuil, 1970).

is to find the logical or rhetorical pattern around which the story is constructed. Certain models make it possible to distinguish between various types of functions. Contributions by Barthes, Todorov, A. J. Greimas, Gérard Genette, and others are gathered in an issue of the review *Communications,* entitled "L'Analyse structurale du récit" (No. 8, 1966).

A distinctive feature of recent French criticism has been an attempt to reconcile the formalistic approach with psychoanalysis and sociology. Here, in this country, this sounds a little like squaring the circle. The aesthetic form is viewed as something absolutely unique and apart from all other reality, which remains nonformal, because in all matters not directly aesthetic the positivistic and naturalistic perspective is still allowed to prevail. In France, many literary critics are used to viewing their work as part of a larger attempt to formalize all the social sciences, at first directly and now via language considered the alpha and omega of all social and cultural reality. People like Lacan and Althusser have tried to show that the best in Freud and Marx is already moving toward their own kind of linguistics-oriented formalization. This means, of course, that the analyses of fiction provided by Freud and Marx themselves are, to say the least, deemphasized. Instead of "decoding" the social implications of Balzac's rhetoric, Marx naïvely read his novels as if they were—blasphemy—almost on a par with *Das Kapital.* How right he was to say that he, Marx, would never have made a good marxist!

Rather than on Marx himself, of course, the formalist structuralists prefer to vent their scorn on closer targets; they deplore the contemporary research that uses the word *structure* and remains as blissfully unaware of language as a fish is of water. Lucien Goldmann certainly lived his sociology of literature as if it were his natural milieu. In his system, writers can directly apprehend social and ideological structures which are already out there in the world but which only a great writer can make fully explicit.

Within this general framework, Goldmann developed more definite views on the novel,[4] also derived from the early Lukacs. In his *Die Theorie des Romans,*[5] Lukacs contrasts the certainties of the epic with the problematic nature of the modern novel and its heroes in a world of collapsing values. Goldmann felt

---

[4] See *Pour une sociologie du roman* (Paris: Gallimard, 1964).
[5] Georg Lukacs, *Die Theorie des Romans* (Berlin: Cassirer, 1920).

that this concept of a problematic hero needed specification and that my own views,[6] read in the light of a marxist theory of value, would provide the right analytical tool. According to these views, the great novel is the revelation of so-called *mediated* desire, of a desire, in other words, which always patterns itself on other desires.

Further research has certainly confirmed the close relationship between the socio-economic development, as represented in the novel, and the systematic unfolding of mediated desire. In his brilliant essay *Structures sociales et vision romanesque chez G. de Maupassant,*[7] Charles Castella shows not only the paramount role of mediated desire in novels where its presence had not been suspected before but also the extraordinary degree of integration between this desire and the social picture provided by Maupassant. Both keep evolving along the same descending patterns. Because of its quality as a theoretical statement as well as practical criticism, Castella's essay transcends the significance of a single-author study.

In his no less remarkable work on the medieval novel, Pierre Galais shows convincingly, I believe, that mediated desire is already fully explicit in *Chrétien de Troyes,* and in a context that looks like an allegory or a prophecy of the modern industrial subjection.[8]

All this proves the continued vitality and real progress of our studies. This progress is such, as a matter of fact, that I doubt it can be contained within the limits of a single genre, or even of prose fiction as such. The drama is certainly involved. The greatest expert on secondhand desire, both in terms of underhanded exploitation and spectacular revelation, may turn out to be William Shakespeare himself.

To go even further: The problematic is so coherent and so harmonious within a group of superior writers, its integrative and structuring power such, that mediated desire deserves to be examined for its own sake. It is not enough to view it as a specification of marxist or modern alienation, or of Freudian identification, as some people have suggested. It simply works better than any of these theories taken separately or together and this, in my view, should be the only criterion of acceptance,

[6] In *Mensonge romantique et vérité romanesque* (Paris: Grasset, 1960).

[7] Lausanne, L'Age d'Homme, 1972.

[8] "Littérature et médiation; réflexions sur la genèse du genre romanesque," *Etudes Littéraires,* 4 (April 1971).

even outside the novels. I see more future, therefore, in rethinking current doctrine through mediated desire than in "reducing" mediated desire to any of these doctrines.

My real interest lies not in "theories of fiction" but in those superior works that are anything but fictional to me, even though a formal literary classification will have to regard them as such. This is a formidable claim, of course, and of unparalleled naïveté from the perspective of all formalism. I will answer formalism by accusing it of not being radical enough. Formalism does not realize that its doctrine is couched in almost the same language as everybody else's, including the novelist's. The question ultimately boils down to which set of texts will be privileged. Which texts can help us most in our interpretation of other texts? We are better off, I am convinced, with Cervantes and Dostoievski than with formalistic marxism, psychoanalysis, and semiology. This conviction is based not on aesthetic fetichism, not on a blind acceptance of tradition, but on a formalization that I believe to be demonstrably superior in all instances. Michel Zeraffa points out that the great novels are no strangers to the *décodage* which is the major occupation of much criticism.[9] Great novels decode many sublanguages including, of course, the bad literature that proliferates around them. If we place the right novelistic texts in the right light, we will find that they also decode or come close to decoding much of what passes for a scientific revelation today. Before we set out to demystify a text, we should make sure we are not already demystified by it. Turning the tables of *décodage* on the decoders themselves will certainly be a lot of fun and it may do more to advance the true interests of science, if not *scientificity*, than just about anything else.

The present distinction between scientific and nonscientific, between the texts that decode everything and the texts that, never being read sympathetically, must patiently suffer this *décodage*, looks to me more and more like one more literary distinction that goes unrecognized, not only because it is novel but because it is based on the most bizarre and improbable aesthetics ever devised, the aesthetics of absolute and ecstatic boredom. To deflate this bureaucratic neoromanticism of ecstatic boredom—alas—we have no new Cervantes, no new Shakespeare, no new Molière, but we do not really need them; the old ones

---

9 *Roman et société* (Paris: Presses Univ. de France, 1971).

will prove quite serviceable once again if we only give them the chance.

One can show concretely, I believe, why the current type of formalization remains totally blind to what is truly decisive in great literature. Structuralism and all its legitimate or illegitimate offspring, always subordinate identity to difference. Meaning comes from the differentiation in the Lévi-Straussian binary structure. In "Du Mythe au roman,"[10] Lévi-Strauss traces the origin of a certain *feuilleton*-like fiction, somewhere in the American Indian world, to the gradual weakening of the difference in his binary opposition, thanks to which repetitions and substitutions can multiply. He views this process as one of impoverishment, which it may well be in that particular case, but he generalizes about all Western fiction in line with his belief that between the "natural and logical order of myth," on the one hand, and his own scientific exploration of it on the other, no cultural achievement ever takes place that deserves the attention of the true-blue structuralist.

The framework provided by Lévi-Strauss is a good one, I believe, to consider the relationship of myth and literature but it is impossible to agree that the weakening of differences which loosens the rigidity of the binary structure must be viewed primarily as impoverishment. The crusade against Western "ethnocentrism" is a noble undertaking, but how can Lévi-Strauss disavow a process without which it is obvious that structuralism, among other things, could never have seen the light of day? More important still, the anthropologist excludes the possibility that the difference, after getting "weaker" and "weaker," might disappear altogether. By unduly limiting the scope of the process, he manages not to see its crucial importance, even for myth itself.

The literary followers have been docile on all these points and they have no excuses, dealing as they do with the greatest literature. All writers, with them, should keep busy weaving their neat little structures and leave the question of meaning per se to the wise structuralists. But great writers, obviously, have always been less concerned with adding more meaning to the existing stock than with the life and death of all meaning, and they are more radical in their approach than their critics since they spell out the dissolving of the differentiated structure

---

10 In *L'Origine des manières de tables* (Paris: Plon, 1968).

into the undifferentiation of pure reciprocity, into the nonsensi-
cal antagonism of the tragic and comic *doubles*. No wonder
structuralism remains mute on comic and tragic effects, both of
which become united in great fiction. No wonder current theorizing, under the influence of Freud, of Rank, and now Lacan,
remains stuck with a solipsistic conception of the *doubles* as
imaginary projections of the individual self.

The superiority of literary "decoding" is based on its explicit awareness of the *doubles,* on the realization that such decoding is not the privilege of an academic élite but that it comes
to pass through the tragedy and comedy of the still unperceived
doubles. This tragi-comic dimension, the specifically Western
and modern dimension, means not less but more "science" than
we now have; it means, among other things, history.

In the hands of the best among the younger researchers,
this unnecessarily limited framework of structuralism now
seems to open up. Taking her departure in the work of still another Russian formalist, Bakhtine, who wrote on Rabelais and
Dostoievski, Julia Kristeva distinguishes two types of works;
those she calls "dialogical" are based on an oscillation between
two poles, on a subversive ambivalence which transcends the
possibilities of Aristotelian logic; the others can do no such thing
and are called "monological." In order to be consistent, Kristeva, I am afraid, will have to confine to the monological dog
house many practices characteristic of the general approach to
which, apparently, she still subscribes.[11] The reliance on hier-
archic meta-languages and the purely differential categories of
most formal-structural research obviously falls short of the "dialogical." In order truly to define this last category, however,
Kristeva will have to go to the end of the "weakening" process
and dissolve the differences entirely. She will have to acknowl-
edge the *doubles* as real. She will have to catch up with Dostoievski himself, in other words.

Everything the current methodologies can do, Dostoievski
can do better. This does not mean current research is insignificant. It will be very significant, indeed, if it can catch up some
day with the superiority of great fiction, not through more fiction, but through a language systematic enough to reach other
disciplines. This means, really, that we have to recover the
lost substance of our studies. Perhaps because this substance

---

11 *Semiotikè. Recherches pour une sémanalyse* (Paris: Seuil, 1969).

has always eluded our complete grasp, we now allow it to slip away from us entirely. We have been plundered by disciplines that still terrify us because they claim a scientific status which is not really theirs. The rest of our treasure we squander away by systematically turning for our prophets to men of great talent, no doubt, but who also are the greatest disparagers of our texts, either openly or in secret: people like Freud, who saw literature as the archetypal lie; people like Bachelard, who sees it as mere day-dreaming; and now Lévi-Strauss, who is convinced nothing really significant has happened between the neolithic and the industrial revolutions.

We must welcome the signs of change, wherever they come from, and it is a hopeful sign they come from all shades of the theoretical spectrum, suggesting, really, that some divisions are less irrevocable than they appear. The future looks promising to me. I see fewer followers behind the four horsemen of our apocalypse—aesthetic fetichism, chatty impressionism, bland scholasticism, and arrogant pseudo-demystification. I see less condescension on every side, a more open dialogue between great fiction and the best in the social sciences. I see a serious attempt to reach the potential knowledge of these great works. I see a decisive effort to make their still half-veiled revelation fully explicit for the first time.

Todorov and the Structuralist Science of Poetics

James R. Bennett

University of Arkansas

James R. Bennett

University of Arkansas

A T the beginning of Aldous Huxley's *After Many a Summer Dies the Swan*, we see Los Angeles through the eyes of Jeremy Pordage, scholar. Jeremy's mind, itself a hodgepodge of irrelevancies (his favorite line in *The Prelude* being "And Negro ladies in white muslin gowns"), records the patchwork chaos that was and is Los Angeles: primitive Methodist churches built in the style of the Cartuja at Granada, billboards advertising jumbo malts, instant cash loans, Jesus Saves, and brassieres—while ominously in the background sound the Spanish Civil War and the rise of a dictatorship. But Los Angeles is no more than the most blatant expression of the intellectual jumble Huxley discerned in the United States. The study of literature is part of that confusion. Huxley's spokesman, Mr. Propter, summarizes the indictment: "Just a huge collection of facts about lust and greed, fear and ambition, duty and affection . . . with no co-ordinating philosophy superior to common sense and the local system of conventions, no principle of arrangement more rational than simple aesthetic expediency."

We recognize this description of the literary "discipline" as all too often true, whether in the United States or in France. The only coherence cementing many literature departments in either country, until recently, has been literary history. John Henry Newman's arguments in *The Idea of a University* are painfully even more appropriate today. A person is intellectual when he grasps what he perceives, takes a view of things, and invests it with an idea. But the student of today often exhausts himself on the particular and external. He has no mental center.

Even those pursuing the doctorate of philosophy in literature seldom assimilate enough accurate general ideas and procedures to allow them control over the multitudinous particular. Loaded with a mass of undigested facts, an unmeaning profusion of subjects, some throw it all up in disgust, or graduate distracted, shallow, and demoralized.

Or if the framework of literary history were complemented by the "new critical" study of individual works (in France the traditional "explication de texte"), the analysis often descended into another kind of particularity sometimes just as bewildering and critically enfeebling—the kind of "mere textual analysis," Leslie Fiedler reminds us, "a-historical, anti-biographical," which does at least provide "a higher remedial reading which an age of lapsing literacy perhaps demands."[1]

Thus we welcome the influence of French structuralism, and critics like Roland Barthes, A. J. Greimas, Claude Bremond, Gérard Genette, and Tzvetan Todorov. If we are to gain understanding, we must reduce to method, we must relate our facts, we must generalize, but we must first examine with rigorous self-consciousness our methods for arriving at knowledge. These critics bring to the study of literature an admirable awareness of reality as models of perception, and a passion for comparison and systematizing essential to reducing to order and meaning the multiplicity of information. They are trying to find methods for connected views of the old and new in literature, the far and near, without which there is no whole and no center. They are brilliant illuminators of coherence in literature.

By his steadfast search for and advocacy of rigorous methodology by which the study of literature might approach a science, Tzvetan Todorov represents a particularly consistent purpose within "structuralism." His criticism has been a continued effort to elaborate an essay in which he outlined the major sources of meaning in literature—from sound to plot structures.[2] During the past decade Todorov has steadily defined the elements of his "poetics" for the study of literature as an autonomous subject for scientific study.

"The bibliographies of stylistics contain thousands of titles," Todorov observes, "there is no lack of observed facts; however,

---

[1] *Love and Death in the American Novel,* rev. ed. (New York: Stein & Day, 1966), p. 9.

[2] "La description de la signification en littérature," *Communications,* 4 (1964), 33–39. See the checklist of Todorov's works in *Style,* 8 (Winter 1974), by Irene Bergal and James R. Bennett.

the polysemy of concepts, the imprecision of methods, the uncertainty about the very goal of this research hardly make for a prosperous discipline."[3] In contrast, "The structural analysis of literature is nothing other than an attempt to transform literature into a scientific discipline," by which he means "a coherent body of concepts and methods aiming at the knowledge of underlying laws."[4] His definition is meritoriously inclusive, at least potentially. "In a positive sense, one could present the task of poetics as one of making an inventory of all the means in the command of a writer (that is, he who is searching for the 'strictly literary effects of the language'), means which the 'poetician' attempts to present systematically."[5] If literary criticism is to become a science it must ultimately include not only "structures narratives," "stylistiques," "rythmiques," and "sonores," but also "l'evolution littéraire" and "la relation entre littérature et société."[6] Our efforts, he insists, "ought to be directed toward the elaboration of a general theory, toward the creation of a coherent and homogeneous framework within which individual stylistic studies could find a place."[7]

In practice, however, Todorov distinctly restricts the "realm of poetics." He speaks favorably of Valéry's awareness of the necessity to "delimit" the content for the science of literature: "This will have two limits. First, it deals with literature rather than with the author or the reader, or with contemporary society. Then, its object is the literary use of the language rather than such-or-such specific text."[8] First, he reduces to a secondary status the historical, cultural, and biographical contexts. This "does not mean a denial of the relation between literature and other homogeneous series, such as philosophy or social life"; rather it is a question "of establishing a hierarchy" of priorities: "literature must be understood in its specificity, as literature, before we seek to determine its relation with anything else."[9]

[3] "The Place of Style in the Structure of the Text," in Literary Style: A Symposium, ed. and trans. Seymour Chatman (New York: Oxford Univ. Press, 1971), p. 29.

[4] "Structuralism and Literature," in Approaches to Poetics, ed. Seymour Chatman (New York: Columbia Univ. Press, 1973), pp. 154, 156.

[5] "Valéry's Poetics," Yale French Studies, 44 (1970), 66.

[6] T. Todorov and Oswald Ducrot, Dictionnaire encyclopédique des sciences du langage (Paris: Seuil, 1972), p. 110.

[7] "The Place of Style in the Structure of the Text," p. 29.

[8] "Valéry's Poetics," pp. 65–66.

[9] "Structural Analysis of Narrative," Novel, 3 (Fall 1969), 73. Todorov defends formalists and structuralists from the charge of neglecting history in "L'histoire de la littérature," Langue Française, 7 (Sept. 1970), 14–19, where he argues that the proper study of literary history is of the evolution of forms.

Then Todorov removes the individual work except as a point of departure.[10] With Saussure's distinction between "langue" and "parole" as his foundation, Todorov would replace the atomism of traditional "explication de texte" with the *"Gestalteinheit"* into which the facts fit.[11] Poetics should focus upon its specifically literary content—"stylistic and narrative devices, themes, and genres in general."[12] Genres assume an important position: "The object of these poetics will then be constituted of a general theory of literature (of the various categories of literary discourse) and of a theory of genres: which actually amounts to the same thing."[13] And the best method is categorical systematization. As procedures of service to this restricted poetics, Todorov especially urges the taxonomic and typological ordering of the literary effects of the language. Succinctly, Todorov believes that the only way to grasp the concrete is to pass through the abstract.

In his numerous books and essays Todorov struggles to establish his poetics in a tone almost always tentative and exploratory. In one essay, for example, he remarks that "It goes without saying that owing to the present state of our knowledge in this area, I will limit myself to remarks of a general character."[14] In another he is "perfectly conscious of the fact that the mere enumeration of these examples does not satisfactorily replace the proofs by which I should back up my initial statement. Not only am I selecting isolated remarks instead of formulating an integrated system of arguments, but the initial terms whose very relationship I am trying to describe, the terms 'language' and 'discourse,' are far from being clear and rigorous."[15] And in another his aim is modestly expressed as a desire "to suggest a certain number of categories for examining and describing plots."[16]

Todorov ranges through an extraordinary extent of literature and scholarship, always driving toward consistent theory and method. Two ideas represent his primary approaches: on the

---

10 In *poetics*, but not in *interpretation*—a distinction Todrov is careful to make. Furthermore, there is no absolute wall between poetics and the individual work, since "neither one nor the other is found in a pure state. To know literature, one always proceeds from concrete works." ("The Place of Style in the Structure of the Text," pp. 29–30.)

11 "Connaissance de la parole," *Word*, 23 (1967), 500–17.

12 "Structuralism and Literature," p. 158.

13 "Valéry's Poetics," p. 70.

14 "Language and Literature," in *The Structuralist Controversy*, ed. Richard Macksey and Eugenio Donato (Baltimore: Johns Hopkins Univ. Press, 1972), p. 126.

15 "Structuralism and Literature," p. 168.

16 "Structural Analysis of Narrative," p. 73.

one hand, the relationship between one discipline (the micro-rhetoric of schemes and tropes) and another (the macro-rhet-oric of chapters in a novel) ; on the other hand, the underlying pattern of a form common to all its individual representatives (open and closed stories). He draws considerable inspiration from the Russian formalists, such as Shklovski, who explored analogies between language (especially rhetorical devices) and larger relationships of character and plot (e.g., antithesis and parallelism), and who in his studies on the typology of the *récit* distinguished two major types of combination among stories.[17] Todorov has explored the "new epistemology" of semiology as a framework for the inclusive study of all signs, from all language codes used for communication to all patterns of social behavior.[18] His essay on "la parole" offers a general plan for the study of a piece of literature: A. Semantic Analysis, B. Syntactic; Five Types of Discourse, etc.[19] "He builds a theory of the structure and operation of the literary discourse" (that is, of literary discourses), in order to "discover in each work what it has in common with others."[20]

Todorov has written several essays and two books on the narrative, a form which has received recently an enormous amount of attention.[21] His method is very helpful in distinguish-ing genres (what is a narrative) and individual modes within genres: the Raymond Chandler thriller versus a Sherlock Holmes mystery;[22] the fundamental pattern and four varieties of the James tale;[23] the "fantastic" story versus the "uncanny" and the "marvelous";[24] and the title of his analysis of the *De-cameron* is *Grammaire du* Décaméron (1969), in which he de-scribes the fundamental patterns of the stories, the narrative deep structures, in homologous grammatical forms.

His approach to style is similarly systematic. He distinguish-

---

[17] "Some Approaches to Russian Formalism," *Twentieth Century Studies*, Nos. 7–8 (1972), 6–19.

[18] "Perspective sémiologique," *Communications*, 7 (1966), 139–45.

[19] "Connaissance de la parole."

[20] "Structural Analysis of Narrative," p. 71.

[21] J. Dudley Andrew, "The Structuralist Study of Narrative: Its History, Use, and Limits," in *Bulletin of the Midwest Modern Language Association*, 6 (Spring 1973), 45–61.

[22] "Poétique," in *Qu'es-ce que le structuralism?* ed. Oswald Ducrot et al. (Paris: Seuil, 1969).

[23] "The Structural Analysis of Literature: The Tales of Henry James," in *Structuralism: An Introduction*, ed. David Robey (Oxford: Clarendon Press, 1973), pp. 73–103 (abridged from "Le Secret du récit").

[24] *The Fantastic: A Structural Approach to a Literary Genre*, trans. Richard Howard (Cleveland: Case Western Reserve Press, 1973).

es "three aspects in any utterance"—verbal, syntactic, and semantic—for the close analysis of a passage, and then breaks down these categories into "categories of utterance" and "categories of the speech act."[25] Following William Empson's *The Structure of Complex Words,* he elucidates the intricate meanings of words, utilizing six ways in which a word is complex and four different associations we attach to a word, concluding in the same essay to inquire generally into "what happens to all these multiple meanings when a word is used in a sentence," and whether there is "some specific literary usage of words and meanings."[26] (His models here are the Eastern European formalists—Tynjanov, Mukařovsky, Jakobson.) He has a long, detailed essay on symbolism, "Introduction à la symbolique." In his introduction to a bibliography of the study of sound symbolism he offers a meticulously outlined structure: Part One, Théories. I. Théories Sémantiques. 1. Théoriques Extralexicales. a) Théories Acoustiques. Etc.[27] And in one essay he divides the problem of the riddle into two parts and then analyzes each exhaustively (metaphor, synecdoche, metonymy, syllepsis, etc.).[28]

We have only to remember the words of Newman and Huxley to remember how important is Todorov's drive for theory and system. He shares the achievement of structuralism in general, the effort to create a consistent philosophy of models constructed on the analogy with language.[29] And by his analytical sophistication, he makes a special contribution to the realization of his belief that the systematic study of any one aspect of literature will furnish a foundation for system elsewhere: "the structural analysis of literature is a kind of propaedeutic for a future science of literature."[30]

Yet in spite of his carefully repeated tentativeness and his reminders that the development of systematic methods for the study of a small part of literary experience is preliminary to an eventual systematization of all, there remain at least four basic

---

[25] "The Place of Style in the Structure of the Text," p. 32.
[26] "Meaning in Literature: A Survey," *Poetics,* 1 (1971), 8–15.
[27] "Le sens des sons," *Poétique,* 11 (1972), 446–62. The essay on symbolism is in *Poétique,* 11 (1972), 273–308.
[28] "Analyse du discours: l'example des devinettes," *Journal de Psychologie,* Nos. 1–2 (Jan.–June 1973), 135–55.
[29] See Fredric Jameson, *The Prison-House of Language: A Critical Account of Structuralism and Russian Formalism* (Princeton: Princeton Univ. Press, 1972), p. 101.
[30] "Structural Analysis of Narrative," p. 71.

objections to his work—terminological, phenomenological, logical, and moral.[31]

First, some of the difficulty in understanding the structuralists derives from their proliferation of jargon. In content Todorov is often not new, as he frankly states in regard to "énonciation": "nous ne prétendons pas jouer un rôle du pionnier."[32] Readers familiar, for example, with Brooks and Warren's *Understanding Poetry* (1938) and *Understanding Fiction* (1943) will experience a sense of recognition in reading Todorov, once they pierce through the specialized vocabulary and greater systematization. Language is action: one aspect of Todorov's "énonciation" resembles Brooks and Warren's *tone*. The "speaker's attitude toward his subject and toward his audience, and sometimes toward himself,"[33] is expressed and categorized in Todorov's *"forcé illocutionnaire"* (derived from J. L. Austin's *How To Do Things With Words*), "l'ordre des mots, l'accent logique, l'intonation, la ponctuation, le mode du verbe, le statut de la phrase, la structure lexicale des verbes, les verbes performatifs."[34] Similarly, Todorov's investigation of plot amounts to a schematic formulation of Brooks and Warren's treatment of plot in *Understanding Fiction*. Brooks and Warren define plot as "the structure of an action," not "the structure of an action as we happen to find it out in the world, but the structure within a story," a "series of events, a movement through time, exhibiting unity and significance."[35] Todorov follows the same reasoning to discover two general plots with subdivisions in the *Decameron*.[36] And like Brooks and Warren, Todorov discovers in every plot a triadic form. Brooks and Warren: an action "is a series of connected events moving through three logical stages—the beginning, the middle, and the end." Todorov:

---

[31] J. Dudley Andrew in "The Structuralist Study of Narrative" has already summarized the "serious charges" against the structuralists including Beret Nathhorst's indictment of the pseudo-impressionism of Propp and Lévi-Strauss, and Paul Ricoeur's rejection of taxonomies by insisting upon Chomsky's "dynamic generative grammatology" to study "structuring operations." Also see Jameson's *The Prison-House of Language.*
[32] "Problèmes de l'énonciation," *Langages*, 17 (March 1970), 3.
[33] *Understanding Poetry*, 3rd ed. (New York: Holt, Rinehart & Winston, 1966), p. 181.
[34] "Problèmes de l'énonciation," p. 5.
[35] *Understanding Fiction*, 2nd ed. (New York: Appleton-Century-Crofts, 1959), pp. 77–78.
[36] "Structural Analysis of Narrative," p. 73.

> Every narrative is a movement between two states of equilibrium, which are similar but not identical. At the beginning there is always a balanced situation; the characters form a configuration which may be in movement but which nevertheless preserves unaltered a certain number of fundamental traits . . . then something comes along to break the calm and creates an imbalance . . . the **equilibrium is then restored, but it is not the same as at the** beginning.[37]

Because students in the U.S. have been suckled on Brooks and Warren and other critics cognizant of the underlying deep structures of plots—Northrop Frye's *Anatomy of Criticism,* Francis Fergusson's *The Idea of a Theater,* E. M. Forster's *Aspects of the Novel*—Todorov's categories will not seem strange. But his terminology is a definite, though not insuperable, barrier to communication. (In extenuation, of course, we should remember that Todorov writes primarily for a French, not an American, audience.)

A second objection relates to the abstractness of Todorov's approach. He virtually eliminates two main areas of the concrete literary experience. The first, the "external"—history, culture, biography, psychoanalysis, Marxism—because it "reduces literature to the status of mere material which illustrates a subject other than itself."[38] But an even more fundamental motive is Todorov's disbelief in the referential connection between literature and the "world": the literary text is "not 'representative' of anything but itself. . . . Literature is created from literature, not from reality."[39] The other area, the particular whole work, is usually omitted from his poetics because it is a matter of "interpretation," which "has its own techniques, its own methods."[40] That is, following Northrop Frye in *Anatomy of Criticism,* Todorov advocates "removing from literary study any value judg-

---

[37] "The Fantastic in Fiction," *Twentieth Century Studies,* 3 (May 1970) , 88. See Andrew, p. 51. Brooks and Warren differ only over the specific nature of the triad: "The beginning of an action always presents us with a situation in which there is some element of instability, some conflict; in the middle of an action there is a period of readjustment of forces in the process of seeking a new kind of stability; in the end of an action, some point of stability is reached, the forces that have been brought into play have been resolved."

[38] "Structuralism and Literature," p. 155. I do not wish to overstate the case. In all his book-length studies (*Littérature et signification; Grammaire du Décaméron; Introduction à la littérature fantastique*) , Todorov does briefly deal with social and ideological structures. As he wrote me, "I just believe one cannot be a specialist of everything simultaneously."

[39] *The Fantastic,* p. 10.

[40] "Structuralism and Literature," p. 159, and "Structural Analysis of Narrative," p. 71. An exception to my generalization is Todorov's study of *Les liaisons dangereuses* in *Littérature et signification.*

ment."[41] Both the author and his milieu and the whole concrete work, then—which most readers have traditionally found most important in literature—are drastically attenuated in value. In their place is an abstract structure of an internal form or aspect of a form. It is literature become pure artifact.

We discern here Todorov's persistent effort to delimit "literature" as an autonomous object for scientific study, and to that extent we can follow him. But his rejection of the "world" and the whole concrete text as elements of the proper study of literature raises issues so fundamental to the whole enterprise of literature that we can wish Todorov had examined his postulates more thoroughly. One of the themes, in fact, of Jameson's *The Prison-House of Language* is the question of the relationship between literature and "reality," and he opens his book with an analysis of Saussure's place in the "vaster crisis in the sciences in general" regarding the relationship of superstructure to infrastructure, of synchrony to diachrony.[42] The subject necessitates Jameson's massive analysis, for there are no easy assumptions here. Todorov has too quickly accepted as final the auto-referentiality of the text, perhaps in despair over the problems involved in containing literary components and their extrinsic reference points within a scientific poetics. In this way he joins company with Robbe-Grillet and Roland Barthes in asserting the identity of form and content, thereby diminishing drastically the traditional mimetic role of literature. Several replies are possible, the one by David Caute in *The Illusion* will serve. The content of a work of art has three elements: 1) subject (world); 2) treatment of the subject (form); and 3) associations stimulated in the audience. "Content always refers to the world (material, mental, associative or whatever) *outside* the work of art mediated and reshaped by artistic form. . . . Literature is not mathematics, or music, or chess."[43]

The other source of Todorov's abstractness—his devaluation of the whole individual work—is characteristic of Eastern European formalism and French structuralism in general. The "phenomenological" and "existential" critics—Eugenio Donato, Georges Poulet, Merleau-Ponty, Mikel Dufrenne—have attacked

---

41 *The Fantastic*, p. 9.
42 See esp. pp. 14–15, 160, 211, 212-13.
43 *The Illusion: An Essay on Politics, Theatre and the Novel* (New York: Harper & Row, 1971), p. 151.

the structuralists on this basis for several years.[44] Jameson iterates their complaint:

> We must here underscore a tendency which we found at work in an analogous moment of Formalism as well. . . . This is the transformation of diachronic events into synchronic categories, the replacement of the event by the static concept. . . . It is for this reason, it seems to me, that the purely classificatory uses of the actantial reduction . . . are unsatisfactory.[45]

The primacy of categories freezes the text and rigidifies response to the dynamic experience of reading.

The "phenomenological" method contrasts sharply. Meaning in art is a joint achievement of artist and reader; writing and reading are both acts, every text dependent upon both for meaning. Todorov does partly defend himself by arguing that "In practice, it is always a question of going continually back and forth from abstract literary properties to individual works and vice versa,"[46] and he follows this practice in *Poétique de la prose* (for example, his analysis of the James tale). But in other instances—notably in the *Decameron* book—he does not move back and forth, the stories "used only to display an abstract literary structure."[47] These stories he reduces to their barest action in order to perceive what they contain in common, and he employs "a schematic formulation which retains only the common elements" of the plots. Clearly, then (as it has been suggested of Lévi-Strauss), Todorov cannot be sweepingly accused of disrespecting stories.[48] He is not interested in narrative merely for the exercise of breaking them down into their minimal structures. But even though there is "a way back" from the abstract schema to the individual tale (back to parts of the diagram of algorithm of action, theme, rhetoric, speaker, speech event, participants, narrated event), the final effect of his approach, by ignoring the relation between text and reader and by his categorical preoccupation, is to diminish our immediate response to literature as a felt experience.

Furthermore, not only is Todorov excessively abstract and removed from the dynamic interaction of story and reader, but his very modesty in limiting his aims in order to perform some

---

44 Briefly summarized by Andrew, pp. 58–59.
45 *The Prison-House of Language*, p. 126. "Actantial" derives from A. J. Greimas' term for any structure underlying the surface content.
46 "Structural Analysis of Narrative," p. 71.
47 "Structural Analysis of Narrative," p. 73.
48 Andrew, p. 47.

work well, one of his most attractive traits, finally betrays him. The self-imposed limitation of his field of study threatens the factual and logical validity of his conclusions. His method should be contrasted to the one well established in the United States, particularly in the study of nineteenth-century English literature, but also formulated by critics as diverse as Leslie Fiedler and (following J. R. Firth) John Spencer and Michael Gregory. It is called the "contextual" approach. Fiedler describes it in this way:

> The best criticism can hope to do is to set the work in as many illuminating contexts as possible: the context of the genre to which it belongs, of the whole body of work of its author, of the life of that author and of his times. In this sense, it becomes clear that the "text" is merely one of the contexts of a piece of literature, its lexical or verbal one, no more or less important than the sociological, psychological, historical, anthropological, or generic. The contextual critic desires only to *locate* the work of art, to point toward the place where his contextual circles overlap, the place in which the work exists in all its ambiguity and plenitude.[49]

The linguists Spencer and Gregory say virtually the same thing:

> A literary text may be said to have a context of situation in the sense in which it was understood by Firth. A text may, that is, be regarded as an "utterance" which is part of a complex social process; and therefore the personal, social, linguistic, literary, and ideological circumstances in which it was written need, as literary scholars have always recognized, to be called upon from time to time when any serious examination of a literary text is being made.[50]

This "contextual" approach has been employed effectively in the study of nineteenth-century writers, for example, by Walter Houghton (*The Art of Newman's "Apologia,"* 1945), John Holloway (*The Victorian Sage,* 1953), and Richard Ohmann (*Shaw: The Style and the Man,* 1962). These critics not only

---

[49] *Love and Death in the American Novel*, p. 10. David Caute in *The Illusion* has also challenged the structuralists for their diminished, crippling conception of "text": "the final text is a purely arbitrary moment in a long process of amendment and revision" (p. 149).

[50] "An approach to the study of style," in *Linguistics and Style,* ed. John Spencer (London: Oxford Univ. Press, 1964), p. 100. Roman Jakobson, who has inspired both formalists and structuralists, also offered a caution to excessive auto-referentiality in his "Closing Statement: Linguistics and Poetics," in *Style in Language,* ed. Thomas Sebeok (Cambridge, Mass.: MIT Press, 1960), p. 353. Jakobson identifies six factors involved in a text: addresser and addressee, context and message, contact and code.

insist upon the importance of considering together history, culture, author, genre, structure, paragraph, sentence, and word, but they follow operational methodologies for relating each context (e.g., Ohmann's "epistemic choices"). By comparison with these critics we can see just how limited are Todorov's aims (though he can teach them much in rigorous thinking), for he not only insists upon studying only the strictly literary context of "a complex social process," but he further limits himself to only some of the possible strictly literary contexts (especially by his tendency to minimize as a subject of concern the converging patterns which constitute a whole work). And this is a serious matter, because if, as the contextual critics claim, meaning derives from the interdependence and interaction of all the contexts, if a text is plural and its reality requires a holistic reading, then Todorov, by his deliberate avoidance of crucial contexts, may misjudge meaning. He is right in arguing that methodology is not a minor area of the larger field, but he does not show us a methodology operational for the whole reality of literature. He would reply, no doubt correctly, that no such methodology exists or can exist in our present state of knowledge. But the contextual model offers a reliable heuristic that potentially contains Todorov's scientific rigor within the wholeness of traditional humanistic literary concerns.

This lack of humanistic wholeness, which a Huxley or a Newman considers inseparable from literature, is Todorov's essential failure. I have concentrated upon his attenuation of the communication act. Of even greater significance is his general omission of the evaluative and judgmental as a part of literary experience. In the matter of esthetic judgment, Todorov would say, with considerable justification, that we must first describe accurately before judging. But since expressed or implied moral attitudes are a part of the system of signs, they therefore deserve at least as much (and I believe more) systematic analysis and tools for understanding as the other elements of the text. Todorov has too easily accepted the arbitrary and conventional nature of language, the intransivity of words, the closed universe of the sign. To say that "literary discourse cannot be true or false, it can only be valid in relation to its own premises,"[51] is both to oversimplify dogmatically and to abandon literature's traditional mimetic and pragmatic roles. By his deliberate with-

---

[51] *The Fantastic,* p. 10. See Andrew, pp. 56–58, on the controversy over truth versus validity.

drawal from esthetic and moral judgment into a methodological preoccupation with a shrunken literature, Todorov reduces the seriousness of his enterprise. Thus he contributes to the continued diminution of the importance of literature to life.

Many of these objections, however, are blunted by the very provisional and initiatory nature of Todorov's investigations. He declared recently:

> Where does language end? and where does the discourse begin? At the present time we are still very unsure. But I believe that in our field the very raising of certain questions is in itself an important step. Good questions are perhaps more necessary right now than acceptable answers.[52]

Todorov's assertion that methodology is the "very center" of poetics, "its principal goal,"[53] offers a way into a larger criticism. For if literature (including criticism) contributes to culture— is significantly involved in interpreting and sustaining life—then the *goal* of poetics includes and ultimately directs methodology. Todorov's great virtue is his rigor. Hopefully we will witness the future enlargement of his criticism to include the coordination of the complex content of literature.

---

[52] "Structuralism and Literature," p. 168.
[53] "Structural Analysis of Narrative," p. 76.

Semiology and Literary Theory

Susan Wittig

University of Texas

WITHIN the last half-dozen years or so, the concepts of semiology have become a focus for discussion in all areas of aesthetic discourse, providing not only a complex paradigm of definitions but a complicated set of new problems—and perhaps reformulations of old ones—as well. The fact that these semiological definitions and methodologies have become current, even fashionable, has engendered a number of questions from critics of more traditional background, who wonder what semiology can offer to the theory and practice of literary criticism. Moreover, semiotics itself stands at something of a crossroads, having arrived at a theoretical development sufficient to serve as a critique of its own basic assumptions, and a critical recognition sharp enough to discern some of the problematic constraints it has imposed upon its own understanding of signification. For these reasons, I would like to examine some definitions within the framework of the theoretical development that has led contemporary semiotics to this critical self-examination, and to suggest how literary criticism is involved, even implicated, in this reevaluation.

Semiotics claims for itself the distinction of being a science of sciences, a theoretical foundation upon which complete and systematic descriptions of social phenomena and forms of human expression may be based. It concerns itself exclusively, and ambitiously, with the study of sign systems and with the production of meaning; it takes as its methodological base some of the methods of linguistics, but it *subsumes* linguistics, for it sees natural language as only one of a very large number of languages. In the semiotic view, all social activities—myth, moral codes, economics, politics, the arts—all these social systems are languages, encoded in various structures: structures of exchange, material structures, verbal structures, tonal structures, and so forth. These second- and third-order communication systems demonstrate the same basic principles as those which characterize the first-order system of natural language: the double articulation of the signifier and the signified; the nature of the relationship of the sign to the referent, whether it is iconic or conventional; the character of the sign, and the character of whole systems, as either denotative or connotative or both; and the constitution of complete sign systems as syntactically ordered patterns of relational components. Insofar as the literary sign is treated in semiology, then, it is viewed within the larger perspective of *all* sign-making activity—as demonstrating the same principles, although to different degrees and with significantly different emphases, that shape all signifying modes.[1]

I would like to trace a major developmental pattern in literary semiology by beginning with the linguistic work of Ferdinand de Saussure.[2] It was Saussure who first asserted the arbitrary nature of the sign, and who first postulated its articulation into two component elements: a signifier and a signified. It was also Saussure who outlined the important distinction between synchronic linguistics (the study of language as a state-system) and diachronic linguistics (the study of language as an evolving system). Concerned that linguistics develop a descriptive component capable of systematically specifying the patterns of any communicative activity, Saussure insisted that only when the functional components of a whole system are described and their relationship to one another clearly defined can the synchronic, or state-system be understood—and only after that synchronic system has been described can the diachronic evolution of systems be discussed meaningfully. For a corollary to this proposition, Saussure developed the concepts of *syntagm*—the developmental, temporal succession of language as speech, chained in a sequential occurrence, *in praesentia*—and of *paradigm,* associational patterns of language, a-temporal, a-sequential, held in potentiality in the mind of the

---

[1] For a review of the distinction between everyday speech and literary language, see Tzvetan Todorov, "Artistic Language and Ordinary Language," *Times Literary Supplement,* 5 Oct. 1973, pp. 1169–70.
[2] Ferdinand de Saussure, *Course in General Linguistics,* ed. Charles Bally and Albert Sechehaye (New York: Philosophical Library, 1966). Passages of particular interest are pp. 7–17, 65–70, and 91–95.

speaker. In speech, Saussure says, the speaker selects an item from the paradigms of similar items that he holds in his mind and inserts that item in the syntagm of his speech—a process of selection and combination. Saussure postulated as well the categories of *langue* and *parole*: the *langue,* the communal storehouse of lexical and syntactical patterns, the coded, regularized system of autonomous social conventions and social values which constrain and control human expression; and the *parole,* the individual, unique, one-time expression of this community possession. It is only because we possess the common code of the *langue,* Saussure says, that we can understand one another; without it, our efforts to communicate would be fruitless. This same concept can be found as well in the semiotic studies of Charles Sanders Peirce and Charles Morris, both of whom view language (both natural and artificial language) as a social system of signs that mediate the responses of individual members of the community to one another and to their environment. In this tradition, the concept of constraints institutionalized by the community upon its signifying systems has taken on a major importance.

Prompted by their discussions of Saussure's principles, some Russian Formalists of the early 1920's were encouraged to see literature itself as a diachronic system of evolving genres, subject to the same developmental principles as natural language— and to treat the single literary work as a synchronic system of individual components, related to one another *functionally,* within a formal code. In these terms, code may mean both the generic expectations established by our acquaintance with other, similar works, and the formal structures of phonological, syntactical, and metrical repetitions within the poem itself. If a sonnet is in French, for instance, we certainly cannot understand it unless we understand the French language-code; we may not be able to comprehend it fully, however, unless we comprehend the sonnet-code, with its formal, generically determined patterns. Other Formalists, for example Vladimir Propp, approached the concept of genre itself as a synchronic system: all works within the genre share similar structural features, related within an identical structure. Propp's work on the Russian fairy tale, which also employed the Saussurian concept of selection-combination as a principle of the creation of the tale, stressed the constraints imposed by the genre upon the individual tale.[3] In this view, the tale is constructed according to the patterned constraints built into the genre to which it belongs; without these affiliations a tale is almost totally incomprehensible, because it is new, strange—it is in a different language, and its audience possesses no cognitive pattern by which it may be decoded. Propp's study, not published in English until 1958, has been of major importance to students of folklore and popular literatures.

The same formative principle has been significant in the work of Claude Lévi-Strauss on myth. Like Propp, Saussure, Peirce, and Morris, Lévi-Strauss contends that the systematization of the code and the constraining forces imposed by the culture upon myth are its most important formational factors; without cultural significance, myth has no meaning—and cultural significance requires the communal understanding and communication of all the elements involved in the creation of the myth.[4]

These studies have two important features which are common to much semiological work: they are linked by their use of linguistic concepts and methodologies, primarily the structural linguistics of Ferdinand de Saussure; and they are consistent in their assertion, in one way or another, that the communal observation of the code, the *langue,* is of primary importance in understanding the work, or sign-system. They are often cited, as well, in the development of the semiologically oriented study of literature and literary signification. It is not difficult to see why this focus should become important in studies of these kinds of community arts, and particularly in anthropology and folklore; however, when this emphasis was subsumed in a general way into the semiotic model, it began to provide some crucial difficulties that we are just now beginning to understand fully. Very recently, and again, under the influence of Russian Formalism and the Prague School, who introduced the notions of foregrounding and estrangement into the vocabulary of stylistics, this emphasis upon the code has been seriously questioned, and the whole continuum of semiological work which

---

[3] Vladimir Propp, *Morphology of the Folktale,* trans. Laurence Scott (Austin: Univ. of Texas Press, 1968).

[4] See particularly Lévi-Strauss's introduction to *The Raw and the Cooked,* trans. John and Doreen Weightman (New York: Harper & Row, 1969), and "The Story of Asdiwahl," in *The Structural Study of Myth and Totemism,* ed. Edmund Leach (London: Tavistock Publications, 1968).

derives from Saussure is now being called up for review—primarily by Julia Kristeva, who has suggested that the signification of a work of art can only be understood in terms of a transgression of the commonly accepted code: that is, even though a work of art is invariably subject to social and artistic codes, its meaning, its significance, lies in the way to the degree that it infringes the code, renovates it, perhaps even endangers it. The work of art, rather than yielding to social and generic constraints, challenges them—although that challenge, paradoxically, has the effect of renewing the social and artistic contract.[5]

This then is one aspect of the dilemma faced by semiotic studies, a dilemma brought about by a long-term adherence to a particular linguistics model and the enforced examination brought about by the development of a competing model. However, this particular challenge involves contemporary literary criticism, particularly American literary criticism, in rather different terms; generally speaking, we have not yet begun to recognize the importance of understanding formal generic influence and individual deviation from the genre, for we have not yet seen how critical is the dominance of the generic code. Most American literary criticism is in the pre-Saussurian state of recognizing only a multitude of evolutionary differences, of uniquenesses, and has not yet begun to develop a systematic concept of the formal relations among literary works. It does not, therefore, articulate fully or appreciate precisely the violations of code, transgressions that make art possible and meaningful. The concepts of semiology, in relation to the notions of code and violation of code, can establish an important forum for discussion in literary criticism.

I would like to make this last statement more explicit by turning to the work of Roman Jakobson, whose studies of linguistics and poetics follow in the tradition of Saussure but who has added several important features to this semiotic model: the concepts of encoder and decoder, or sender and receiver, and the notion of the coded message, transmitted by means of a communications channel, the physical and psychological connection between sender and receiver.[6]

5 Julia Kristeva, "The System and the Speaking Subject," *Times Literary Supplement,* 12 Oct. 1973, pp. 1249–50.

6 Roman Jakobson, "Linguistics and Poetics," in *Style in Language,* ed. Thomas A. Sebeok (Cambridge, Mass.: MIT Press) , pp. 350–77.

This semiotic model, which is also outlined by Charles Morris,[7] may prove useful in the study of literature in several important ways; it will provide in this essay a very brief and sketchy typology of literary forms and of kinds of literary criticism. Based on the dyadic distinction between sender and message, receiver and message, and message and referent, six basic functions can be distinguished within the communications act—functions that may be common to all communications events. The relationship between message and external referent, the *referential* function (or, in Morris's terms, the *semantic* dimension) becomes dominant in scientific language or in other heavily denotative systems. In mimetic and representational theories of literature, the semantic dimension has been considered to be the dominant feature of the literary sign; literary critics who are concerned with the referential function are likely to explain the work with reference to the external context in relation to which the meaning is said to be produced: in relation to the social or political or psychological "truth to life" of a novel, or play, or poem.

Two other functions outlined by Jakobson, the conative and the emotive, are both described in Morris's pragmatic dimension, the relation of the sign to its interpretants. In the emotive function, the dominant features of the message focus attention upon the sender's attitudes toward what he is speaking about. For example, the simple statement "Unfortunately, he couldn't attend today's meeting," is partly referential, but also partly emotive, because it is an expression of the speaker's regret, as well as a statement of fact; a narrator who deliberately lies to us in the face of contradictory evidence is employing a similar device—calling attention to himself as narrator, to his own veracity or lack of it, and to the emotive function. Considerations of this function *within* the work have led us into problems of point of view in literature, and into the careful treatment of modes of narratorial intervention and manipulation of the referential function, particularly in first-person novels: Wayne Booth's *The Rhetoric of Fiction* may be seen as a study of the emotive function. In terms of the creation of the work, concern with the emotive function has also led us to adopt psychoana-

---

[7] Charles Morris, "Foundations of the Theory of Signs," in *Foundations of the Unity of Science*, ed. Otto Neurath, Rudolph Carnap, Charles W. Morris (Chicago: Univ. of Chicago Press, 1969), I, 78–137.

lytic and psychological approaches to the study of the artist's emotional and cognitive states. And in search of a larger understanding of the emotive function, we may move beyond the immediate author to the "collective unconscious" that has had a shaping hand in the formation of the literary work.

Orientation toward the receiver of the message, on the other hand, toward the conative function, can be most clearly seen in the emotional appeals of sentimental or didactic literatures, which attempt to move the reader to certain attitudes—although the argument can be and has been made that all literatures work toward this end. Correspondingly, there is the audience-oriented school of literary criticism—Stanley Fish's *The Self-Consuming Artifact* provides an articulate defense of this position—which finds the meaning of the literary work in the audience's engagement with it, and views the seekings of the reader's mind as he makes his way through a Baconian sentence or down the labyrinthian ways of *Paradise Lost,* as the final interpretant of literature—in fact, the real *meaning* of the literary event. This particular critical approach is very much in line with Morris's semiological work—a behavioralistic view of the signifying process that led him to postulate the interpreter's response as the final interpretant of the sign.

But in addition to these three functions, there are three others which are perhaps of greater interest to students of literature, and to contemporary semiologists, because they call into question considerations of literary form. There is first of all the phatic function, in which attention is drawn not to the message, but to the medium of communication, to the channel itself. In everyday language, the sender may attempt to determine whether the communication is being received ("Are you listening?") or the receiver may assure the sender that the message has gotten through ("I understand . . . uh hu . . . right"). A similar technique is used in oral genres, when the minstrel commands his audience's attention by saying, "Lords, be quiet and listen to me"—or even by a modern novelist who numbers the pages of his book out of order, or inserts blank pages, calling our attention to the actual book we have in our hands, to the channel through which the communication is made. In these brief communication sequences, whether spoken, or graphic, or gestural, very little information is exchanged, if we take information to mean reference; the essence of the communication is to make us acutely aware of the communication link, the channel.

But even more important for the purposes of literary criticism is the *metalingual* function, where features of the code are employed to call attention to the nature of the code itself, or to the problems involved in decoding the message. This function occurs often in everyday conversation ("You have an interesting accent,"—or, said to a child at the dinner table, "Don't talk with your mouth full; we can't understand you"). In a literary work, the metalingual function often serves to call attention to the conventions of the code, which become invisible to us because we are habituated to them. Take, for example, the long-winded *occultatio* near the end of Chaucer's *The Knight's Tale,* where the Knight spends nearly fifty lines describing to us exactly how he is going to *abridge* his description of Arcite's funeral—by telling us in minute detail all the items he is going to leave out—that is, by leaving all of the omissions *in.* The same effect achieved by the over-extension of the rhetorical convention in this instance is achieved in other instances by omission: in an unrhymed sonnet, for example, where a crucial formal convention of the sonnet-code, the rhyme scheme, is violated, and we are made sharply aware, because the rhyme is absent, of its function within the sonnet form. The referential importance of these features is minimal; their primary function, rather, is to make us aware of the rhetorical and formal conventions of the code to which we have become habituated to the point of having ceased to perceive them.

Finally, there is the poetic function, the "set to the message," in Jakobson's famous phrase, the focus upon the message for its own sake. All poetry, most novelistic prose, calls attention in one way or another to itself, as language-play, as conceptual play; the language is not primarily referential, although it may refer to some "real" object or event; it is not, in this view, even primarily emotive or conative, although those functions may play a role in our understanding of its causes and its effects. The literary sign rather is primarily reflexive; that is, the sign turns back upon itself, to examine its own sign-form and its own sign-function. The system becomes, as Hjelmslev suggests, a connotative, rather than a denotative system—with this crucial difference: that what the poetic sign connotes is its own nature as poetic sign.

These matters are the specific concerns of Formalism, which attempts to establish beyond question the autotelic nature of the literary event. Here, we can see Formalism directly opposed to those species of literary criticism which focus on the semantic dimension, on the relation of the work to some external referent, and opposed just as strongly to pragmatic theories of literature, to the study of the psychological state of the artist, or to the cognitive processes of the reader.

This opposition is very near, these days, to the center of the critical predicament in which we have once again found ourselves, as we periodically do, hung upon the horns of the dilemma of reference. It seems to be a general human tendency to attempt to break down the semiotic process and to name some ultimate referent which is not a sign, which is a *thing,* a "real" object in the "real" world. This participation in external reality, this "representational" quality of the sign seems to impart to it whatever value it may have as a social, a communicative, even an artful object. Especially in this era of Watergates, as we are confronted by the consequences of political sign-making—the substitution of the public sign for the private act, the use of words to befuddle rather than to clarify—we have come to distrust mediated realities, and to look for immediate ones; we have turned again, in a new kind of Platonic fervor, away from the sign-world to a world where, we hope, things undeniably exist, where the expression of ideas is unambiguous, where literature and our activities as literary scholars have social relevance. But Formalism, in its pure state, resists these temptations, and maintains that the value and meaning of the work of literature is in itself. This position, as we all know, has earned for the Formalist critic the charge of reductionism, of solipsistic self-indulgence; as Paul de Man has pointed out, Formalism nowadays is mostly described in terms of imprisonment and claustrophobia: "the prison house of language," "the sterility of Formalism," and so on.[8]

But there is another view of this problem of reference, a larger, more specifically *semiological* perspective, which may allow us to resolve this difficulty—or at the very least, may help us to come to terms with it. In this view, which can be traced to the seminal work of Charles Sanders Peirce, the ultimate

---

[8] Paul de Man, "Semiology and Rhetoric," *Diacritics,* 3 (Fall 1973), 27–33.

referent, or interpretant, of any sign is *another* sign.[9] According to Peirce, we cannot *de*construct the semiotic process by looking for a sign-referent in external reality; in point of fact, Peirce says, we inevitably interpret one sign by translating it from its original medium into another sign, in another medium. For instance, the social world portrayed in a nineteenth-century novel does not have a referent in nineteenth-century "reality"; what that literary sign-system refers to, in Peirce's terms, is *another* set of signs, the highly patterned, carefully coded signs of the social system, embodied in linguistic patterns, in gesture, in costume, in hair style, in furniture style, and so forth. We may, if we choose, interpret these social signs by a commentary in the first-order system of natural language, in which we explain how these social systems work, but that *too* is a sign system.

And another example, perhaps a little closer to our immediate concern: in the act of critical analysis, we translate the literary work from its own medium (which is itself a translation of several congruent sign-systems, as we have just seen) into the axiological categories of whatever theoretical approach we have adopted. We do not come closer to the work in so doing; we have simply reevaluated it—have translated it into the signs of another sign system. The danger in this process, obviously, is that we often deceive ourselves; we believe that our literary theorizing takes us closer to the work; we forget that we have committed the novel or play or poem to a translation, and that

---

[9] Charles Sanders Peirce, *Collected Papers*, 8 vols. (Cambridge: Harvard Univ. Press, 1931–35), esp. II and V. However, the discussions of the particular problem are scattered throughout Peirce's writings. A very good, brief review of the concepts outlined here may be found in John Dewey's discussion of Peirce and Morris, in "Peirce's Theory of Linguistic Signs, Thought, and Meaning," *The Journal of Philosophy*, 43 (Feb. 1946). Dewey says:

> Peirce uniformly holds (1) that there is no such thing as a sign in isolation, every sign being a constituent of a sequential set of signs, so that apart from membership in this set, a thing has no meaning—or is *not* a sign; and (2) that in the sequential movement of signs thus ordered, the meaning of the earlier ones in the series is provided by or constituted by the later ones as their interpretants, until a conclusion (*logical* as a matter of course) is reached. Indeed, Peirce adheres so consistently to this view that he says, more than once, that signs, *as such*, form an infinite series, so that no conclusion of reasoning is forever final, being inherently open to having its meaning modified by further signs. (p. 88)

What Peirce has done here, it would seem, is to project the semantic dimension upon the syntactic dimension, excluding almost entirely external reference—except insofar as that external reference becomes a component within the syntactic dimension.

it is likely to have suffered in the process. And we forget—or do not realize—that our particular sign system may have deficiences which do not permit us to see all the crucial aspects of a particular work or group of works.

In a sense, then, as Peirce has implied, there is no referential function, as it is usually thought of—neither in ordinary language nor in the languages of art—for the interpretant of one sign is always and necessarily another sign, and semiology becomes the study of an infinite semiosis, rather than the study of an immediate—or even mediate—reference: the study of signs which refer to signs which refer to signs, and so on, *ad infinitum*.

However semiology reconciles these differences of opinion, it does appear that it can provide literary criticism with—at the very least—a framework which can allow us to see our own critical approaches, our own signifying practices, in a broader perspective; in other words, it may enable us to construct a typology of literary criticism. Beyond that, a clear understanding of the process of signification and of the production of meaning is vital to all students of literature, and a sharper sense of how the literary sign is similar to, and different from, other forms of social sign-making is crucial to a broader perspective upon human creativity.

B. The Social Sciences

Cultures as Systems: Toward a Critique of Historical Reason

Ludwig von Bertalanffy

THE topic presented here is ancient, but still hotly debated. Given modern expression, it may be formulated thus: The consideration of cultures as "systems" is a useful model which can form the basis of a science of "culturology," opening new vistas and approaches toward understanding the phenomenon of civilization.

This proposition is in one sense very old. As Oswald Spengler stated in his *Decline of the West*,[1] the usual view of human history is that of a linear progress, starting somewhere in the neolithic age and leading, via the cultures of antiquity and the Middle Ages, up to our modern civilization and into a future of inexhaustible potentialities. Opposed to this is the view of history as a sequence of great cultures, each showing a sort of life cycle, with birth, growth, maturity, and final decline. Spengler was neither the first nor the last Western protagonist of a cyclic view of history. Giambattista Vico was possibly its first proponent in the West, with precursors in ancient and even Indian cosmologies. More recently, this basic view found expression in the work of Toynbee, Sorokin, and others, and in a certain sense also in Marxian dialectic materialism.

Such "philosophy of history" is not in high regard among professional historians, but the same problem appears in mod-

---

1 Oswald Spengler, *Der Untergang des Abendlandes* (Munich: Beck, 1922). Abridged English translation: *The Decline of the West*, trans. C. F. Atkinson (New York: Modern Library, 1965). See also: Ludwig von Bertalanffy, "Einführung in Spenglers Werk," *Kölnische Zeitung*, Literaturblatt No. I–VI (May 1924).

ern, empirical investigation, as, for example, the origin of pre-Columbian cultures. Thus to Alfred L. Kroeber, the dean of American anthropologists, American and Eurasian cultures did not appear to be "parts of the same plot," while other recent writers such as A. Ford consider "human history as a single connected story."[2] The identical problem is expressed in different ways. Are cultural change and evolution essentially an expression of an inherent and autochthonous dynamics, or are they brought about by cultural diffusion? Is history a sequence of individual, unrepeatable and therefore merely describable events, or does it show recurrences and regularities as, respectively, the opposing "idiographic" and "nomothetic" views of history contend? Is it the case that events entirely different in content but comparable in structure reappear in widely different geographical and temporal locations? These and other formulations are different aspects of the very same problem.

We are all aware that the views of so-called "cyclic historians" were refused by the great majority of professionals. The great "Debate on Spengler" in the 1920's[3] was repeated in the "Debate on Toynbee" in the 1950's,[4] often in identical words. Some of the principal objections can be disposed of quickly by admitting that they are correct. It is generally agreed that the great world constructions by Spengler or Toynbee rest on insufficient facts and arbitrary selection of data that put them into a procrustean bed of preconceived notions. Pieter Geyl's debate with Toynbee[5] is typical of this critique and hardly needs further elaboration. But, on the other hand, as Kroeber[6] and Sorokin[7] have pointed out, there is a broad area of agreement among the theoretical historians, and a general acceptance of the facts of "ups" and "downs" in the history of civilizations. The factual content of cultural history is essentially the same whether we label it, with Spengler, as "Decline," or with Mac-Neill as the "Rise of the West." Spengler's oversimplified scheme of eight "high cultures," or Toynbee's scheme of some thirty, was exploded by the exploration of many "lost" or "forgotten"

2 See Caroll L. Riley, et al., eds., *Man Across the Sea* (Austin: Univ. of Texas Press, 1971), pp. 221, 455.
3 Manfred Schröter, *Metaphysik des Untergangs* (Munich: Leibniz, 1949).
4 Arnold Toynbee, *A Study of History.* XII: *Reconsiderations* (New York: Oxford Univ. Press, 1961).
5 Pieter Geyl, *Debates with Historians* (New York: Meridian Books, 1958).
6 Alfred L. Kroeber, *Style and Civilization* (Ithaca: Cornell Univ. Press, 1957).
7 Pitirim A. Sorokin, *Social Philosophies of an Age of Crisis* (Boston: Beacon, 1950).

cultures in the short period since their books were written; but the general scheme of Rise and Fall was reinforced rather than refuted by these discoveries.

A second criticism of theoretical history is directed against the so-called organismic analogy. Civilizations obviously are not "organisms" like plants or animals; and it seems to attribute to the theoretical historians a somewhat infantile naïveté to presume that they took a poetic metaphor literally. It is worth noting, however, that while the organismic analogy is passionately attacked in history, it is used without qualms in sociology. It can be said that the concept and model of "system" is central in recent developments of the social sciences, as shown by American functionalism in sociology and French structuralism in anthropology. Rather prosaic phenomena such as business enterprises, professional specialization in tribes and nations, and urban development appear to follow life cycles and system laws which can even be stated in mathematical equations, e.g., the law of allometric growth.[8] The problem of a theoretical history, it seems, can be defined by the question of whether the model of "system," which is accepted in the synchronic considerations of sociology, may also be used in the diachronic considerations of history; whether it applies not only to the temporal cross section of present societies but also to the longitudinal study of their becoming and history.

Of deeper impact is the third, or epistemological objection against theoretical history. Spengler, for example, was accused of unscientific, subjective, intuitive procedure, and of wild metaphysical speculations. Toynbee, rather touchingly, defends himself against the reproach of considering cultures as "organisms" and refers to his "well-proven empirical method," while obviously his constructs, including parentage and affiliation of civilizations, are just as speculative and thrive on the organismic metaphor he condemns.

The answer to these questions of method is in the concept of "model," which only recently has found the attention and clarification it deserves. For example, we may strip away from Spengler's work all metaphysics, philosophy, and artistry. This robs him of much of his poetry and attraction; but what remains

---

[8] Raoul Naroll and Ludwig von Bertalanffy, "The Principle of Allometry in Biology and the Social Sciences," *General Systems*, 1 (1956), 76–89. Mason Haire, "Biological Models and Empirical Histories of the Growth of Organizations," *Modern Organization Theory*, ed. Mason Haire (New York: Wiley & Sons, 1959), pp. 272–306.

is a conceptual model; that is, a construct of cultures as "systems," with general principles or laws applying to such entities. The question, then, is empirical, i.e., whether such a model is useful and leads to explanation of facts, to synthesis of otherwise unconnected data, and to verifiable predictions.

Such model construction is not particular to theoretical history. First, it is to a degree irrelevant in which way it was obtained: by intuition, speculation, or empirical generalization.[9] The history of science shows that models and laws of extreme importance were not infrequently reached by wild speculation. Kepler, for example, derived his astronomical system and laws from fantastic Neoplatonic constructions. Furthermore, conceptual models—paradigms is Thomas Kuhn's term[10]—are basic in any science and in ordinary cognition as well. Models of different generality are used throughout history. A biography of, say, Napoleon, by the most "empirical" and "unphilosophical" writer is determined by a "model" of that person which guides him in the selection, arrangement, and interpretation of data, models which in this particular case range from Napoleon the Corsican bandit to Napoleon the philosophical pioneer of a unified Europe, with any number of intermediates between.

Thus no historical description or narration is possible without conceptual models. We could not even speak of wars or revolutions if such terms did not refer to conceptual schemes which are based on commonalities, analogies, and recurrences. The difference between conventional and theoretical history is only one of degree. The orthodox historian writing on the Greek polis or the American or Russian Revolutions uses commonsense constructs or models which, as experience shows, are only too often tainted by his national, religious, social, and other biases. The theoretical historian consciously attempts a construct of history, with explicit delineation of his model and the consequences derived therefrom. Obviously this is an ideal, far from being realized in the series of thinkers from Vico to Spengler and others. But such considerations are apt to show that the attempt at theoretical history is not an irregularity. It is not in contrast to the "historical method," and not empty speculation, but rather an expansion of ordinary ways of thinking. "Cultures as systems" is, admittedly and emphatically, a more general

9 Arthur Koestler, *The Act of Creation* (London: Hutchinson, 1964).

10 Thomas S. Kuhn, *The Structure of Scientific Revolutions* (Chicago: Univ. of Chicago Press, 1962).

and abstract scheme than those in conventional historiography. But its validity depends not on a priori decisions about the historical method but on the criteria of appropriate models as used in ordinary life and in science.

This brief introduction cannot attempt to define "culture."[11] It seems more interesting to express, rather dogmatically, a few theses of a "system theory in history."

(1) History takes place not as an evolution of an amorphous humanity or of the species, Homo sapiens, but as the evolution of holistic entities or systems called cultures or civilizations, localized in space and time.

(2) Cultures show autonomous development in the sense that their changes are not completely accountable to changes of the environment, physical or cultural. They are "inner-directed," to use the term of Riesman, not merely "reactive" in response to stimuli, but "active" or creative systems.[12]

(3) The latter proposition relates to the question of autochthonous evolution and cultural diffusion. Clearly, cultural diffusion is far more extensive than was realized even a few decades ago. But significant cultural change is never passive reception, and is always active assimilation in the "open system" of culture. Cultural diffusion, even if patent and undisputed, contributes nothing to explain the "style" or origin of a culture. Christianity obviously was diffused over a large part of the ecumene but "in spirit" or "style" (to be discussed later) paleo-Christianity, Latin Catholic, Greek Orthodox, or Anglo-American Puritan Christianity are vastly different. Buddhist images go back to the diffusion of Hellenistic art in ancient Gandhara, but no one mistakes a Chinese Buddha for an Olympian deity. Classic Latin became a new language in vocabulary and structure when absorbed by Celtic and Germanic tribes, or converted into Church Latin and the Romance languages. Conversely, mere adoptions in cultural diffusion do not make for culture change—they are comparable to the imported silk hats which were sported by some African chiefs of the nineteenth century.

(4) "Culture traits do not a culture make" may be a *bon mot* for a system conception of culture, and the criticism it implies for much of conventional research. Take the example of

---

11 See Alfred L. Kroeber and Clyde Kluckhohn, *Culture. A Critical Review of Concepts and Definitions* (1952; rpt. New York: Vintage, 1963), which includes some 260 definitions of culture.

12 Ludwig von Bertalanffy, "General Systems Theory and Psychiatry—An Overview," *Psychiatric Spectator*, 4 (1967), 6–8.

the relation between Old-World and New-World cultures, discussed for centuries and reviewed in *Man Across the Sea*. It may well be that arrowheads, stone axes, and pottery show remarkable similarities in the Old and New Worlds (p. 271), and that long lists of cultural features shared between ancient Mesopotamia and Mesoamerica can be elaborated upon (pp. 266 ff). But this does not help in the understanding of the specifics of Maya or Aztec cultures—say the hundreds of rain gods in Uxmal and Kabah, or the 20,000 human victims sacrificed at the consecration of the great Teocalli in what today is Mexico City.

(5) When applying the system model, two aspects always have to be distinguished, and consequently also in historical entities. As was clearly recognized by Spengler and Vico, these are (a) commonalities of structure found in different systems and expressed in their so-called isomorphics, and (b) the specifics of systems, called "style" in culturological consideration.

As mentioned, general system laws can be stated in the sociocultural realm, as is demonstrated by mathematical equations found to apply to many phenomena such as population growth, urbanization, social differentiation, and others. On the other hand, specifics of individual systems make for the idiographic character or "style." This dichotomy is of a quite general nature. In biology, for example, there appear to be general laws of evolution and of adaptation to different environments; on the other hand, there are anatomical "types" or "styles," such as reptiles and mammals, marsupial and placental mammals. Different taxonomically and anatomically, they often show surprising "convergence" when adapted to similar environment, so that a true wolf and a marsupial "wolf" appear almost the same to a naïve observer. Similarly, there are basic functional demands, as for example in architecture: a place to live in, a place to defend, or to worship in—that is a "house," "a citadel," a "temple"—which, while common to all cultures as systems, may be erected in different "styles" in each.

The question, in biology, of "homology" and "analogy," is paralleled in culture by the question of convergence of independent developments or cultural diffusion. There seem to be certain prototypes, as it were, which appear in different and independent cultures. In other terms, there appear to be basic "structures" as described by Chomsky in linguistics, but probably also active in other fields of culture. For example, the primitive oval house or hut is common to Romans and Mayas; the "false arch" is found in Mycenean and pre-Columbian architecture; the archaic smile as a first attempt to give expression to sculpture occurs in archaic Greek statues, in the *Sourire de Reims,* and the Maya Corn God. On the other hand, there are "idiographic" or idiosyncratic features of the individual cultures and periods.

(6) That there are regularities in cultural evolution which are roughly comparable to a biological life cycle is, to an extent, trivial. We speak with facility of primitive, mature, and decadent stages in Greek plastic art or German music, of a "classic" stage in pre-Columbian art, of Greek Baroque in Pergamon. Even the biologist speaks of primitive, mature, and baroque species in the evolution of ammonities (cephalopods). (The statements on biological evolution given in von Bertalanffy's *Problems of Life,* can, to a large extent, be "translated" into description of cultural evolution). Trying to establish structural principles common to culture change or evolution is, therefore, but an expansion of a widely applied model or paradigm.

(7) In a survey of the variety of cultures explored by history, archeology, and anthropology, two principal types can be distinguished. They may be termed "anthropological" and "historical" cultures, primitive cultures and civilizations, or by similar terms. Among the hundreds of cultures known, only comparatively few had and made "history," that is, underwent significant changes in historical times. Others remained more or less stationary at a primitive level.

The exact number of high cultures or civilizations is uncertain, their delimitations are debatable, and intermediates may occur. It should be emphasized that the distinction just noted has nothing to do with adaptiveness or intelligence. Primitive cultures are outstandingly adapted to their frequently inclement environment, as the mere fact of their survival over immense periods of time demonstrates, while high cultures have vanished, and the fate of our own civilization is problematical. Similarly, the natural "intelligence" required of a bushman or Australian aborigine probably exceeds that of the average American in a routine job of our specialized society. Certain aspects of "primitive" cultures—such as language and kinship relations—are more complex than in our civilization. (Note, as an example accessible to the layman, the simplification occurring in Greek grammar from Homeric to Attic Greek, to the koine and modern Greek; or from Chaucerian to modern English.) Nevertheless,

the difference remains in cultures that, to the best of our knowledge, are stationary, and those which underwent—or perhaps
suffered—rapid cultural change within short periods of time.
Remember not only the few centuries of industrial technology
and the few decades of atomic energy; remember also the mere
fifty years of classical Athens, or the 150 years leading from the
first, pre-dynastic stone graves to the great pyramids of Egypt.

Neglect of this fact has serious political consequences.
United Nations members have an equal vote, whether they represent some primitive tribe (or rather ethnic splinters created
by the whimsy of colonial policy) or the historical "civilized"
nations. Speaking more generally, what, in a time of change
and paranoiac nationalism, does "culture" mean? When linguistic or religious groups, as in Canada or Ireland, make claims for
different "cultures," it becomes apparent that the definition of
"culture" and cognate words has immediate political impact.
What is "youth" or "counter culture"—a passing fashion, a sub-
culture, a new developmental phase? A word or label, as is all
too often the case in history, may become "reality," with dire
or sanguinary consequences.

(8) "Style" is hard to define and so is, consequently, the
number of distinct civilizations and periods that are enumerated.
We may remember, however, that similar difficulties are frequently encountered in taxonomic enterprises of natural science.
The zoologist or paleontologist relies on a somewhat mystical
faculty called "systematic tact." Depending on whether he is a
"lumper" or a "splitter," he may attribute the very same bones
to one or many species. So far as higher systematic units (such
as families, orders, classes, taxa) are concerned, hardly two text-
books of zoology are in full agreement. Hence the definition of
"style" and of "culture" in general (comparable to the species
concept in biology) always contains a conceptual model, and is
not simply derivable from "facts." Nevertheless it appears that
Mozart's music, Watteau's paintings, the "conquest of space" in
Western civilization, or Greek statuary, the polis, and the Platonic bodies, in some way "belong together" and are expressions
of the same "spirit of culture." Spengler was the past master in
the art of exploring that "spirit." His ur-symbols, by which he
tried to epitomize various cultures, are certainly not to be taken
as unique or irreplaceable, but they are brilliant insights into
their essentials.

(9) In the last resort, the "spirit of culture" appears to
derive from categories of experience, that is, the ways—percep-

tual and conceptual—by which humans bring order into what William James described as the "blooming, buzzing confusion" of sense impressions they receive. This order depends, first, on biological factors, specifically, the sensory-neuro-motor equipment of the species. As we know from von Uexkull's *umwelt* doctrine, the experienced world of an animal depends on its receptor and effector organs and therefore is different in different species. Perception never consists of mere "sense data" but is the organization of informational data by psychophysiological mechanisms. In human cognition, activities are added which may be subsumed under the term "symbolic," including cultural, linguistic, historical, and other factors. The idea that knowledge progressively leads to "truth" or "reality" is obsolete; knowledge is a tool which enables man (or any other animal) to find his way in the world and so to survive by selecting schemes or perspectives, both in immediate experience and in conceptual models, which adequately serve this goal but do not simply mirror the universe "as it is."[13]

It was a stroke of genius when Spengler chose mathematical paradigms as primeval or *ur*-symbols of civilizations, such as "plastic body" for the Apollonian, "cavernous space" for the Magic, and "infinite space" for Faustian culture, for the culture-dependent categories of experience find their most formalized expression in the mathematics which a civilization or period produces. The historical forms of mathematical development are therefore a fine indicator of the forms of experience in different cultures without, of course, admitting any monopolistic claim of the Spenglerian *ur*-symbols, or deriving from them metaphysical speculations.

(10) As to the position of our own culture in the present time, it appears that this, too, has followed the general scheme of cultures as systems, with one important difference. The obvious difference between the great civilizations of the past and ours is in the global and technological character of our own. Past civilizations—the classic, the so-called Magic, the West European, pre-Columbian America, and so forth—covered only limited areas of the earth, while the present is *global,* and even extends beyond this planet. Furthermore, past civilizations were limited in their resources and essentially restricted by an economy of needs. In contrast, modern technology would, in principle, provide for an increasing humanity and even an economy

---

13 Ludwig von Bertalanffy, "An Essay on the Relativity of Categories," *Philosophy of Science,* 22 (1955), 243–63.

of abundance, far distant as we may actually be from such a goal in the schizophrenic competition of vested interests, parties, nations, and superpowers.

There seems to me little doubt that the "Decline of the West" rather than being a dire prophecy is a historical fact. The splendid cultural development which began in the European countries around the year 1000 and produced Gothic cathedrals, Renaissance art, empirical science, Shakespeare and Goethe, and modern technological industry and wealth for the common man —this enormous cycle of history is accomplished. Not, indeed, that the "Decline of the West" means extinction of Western people, although this is a distinct possibility; but the "Decline" essentially means fulfillment and hence the end of creative potentialities. The following quotation points up this fact very concisely:

> We note the psychological change in those classes of society which had up till then been the creators of culture. Their creative power and creative energy dry up; men grow weary and lose interest in creation and cease to value it; they are disenchanted; their effort is no longer an effort toward a creative ideal for the benefit of humanity; their minds are occupied either with material interests, or with ideals unconnected with life on earth and realized elsewhere.

One may easily assume that this is taken from an editorial of yesterday's newspaper, decrying the modern decay of art, the loss of values, the commercialism of our time, its counterculture, the flight into Oriental religions, the Jesus freaks, and the like. In fact, it is a description of the late Roman Empire, by a solid and well-known historian, Michael I. Rostovtzeff.

Here, however, appear those two singularities of our civilization, globality and technology, which, in a way, explode the cyclic scheme and place our civilization at a different level from previous ones. Affluence is reached in a sector of the Western world; and technology could, in theory, provide the means of clearing the pockets of poverty left in our own society and advance the presently "under-developed" nations. If so, and presuming that catastrophes such as atomic war, urban decay, crime, racial strife, etc., can somehow be stemmed (quite an optimistic presupposition), the prediction would probably be of a global, technological, mass society in which old cultural values and individual creativity are replaced by novel devices, and a sort of social entropy is reached, leveling out individual, social, racial differences in a Brave New World of affluent mediocrity. This is probably what is meant when it is said that we are entering a "post-historical age." This is not a gratifying outlook for a Westerner, but it is more realistic than the philosophy of counterculture or that of progress toward a technological paradise.

These are a few, and admittedly superficially reviewed, aspects of a system model of culture. In conclusion, two points should be reemphasized. First, that the system model, compared to the conventional procedure of historiography, allows for new insight into civilization in general and specific civilizations in particular, permitting a clearer view into problems like growth and decay, cultural autonomy and diffusion, civilization and primitive culture, and the like. Second, there are a number of trends, different in origin and terminology but nevertheless based upon the same model: the old idea of cyclic history from Vico to Spengler, Toynbee, and Sorokin; American functionalism in sociology and ethnology; structuralism in anthropology of the French school as in Lévi-Strauss, and in Chomsky's linguistics; general system theory as interdisciplinary model, and others. These differ in their formulations owing to the field of origin, individual authors, and so forth. They agree, however, in the basic holistic or system viewpoint. Of these, general system theory is probably most advanced in its formulations and definitions of fundamental aspects. It may therefore be apt to provide a common "language" for these different movements and give them a unity previously lacking. It is in this sense as a working hypothesis, leading to new empirical research and providing a conceptual framework, that the concept of "cultures as systems" has been offered in this essay.

To explore the problems of historical method in depth would necessitate an investigation into what are historical (and scientific) facts, and what are the principles of historical selection, interpretation, and "truth." This would need a separate and lengthy presentation. However, insofar as the prevailing modes of historical thought are to examine parts rather than wholes, to take a monocultural focus rather than a transcultural one, to be linear rather than cyclical in presumption, and to take events as unique rather than to look for common structures and isomorphic trends—insofar as that is true, the conceptual framework discussed here is implicitly a contribution toward a "critique of historical reason."

Myth and the Ethnographer: a Critique of Lévi-Strauss

Erik Schwimmer

University of Toronto

THE relationship between mythology and ethnography has so far been like an unending but never very satisfactory love story. From the earliest days of ethnography (Herodotus), myths have been collected as a means of informing the scientific world of the culture of exotic peoples. From the very early days, mythology has been the subject of theoretical anthropological discourse (Plutarch). Enlightened colonial administrators who wished to 'understand' the natives and had a good classical education often turned to the study of myths for their special enlightenment.[1] The classical evolutionary schools of anthropology used myths as evidence (now recognised as more than dubious) for the prehistory of illiterate populations. When it began to be recognised that myths were not a reliable guide either to actual or past customs or to the facts of history, and when anthropology began to rely largely on data collected in the field and interpreted by functionalist theory, mythology went into a temporary decline. But even in this dark period, ethnographers continued to collect myths, either because they were not fully adhering to functionalism or else simply because myths are easy and pleasant to collect, and because they offer incidental information on various topics. Besides, Malinowski himself had a great interest in myth, as well as a theory of myth. It was really only the firm Radcliffe-Brownians who had little use for them at all.

Around 1960, myth collecting again became a highly respectable practice, in the context of several specialised anthro-

---

1 See Sir George Grey, *Polynesian Mythology* (Christchurch: Whitcombe & Tombs, 1956), Preface.

pological pursuits: the study of oral literature, cognitive systems, and ritual. In all three fields, the influence of Lévi-Strauss began to be felt.[2] Yet one cannot say that Anglo-Saxon work in any of the three was basically structuralist except in a few rare instances. Most work on oral literature would, in an anthropological context, be classifiable as 'formalist,' certainly by the criteria of Lévi-Strauss 1960, while most work on ritual would, by the same criteria, be classifiable as functionalist.

With regard to cognitive systems the position is more complex. The American schools (ethnoscience, cognitive anthropology) made an immense contribution to the analysis of the concrete symbols out of which primitive systems of thought are constructed, while the Evans Pritchard school in England, using a different kind of equally exacting semiotics, was more concerned with the relations holding between levels (religious, social, ecological) of systems of thought and action.[3] Here myths were used as sources for conceptualisations present in the minds of the population but they were not usually analysed in an attempt to discover the deep structure of the myths themselves. Towards the end of the decade, as the volumes of Lévi-Strauss's *Mythologiques* successively appeared, anthropologists interested in cognitive structures began to focus more on the actual texts of the myths that had been collected and a number of interesting analyses appeared in the Anglo-Saxon world.[4]

---

[2] See especially "The Structural Study of Myth," *American Journal of Folklore*, 68, No. 270 (1955); "La Structure et la forme," in *Anthropologie structurale deux* (1960; rpt. Paris: Plon, 1973), pp. 139–73; *Le Totemisme aujourd'hui* (Paris: Plon, 1962); *La Pensée sauvage* (Paris: Plon, 1962).

[3] For this school, see E. E. Evans Pritchard, *Nuer Religion* (London: Oxford Univ. Press, 1956) and *Theories of Primitive Religion* (London: Oxford Univ. Press, 1965); John Middleton, *Lugbara Religion* (London: Oxford Univ. Press, 1960); Victor W. Turner, "Ndembu Divination: Its Symbolism and Technique," *Rhodes Livingstone Papers*, No. 31 (1961) and "Ritual Symbolism, Morality and Social Structure among the Ndembu," *Rhodes Livingstone Journal*, No. 30 (1961).

[4] Some examples are: Catherine M. Berndt, "Monsoon and Honey Wind," in *Echanges et communications*, ed. J. Pouillon and P. Maranda (The Hague: Mouton, 1960), pp. 1306–26; Roy F. Ellen, "The Marsupial in Nuaulu Ritual Behaviour," *Man*, 7 (1972) 223–58; R. Layton, "Myth as Language in Aboriginal Arnhem Land," *Man*, 5 (1970) 483–97; E. R. Leach, *Genesis as Myth* (London: Jonathan Cape, 1969); "The Structure of Symbolism," in *The Interpretation of Ritual*, ed. J. S. La Fontaine (London: Tavistock, 1972), pp. 239–76; Marguerite S. Robinson, "The House of the Mighty Hero," in *Dialectic in Practical Religion*, ed. E. R. Leach (Cambridge: Cambridge Univ. Press, 1968), pp. 122–52; Andrew and Marilyn Strathern, "Marsupials and Magic: A Study of Spell Symbolism Among the Mbowamb," in *Dialectic in Practical Religion*, pp. 179–202; Andrew Strathern, "The Female and Male Spirit Cults in Mount Hagen," *Man*, 5 (1970), 571–85; Evon Z. and Catherine C. Vogt, "Lévi-Strauss among the Maya," *Man*, 5 (1970), 379–92; R. J. Willis, "The Head and the Loins," *Man*, 4, (1969), 519–34; Dell Hymes, "The 'Wife' Who 'Goes Out' Like a Man: Reinterpretation of a Clackamas Chinook Myth," in *Structural Analysis of Oral Tradition*, ed. Pierre and Elli Maranda (Philadelphia: Univ. of Pennsylvania Press, 1971), pp. 49–80.

While this work has undoubtedly been influenced by Lévi-Straussian research on myth, it has not adopted the theoretical approach of *Mythologiques*. It has been supported by a great deal of theoretical writing, usually rather sceptical about basic assumptions made in structuralist myth analyses. In the French-speaking world, meanwhile, some major studies of mythological systems have been made along structuralist lines. Two works of exceptional brilliance, which illustrate the results of which the method is capable, are *Les Jardins d'Adonis* and *Le Roi ivre*, both devoted to cultures of far greater complexity than the American Indian cultures analysed in *Mythologiques*.[5]

We are still left with formidable impediments to a happy marriage between French structuralist myth analysis and Anglo-Saxon empiricism. The impediments are roughly of three types: most oral literature analysis, as summarised recently in Maranda's excellent volume of selected readings (*Mythology*, 1972), tends to cut up myths into constituent units on the basis of purely formal criteria (terms and functions) or of purely content criteria (motifs). On the other hand, it is a necessary condition of the Lévi-Straussian method that the smallest unit be, like the "mytheme," selected by some combination of formal and semantic criteria: a mytheme "will consist of a relation." Even writers such as Maranda, in general committed to 'structuralism,' find the mytheme (at least for now) a difficult unit to handle in analysis. Yet if the mytheme be abandoned, it will become almost impossible to relate the findings of myth analysis to our other ethnographic data. Thus mythology might remain outside the mainstream of anthropological enquiry.

Second, the study of ritual has gradually become deeply involved in mythological themes, as anthropologists became progressively more sophisticated in the exegesis of rites.[6] The tendency for this school has been to separate 'pure' mythology from the study of rites and their exegeses, treating the former as being

---

[5] See Marcel Detienne, *Les Jardins d'Adonis* (Paris: Gallimard, 1972) ; and Luc de Heusch, *Le Roi ivre ou l'origine de l'état* (Paris: Gallimard, 1972). Claude Lévi-Strauss's *Mythologiques* were published in four volumes by Plon under the following titles: I: *Le Cru et le cuit* (1964) ; II: *Du Miel aux cendres* (1966) ; III: *L'Origine des manières de table* (1968) ; IV: *L'Homme nu* (1971). The first two volumes are available in English translation; publication of translations of the other two volumes has been announced.

[6] Among the pioneering works of this approach are Audrey Richards, *Chisungu* (London: Faber & Faber, 1956) ; Mary Douglas, *Purity and Danger* (London: Routledge & Kegan Paul, 1966) ; Victor Turner, *The Forest of Symbols* (Oxford: Clarendon Press, 1967) ; *Drums of Affliction* (London: Oxford Univ. Press, 1968) ; *The Ritual Process* (Chicago: Univ. of Chicago Press, 1969).

purely intellectual whereas the latter combined the cognitive and the affective, thus supposedly offering far richer material for the anthropologist. Lévi-Strauss has argued, in *L'Homme nu* (pp. 597–611), that Turner's type of ritual study failed to make a distinction between two aspects: the study of observable ritual behaviour (which he would place in the category of *l'ordre vécu*[7] and the study of what he calls implicit mythology, essentially similar to the explicit mythology he mainly studies himself. As such data are not susceptible to any verification except from informants' statements, he would classify them as part of *l'ordre conçu*. He would therefore reduce the study of ritual to words spoken, gestures performed, objects manipulated, independently of any gloss or exegesis. The problems in the study of ritual would then become: why these actions are necessary to achieve the objectives of the ritual; in what respect they differ from analogous actions in ordinary life. He would study the meaning to be assigned to these actions by the type of procedures demonstrated in *Mythologiques*. Lévi-Strauss justifies this plan of operations with reference to an important distinction he made between ritual and cognitive systems in *La Pensée sauvage* (pp. 294–302).

Third, and perhaps most important, there is a wide gulf, often not recognised, between the study of cognitive systems and of mythology. Certainly Professor Lévi-Strauss made a useful suggestion by telling students of ritual to distinguish analytically between their proxemics and their cognitive analyses, and no doubt some English and American anthropologists will take this up. Only recently, Raymond Firth, a doughty non-structuralist, has made some very fascinating incursions into proxemics and laid fascinating connections between proxemics, the Tikopia cognitive system, and the ritual level.[8] Furthermore, he has a venerable predecessor in Marcel Mauss.[9]

The difference between virtually all studies of cognitive structure and of mythology is that descriptions of cognitive systems assume, as a preliminary article of faith, that cultures *have* cognitive systems, i.e., that there is a single formulation in which conceptualisations about the nature of various levels of

---

[7] See Lévi-Strauss, *Anthropologie structurale* (Paris: Plon, 1958), Chap. XV.

[8] See "Postures and Gestures of Respect," in *Echanges et communications*, and "Verbal and Bodily Rituals of Greeting and Parting," in *The Interpretation of Ritual*, pp. 1–38.

[9] See *Sociologie et anthropologie*, 3rd ed. (Paris: Presses Univ. de France, 1966), Part 6.

the culture (cosmological, biological, geographical, social, religious, etc.) can be summarised. Certainly this is true to a significant degree. Superior recent ethnographies (e.g., Wagner, *The Curse of Souw* and Strathern, *One Father One Blood,* to give only two examples) state their informants' social philosophy on topics like clanship, and there can be no doubt that they correctly state what is generally believed in those societies.[10] If, however, we look at the myth underlying Wagner's analysis[11] (pp. 38–41), we are aware that his analysis leaves a vast number of questions about the myth unexplained. Strathern provides the analysis without quoting any myths. In both cultures, one may be sure there are myth cycles posing semiotic questions about heroes and their actions over and above what is contained in the coherent and interesting summaries of these cognitive systems.

In my own field material on the Orokaiva of Papua, I have three types of data. First, some data on the 'cognitive system,' resulting from direct questioning, which are similar to the key passages of the two books just mentioned (especially Strathern, p. 20). Second, a collection of myths partly analysed in my book on the social structure of the Orokaiva. But third, answers to some general questions I asked about cognitive structure which I recorded on my tape recorder, by now a familiar toy to my informants who were, in addition, familiar with broadcast dialogues heard on their transistor sets. My informants told me not to turn on my tape until they had prepared the answer they would give to my question. Then they set up a kind of dialogue in which one man asked abstract questions but the other very soon began to tell a myth that would answer the question properly. It was immediately obvious that this myth was a direct answer to my question. They told me that they always taught their children this myth to bring home the very point about which I was asking. They then proceeded to give a second myth, a more adult answer, which took me a little while to see as related to my question; but as soon as I realized that it had the same armature as a group of tales I had collected on my first visit I saw that the second myth restated the message of the first but on a much more profound level. It would take too long to present these tales in the present paper.

---

10 Wagner, *The Curse of Souw* (Chicago: Univ. of Chicago Press, 1967); Andrew Strathern, *One Father One Blood* (London: Tavistock, 1972).
11 *Exchange in the Social Structure of the Orokaiva* (London: Hurst, 1973).

I would suggest, however, that many cognitive questions can be answered in two ways: directly, and in the form of a myth. It would also seem that the answer in the form of a myth is as indispensable to the field worker as the direct answer because the metaphoric language of the myth greatly enriches the information that is given in a direct answer. The direct answer, in this instance, was concerned only with the exchange of goods, whereas the myth involved also marriage relations, relations between bush and village, between pig and man, between pig, man, and ornaments, while it also contained two of Lévi-Strauss's old favorites, the origin of fire for cooking, and *le dénicheur d'oiseaux*, the latter in a transformation even he has not yet encountered. Thus, if one really wants to know how the Orokaiva think, their myths are undoubtedly the most hopeful source.

Unquestionably the work of ethnoscientists such as Conklin, Frake, and Metzger offers a more easily verifiable method of establishing cognitive categories.[12] On the other hand, comprehensive cognitive systems can often not be reconstructed by direct questioning and the building of taxonomies. Myth analysis provides a further method of establishing relations between semes. If this analysis uncovers codes, messages, armatures, and paradigms, a systematic and reasonably objective ordering of semes undoubtedly results.

Such systematic ordering does not, however, yield a description of the 'world view' or 'system of thought' as found in traditional ethnographies. I can most conveniently illustrate the difference by comparing Mauss's analysis of North-West Coast gift exchange in *Essai sur le don*[13] and Lévi-Strauss's analysis of the same exchange in *L'Homme nu*. One might conceivably fit the material contained in the latter work somewhere within the framework of the former, but the opposite operation would be impossible. Structure on the level of myth is not necessarily homologous with structure at other levels (economic, social ritual) introduced by Mauss. Furthermore, even on the level of myth, not all the symbols involved in potlatch appear in *L'Homme nu* or could be built in. Some belong to myth cycles

12 See, for instance, H. C. Conklin, "Hanunoo Color Categories," *Southwestern Journal of Anthropology*, 11, No. 4 (1955); Charles O. Frake, "A Structural Description of Subanun Religious Behavior," in *Explorations in Honor of George Peter Murdock*, ed. Ward H. Goodenough, (New York: McGraw-Hill, 1964), pp. 111–29; Duane Metzger and Gerald Williams, "Tenejope Medicine. I: The Curer," in *Southwestern Journal of Anthropology*, 19 (1963), 216–34.
13 See *Sociologie et anthropologie*, Part 2.

not covered in the book; some do not appear in known myth cycles. Thus, cognitive systems are apt to be far more inclusive than myth paradigms. Also, they tend to be culture specific, while a myth paradigm typically involves a number of more or less contiguous cultural groups.

We conclude that if the attempt to understand the 'system of thought' of a culture leads the ethnographer to myth analysis, myth analysis in turn leads him almost inevitably to question the usefulness of culture specific 'systems of thought' as units of analysis. The basic unit becomes the paradigm, built in order to establish relations between myths. A so-called system of thought is a unique combination of such paradigms, most of which are also found in neighboring cultures, though in other combinations. Thus the ethnographer is led to widen the range of his investigations to units larger than single cultures, perhaps to what Barth has called "poly-ethnic systems," perhaps to even more comprehensive "culture areas."[14]

But does such a procedure reify the cognitive aspect of culture at the cost of the anthropological shibboleth "affectivity"? To clarify this issue, let us briefly return to the instance I gave from my own field work. Starting with a question about the exchange of goods (on the level of a direct answer), my informants had moved to a highly poetic recital for all the symbols which to them have the heaviest affective load and engaged them all in the most dramatic conflicts. One can hardly call that phase of the inquiry a loss of affectivity. But I could hardly have done anything with this tale if I were unable to subject it to a decoding operation so that it could be related to cognitive structure. Thus I was forced, right there in the field, to ponder the questions of the *Mythologiques*. Are there resemblances between this myth and the ones I know? If there are bits of about half a dozen that I recognise, what transformations have been made in each, what do the bits mean now that they have been transformed, and what sense does one get after putting them together? Again, I was not trying to reduce the affectivity of this material, which was strongly enough charged, but merely to make sense of what I had been told.

To me, the meaning was difficult because I had no other

---

14 For his notion of poly-ethnic systems, see Fredrik Barth, *Ethnic Groups and Boundaries* (Oslo: Universitetsvorlaget, 1969) ; "Tribes and Intertribal Relations in the Fly Headwaters," *Oceania*, 41 (1971) , 171–91. Not enough work has been done on the combination of paradigms in a single culture, but see F. E. Williams, *Drama of Orokolo* (London: Oxford Univ. Press, 1940) .

access to it except the intellectual one. I could not trust my intuition. To my informants, the cognitive problem was much less abstruse. They were speaking a language they knew and they were conveying a message charged with affectivity. We may well accept Lévi-Strauss's favourite simile and say they played the myth like music, fully aware of what would be a right or a wrong note, while the whole expressed a feeling of that moment. The problem of the anthropologist is that even if he understands these myths perfectly, it is the other academics who aren't tuned in. For their sake, one is obliged to give abstruse explanations so that they will understand the obvious.

II

Let us, as a first exercise, translate what I have just said into suitably academic language. The analysis of myth certainly introduces us to a way of seeing the world, but not to what is commonly known as a 'cognitive system.' Precisely because of the emotional load it carries, it is untranslatable, in toto, into another universe of discourse. The ethnographer will use it as the best possible guide to the semiotics of the culture, the 'meaning' of notions like pig, wife, ornament, fire, and so on. Hence, as Lévi-Strauss has argued, he is well placed to interpret the otherwise elusive proxemics of ritual. Furthermore, he can understand fully the implications of rhetoric, abuse, and political speeches. In other words, knowing the mythology, he can decode all kinds of communications at the price of having to tell his colleagues how he has decoded them, whereupon his colleagues, if Anglophone, accuse him of having no heart.

The semiotic analysis of myth, which will undoubtedly be a valuable ethnographic tool, requires some theoretical and methodological innovations. Perhaps discussion and criticism have overstressed the former at the expense of the latter. The starting point of enquiry does not lie in the philosophic realm but in the empirical facts of the use of symbolism in the populations we study, and, indeed, in all social groups. It emerges rather clearly from a reading of *L'Homme nu* (and most of the rest of the Lévi-Strauss corpus) that he is supremely concerned to find a method to make sense of myths and symbols and that whatever theory he offers is essentially heuristic, i.e., it fulfills its purpose if it brings order into the material. Authors such as Barnes, who have been disturbed by the philosophical tone of certain writings by Lévi-Strauss, have been insufficiently aware of the peripheral nature of notions such as "fundamental mental structures" in the total system. In a recent essay, these fundamental structures have been reduced unequivocally to neurophysiological processes, very much in the same way that Leach showed how the operations of the human mind essentially resemble those of a computer.[15] Anyone who reads through Lévi-Strauss's investigations with that idea in mind will find that it is perfectly consistent with his method of analysis. If Lévi-Strauss is interested in philosophical questions, these are not framed in the terms of any current Western school; his underlying assumptions are those of *la logique du concret* and of computer technology.

It may be useful to summarise the picture that would emerge. The computer may be either digital or analog.[16] The programme is very complex, consisting of several culturally determined languages called *codes*.[17] The lexicon consists of signs derived from nature and used for the construction of systems of thought. Remaining solidly anchored in nature, they are intermediate between a percept and a concept.[18] On the grammar, our information is still incomplete. It was described in some detail as a special kind of logic, *la logique du concret,* but more recently Lévi-Strauss has despaired of describing it in any philosophic terms now current.[19] He makes some illuminating general remarks about this logic in a recent essay[20] and in the conclusion to *L'Homme nu,* but nothing resembling a systematic exposition or pretending to be such.

Structuralist analysis is interested in three basic operations. The first of these is the encoding of percepts. This is an operation whereby specific and concrete objects (plants, animals, heavenly bodies, geographical features, etc.) tangible qualities (raw and cooked, fresh and rotten, etc.), principles of good manners and propriety, and basic essential problems (to be or not to be?, etc.) are given a semantic value by indigenous actors, i.e., within a culturally bounded system of signification. Encoding is a continuous process, as every change occurring

15 Lévi-Strauss, "Structuralism and Ecology," *Barnard Alumnae* (1972), pp. 6–14: E. R. Leach, *A Runaway World?* (London: Oxford Univ. Press, 1968).
16 *L'Origine des manières de table,* p. 85.
17 *Le Cru et le cuit,* pp. 205, 246.
18 *La Pensée sauvage,* pp. 28–33.
19 *La Pensée sauvage,* Chap. 2; *L'Homme nu,* pp. 569–70.
20 See *Anthropologie structurale deux,* pp. 77–85.

within the infrastructure necessitates additions or modifications to an existing code.

The second operation is the indigenous decoding of messages derived from the superstructure. These messages are contained in myths, i.e., in "stylistically definable discourses that express the strong components of semantic systems."[21] Myths have messages because the encoded material contained in the superstructure includes basic existential problems, i.e., questions to which a totally satisfactory answer is possible only in thought.[22] Myths are told in an encoded form so that they cannot provide practical guidance to the indigenous actors unless they first interpret the messages. These may be as ambiguous as the Delphic oracle. The interpretation adopted will tend to conform, by design or "unconscious rationality," to the interests of the actors. When Malinowski regarded myth as a charter for custom, his argument was not without validity, as members of a society do treat the decoded version of a myth as a charter for action. But Malinowski's method of analysing myth suffered from the drawback that the recorded versions of most myths, being in encoded form, contain many elements ignored by their indigenous interpreters.

The third operation involved in structuralist analysis is the decoding of messages by the anthropologist. This decoding will go beyond that of the indigenous interpreters and account for the elements they have ignored. The anthropologist can, at least in principle, make myths intelligible because he is not constrained in his interpretations by the practical purposes of the members of the society and because he has at his disposal a larger corpus of mythical texts and an analytical method, to be described below. In order to analyse myths, he will require the fullest possible knowledge of the ethnography, ecology, and history of the groups involved.

---

21 Pierre Maranda, ed., *Mythology* (Harmondsworth: Penguin, 1972), p. 13.

22 This idea, found throughout Lévi-Strauss's work, was first developed in "La Structure des mythes" (*Anthropologie structurale*, Chap. XII). It is expressed, at the highest level of generality, by what he called "the canonical relation," i.e., a formula of the following type to which every myth corresponds:

$$F_x \ (a) : F_y \ (b) :: F_x \ (b) : F_{a-1} \ (y)$$

"Here, with two terms, *a* and *b*, being given as well as two functions, *x* and *y*, of these terms, it is assumed that a relation of equivalence exists between two situations defined respectively by an inversion of *terms* and *relations*, under two conditions: (1) that one term be replaced by its opposite (in the above formula, *a* by $a-1$); (2) that an inversion be made between the *function value* and *term value* of two elements (above, *y* and *a*)." The Oedipus complex is an example of this formula.

The three operations above are made possible in structuralist theory by the existence, in objective reality, of mental constructs termed *paradigms*.[23] These paradigms, or images of the world, determine how new percepts are encoded in a culture. Famous examples are the tendency, in Oceania, to regard the white man —when he was first met in the region—as a god, ghost, or returned ancestor; and likewise to describe unknown artifacts such as nails by the terms used for supernatural beings (e.g., Maori: *atuà*). We may explain such classifications if we recognise that new percepts, in order to become intelligible to bearers of a culture, have to be related in some way to an already existing paradigm. This cognitive act of relating to a new percept, to a paradigm, i.e., making sense of it is an act of encoding.

The practical consequence of this act of encoding is that bearers of the culture can now 'think' about the new percept and decide on appropriate actions to take with regard to it. Action is based on the postulated relation of the (unknown) percept to a (known) paradigm. Having categorised a certain white man as a returned ancestor, actors proceed to survey available myths which may provide a 'charter' for proper behaviour towards what has been defined as a returned ancestor. The derivation of this charter would be a 'decoding' operation by indigenous actors.

I shall discuss later the question whether the anthropologist can establish the existence, in objective reality, of the paradigm underlying such categorisations by using a methodology elaborated in Lévi-Strauss's *Mythologiques*. At present, I wish to make only a few general remarks. It is clear that the primary source of a paradigm lies in the infrastructure, as continuous feedback occurs to and from the superstructure. Thus, if the behaviour towards the white men mentioned above has undesirable results, this constitutes a new percept which somehow must be encoded. If this can be done only by transforming the existing code or by adding to or modifying the paradigm, this will be done. Similarly, if a myth is borrowed by a population living in a different environment, it will be modified to allow for the difference. On the other hand, it would be impossible to predict the form this modification would take unless the relevant paradigm was known.

The paradigms established by Lévi-Strauss are basically

---

23 *L'Origine des manières de table*, pp. 80–91.

made up of binary oppositions, though these are often arranged in triads and other such figures. The question has often been raised whether any objective justification can be given for this use of binary oppositions, a criticism Lévi-Strauss tends to answer by appealing to certain neurophysiologically established facts about the structure of the human brain.[24] While arguments of this kind may still be regarded as hypothetical, there is no justification for claiming that these binary oppositions are mere formal antonyms.[25] Where a binary opposition is postulated, there tends to be a mesh of demonstrated interrelations, mediators, incomplete forms, actions aimed at changing unendurable situations, and the like. Certainly terms such as life and death, viewed as a binary opposition, would raise such questions as life after death, rebirth, communications with the dead; there might be a bird with one 'live' and one 'dead' eye; a fish with a 'live' and a 'dead' side, and similar types of evidence related to ritual prohibitions which would indicate that in the cultural context the opposition had more than formal significance. Furthermore, the postulation of a binary opposition in a paradigm is never, in *Mythologiques,* a hasty hypothesis, but tends to be validated by many pages of close argument based on empirical material, as I shall show. Finally, a paradigmatic binary opposition is usually tested for a number of separate codes, e.g., ritual, social, botanical, meteorological, astronomical.

The fact remains that the use of paradigms is the most controversial aspect of *Mythologiques.* In *L'Homme nu* we find paradigms which apply simultaneously to myths found throughout South and North America. While traditional culture history will accept proofs of such diffusion when myths resemble each other, or when an obvious syntagmatic chain can be traced, the boldness of the postulated relationships, however carefully documented, is bound to raise scepticism. The final test, however, does not lie in the credibility of every single operation performed but in the question whether the study has improved the overall intelligibility of the corpus of myths, i.e., whether the type of operations Lévi-Strauss performs offers an illuminating guide to a field worker concerned with the semiotics of a culture.

---

24 See *L'Homme nu* and "Structuralism and Ecology."
25 As was done by K. O. L. Burridge in "Lévi-Strauss and Myth," in *The Structural Study of Myth and Totemism,* ed. E. R. Leach (London: Tavistock, 1967), pp. 91–105, and Robert F. Murphy in *The Dialectics of Social Life* (New York: Basic Books, 1971).

III

Far more challenging than the theoretical arguments are the methodological problems involved in making sense of encoded documents notoriously reluctant to yield their secrets. If, in our discussion of these problems, we shall concentrate mostly on the last volume of *Mythologiques, L'Homme nu,* this is because it is perhaps more interesting to enquire whether the decoding process can have an end rather than whether it can have a beginning.

The last volume does not add greatly to the discussion of the basic methodology of myth analysis. The reader is expected to be already familiar with the technique of establishing transformations and with the building of syntagmatic chains and paradigms. The surprise of *L'Homme nu* lies mainly in that it carries the analysis from truly primitive into complex societies, with a market economy and a rather sophisticated religio-philosophic system. We seem to ascend gradually along an evolutionary ladder from the Klamath and Modoc to the Sahaptin traders of the Columbia River and finally to the various divisions of the Salish. Critics had previously assumed that the paradigms of the previous volumes would lose their force when confronted with extraordinarily rich and profound material such as may be found in British Columbia, but in *L'Homme nu* we find the *dénicheur d'oiseaux,* who had been climbing hundreds of trees and cliffs in the three previous volumes, to be symmetrical to the Salish sky visitors. The trading tribes had, as might have been expected, myth cycles dealing with the origin of exchange and of sharing in a highly systematic way. But on the level of myth, we find no basic structural change: the bird-nester tale transforms equally well into the origin of hunting, fishing, competitive games, and commercial exchanges. Lévi-Strauss spares us theoretical discourse on the theme that socio-economic evolution leaves the "fundamental mental structures of the mind" unchanged; this is the clearest evidence that he is not principally concerned with questions of that order.

Instead, he ends the book with a brief survey of the bird-nester myth over a wide sweep across Canada, in which he shows that commercial exchanges form part of the precontact conceptual world of most of this area, a finding of major importance in American culture history. He concludes with a reduction of all previous paradigms to one single one: man's invention of the technique of fire-making by friction and of the earth oven. This was the event symbolised in innumerable ways in the hundreds of myths that were examined, and represented as the resolution of the opposition of sky and earth, man and woman, affinal groups. As further clarification, Lévi-Strauss quotes a passage from Engels in which the latter calls the invention of fire-making friction as exceeding all other inventions in universal liberating efficacy. Thus, the whole system of mythology developed in the four volumes of *Mythologiques* turns out to be firmly rooted in the infrastructure.

It will be seen that the distinctive achievement of *L'Homme nu* lies in the merciless reduction of a dazzling wealth of mythology of poetic and philosophical magnificence to one event of humiliating simplicity. At the outset we had been promised that the form of *Mythologiques* was to be circular, like a symphony. Neither the reader nor indeed the writer could have supposed that the circle would have been closed in this definite and concrete manner: starting with a myth of the origin of fire, we find ourselves back with the origin of fire again, after traversing over wide areas of mythology, but with the additional knowledge that the supposedly accidental starting point of the series was in fact the actual starting point of human mythological reflection.

Yet, even if the captain of the canoe knew his intended destination in these volumes, the problems of navigation must have been entirely unpredictable and must have been faced simply as they arose. The methodology of the reduction of paradigms, demonstrated in this volume, is in fact extremely exacting. Moreover, reduction was not the only task, as it was also important to thicken the web of pathways between the myths and thus strengthen the force of proof of the method. Finally, it was important to show that the analysis holds over as large a part as possible of North and South America, and to relate it to the culture history of that vast area.

I shall exemplify the complexity of the reduction process by summarising the steps of the first major reduction (pp. 23–219): 1) After ecological preliminaries, it is shown that the Klamath-Modoc area has bird-nester myths. 2) The basic myth M_1 is compared with M_{530} and M_{531} mytheme by mytheme. We find that the South and North American bird-nester myths have a common armature and code, but there are interrelated changes in lexicon and they differ both in their overt and hidden messages. 3) A syntagmatic chain is construed out of a number of myths on a new theme, the "hidden child." 4) The hypothesis is proposed (p. 53) that the myth cycles of hidden child and bird-nester are symmetrical.

At this point, I should explain the purpose of the hypothesis. It is true, but insufficient, that the hypothesis is a necessary stepping-stone to the demonstration with which the book ends 500 pages later. It is also true, but insufficient, that the hypothesis is a contribution to American culture history. For if such were the objectives, the form of the book—in which methodological and historical discussion is mostly offered as a brief respite from the rigours of myth analysis—would be aberrant and inexcusable. I would suggest that the purpose of the hypothesis is first to make sense of the tales about the hidden child, as the syntagmatic analysis preceding page 53, though interesting, leaves them obscure. On the other hand, after three volumes of *Mythologiques,* we are immensely familiar with the bird-nester, who has been elucidated in many paradigms. If the two sets of tales are symmetrical, we can attempt building a paradigm relating them to each other, thus not only making sense of the hidden child, but also deepening our understanding of the bird-nester.

The testing of the hypothesis involves: 1) The North American hidden-child myths must now be related to South American ones at all the relevant levels: social, geographical, meteorological, astronomical, shamanistic, etc. 2) It must be shown that the hidden-child myths are relatable to the myths about Lady Diver. 3) It must be shown that the Lady Diver myths are relatable to the very complex paradigm[26] that has been previously established for the bird-nester myths. 4) In order to do this the paradigm has to be made twice as complex as it was before. Thus, in the bird-nester myths, meat is a means to bring about the origin of tobacco; in the Lady Diver myths it can be the other way about: one needs tobacco before one can hunt for meat. This conforms to common shamanistic practice in the area. 5) At every point, pathways must be traced between the myths whereby the bird-nester, hidden-child, and Lady Diver myths validate the paradigm. It is not enough that transformations hold within each of these syntagmatic chains; they must be cross-linked. 6) At page 143, the demonstration is complete

---

26 *Du miel aux cendres,* p. 25; *L'Homme nu,* p. 87.

for the sociological and meteorological codes. The astronomical code takes a further 77 pages.

All this rigour does not make the demonstration tedious. The study of the astronomical code leads the author to some of his most charming stock characters, such as the libertine grandmother, while Lady Diver takes on a variety of characters according to the habits of the bird in various parts of Canada— from the Micmac to the Eskimo to the Salish. The myths are related not only to each other but to variations in ecology. The mythologies of the tribes involved are distinguished from each other, and the character of each is related to ethnographic and environmental data.

In this epistemology, the direction of the enquiry is to some extent arbitrary, as Lévi-Strauss explicitly recognises. At several points in his demonstration, several fruitful directions are open to him. While mentioning this fact, he does not feel bound to give arguments why he pursues one of these and leaves the others aside. It follows that the paradigms Lévi-Strauss establishes are themselves arbitrary in the sense that he might just as well have established some others. If Lévi-Strauss had wished to account for the whole corpus of American mythology, he would have needed far more paradigms. But this fact does not necessarily invalidate the relevance of the paradigms he did establish. The final test can only be intelligibility: does a paradigm help us to understand the myths to which it refers? Is this understanding consistent with facts in the infrastructure on which the myths are based?

To what extent do the paradigms have implications for the wider question stated by Lévi-Strauss in the untranslatable phrase: "comment les mythes se pensent dans l'esprit humain?" I would suggest they do so at several levels. First, a descriptive level: the reader becomes extremely familiar with a set of stock devices man uses in encoding the facts of the infrastructure in mythological terms. Second, an analytical level: we learn that these devices rely on a quite limited number of basic logical operations. Each of the first three volumes is devoted to one set of these operations: the logic of tangible qualities (1964); the logic of forms (1966); the logic of periodicity (1968). Third, a theoretical level: the universality of these logical operations is proposed on the grounds that they endure in culture history and are distributed over a very wide culture area. Finally, their objective existence is proposed on the ground that the paradigms can be reduced to one master paradigm, the terms of which refer to the paramount invention of primitive man: the making of fire. The epistemological process of reduction of the data thus leaves intact the crucial relation between myths and the infrastructure.

An important methodological question is the handling of time in myth analysis. Periodic time is one of the main themes of the *Mythologiques; L'Origine des manières de table* is entirely devoted to it. Nonrecurring time also appears now and then, when myths are related to each other in such a way that one is logically prior to the other. But mostly the sequences are reversible. A syntagmatic chain can usually be read in either direction. Nonetheless, a syntagmatic chain of necessity reconstructs a diachronic sequence, as we must assume that a transformation occurs in time as a myth is diffused from one area to another, or is locally composed after the analogy of an earlier myth.

On the other hand, paradigms have no time reference at all. They express a purely logical relation. This relation is not usually known to informants, and there is no way of empirically testing it. A striking instance is the obscure cycle of myths on the 'Anus Wiper' (p. 290), which is shown to be transformable into a cycle of myths on the origin of exchange and also into another cycle on the origin of sharing. It is, in fact, intermediate between the two cycles. Lévi-Strauss offers a paradigmatic analysis which explains the Anus Wiper as a logical mediator between the two cycles. Yet this exercise cannot be dismissed as purely formal because ethnographic and ecological evidence is quoted in corroboration.

It may likewise be argued, in principle, that paradigms have no direct relation to space, as they express purely logical relationships. Yet Lévi-Strauss is very careful about spatial variables —distances between groups, relations with environments, faunal and floral distributions, astronomical and cosmological phenomena related to space, and the like. I do not believe that relations in space are more important than relations in time, but in general the former happen to be much easier to ascertain from available sources. While an ethnographer can easily widen the range of cultures included in myth analysis, temporal depth is obtainable only in the rare instances where written records exist over a lengthy period during which myth creation continued

without undue disruption. I shall refer below to a few such instances in Oceanic studies.

IV

Mythologiques has given rise to many criticisms, explica-
tions, debates, and new experiments. In reviewing these, I shall
as much as possible limit myself to the viewpoint of the ethnographer. This is not easy, as the basis of much of the criticism is
philosophical, especially criticism coming from avowed phenomenologists and functionalists.[27] Here debate can often be
reduced to an epistemological level: what kind of sense do descriptions need to make in order to constitute 'knowledge'?

This applies for example to questions such as: Can we hy-
pothesise that any part of a myth is arbitrary? Is a myth adequately explained if we can demonstrate the affective function
of its symbols? Is a classification of mythical functions into narrative, validatory, and explanatory meaningful? Answers to such
questions clearly depend on our definition of myth. If we are
to accept the definitions of Lévi-Strauss[28] and Maranda,[29] as I
have done, the three questions above must be answered in the
negative. Here I shall attempt only to explore to what extent
the definitions are useful and to what extent they may be bar-
riers to empirical research.

The first question is how we are to decide whether or not
a given text is a myth. There is obviously a boundary beyond
which structuralist analysis of a tale is no longer appropriate.
This boundary needs to be ascertainable even between two
tales similar in content, if one but not the other expresses the
'canonical relation' or the "strong components of semantic systems." This line might be drawn either in time ('degeneration'
of a myth into a folktale) or in space (diffusion to an area where
its mythic character is lost). Beyond this line, a tale ceases to
be serviceable for the expression of basic contradictions in the
culture. These contradictions will then be expressed in other

---

27 For G. S. Kirk's phenomenological approach, see his *Myth: Its Meaning and
Functions in Ancient and Other Cultures* (London: Cambridge Univ. Press, 1970),
p. 172. The functionalist presuppositions emerge from Meyer Fortes, "Totem and
Taboo" in *Proceedings of the Royal Anthropological Institute of Great Britain
for 1966* (1967); T. O. Beidelman, "Swazi Royal Ritual," *Africa*, 36, No. 4 (1966);
Victor Turner, *The Ritual Process.*
28 For the canonical relation, see my discussion in n. 22 and in the *Postscript.*
29 See n. 21.

myths or in forms other than myth. The tale may survive as 'folktale' or in a 'romanesque' form, in which it will lose the characteristic ambivalence of myth and acquire a wholly tragic or happy ending, or a pseudo-historical ideology.[30]

Though this boundary has not yet been surveyed, it has been mapped. Lévi-Strauss gives one instance in which a tale leaves the mythical realm when it ceases to be inspired "by a notion of distributive justice" but becomes a tragedy; in another instance, it ceases to do more than "justify certain clan privileges"; in a third, it "validates relations with white people." Perhaps Lévi-Strauss is moving here towards something akin to Kirk's functional classification, though the purely narrative and entertaining and the purely validatory tales are placed outside the mythical realm, i.e., outside the realm where fundamental mental structures are revealed.

This raises several problems to be dealt with at a later stage of my argument: whether literary works ought to be classified as 'myths,' whether the structuralist definitions admit myths in literate societies, and whether there can be structural analysis of mythical accounts of historical changes.

A second, closely related question is whether a myth necessarily has meaning at multiple levels. By Lévi-Strauss's and Maranda's definitions, this must be so as mythic discourse unfolds at a more fundamental level than any specific code to which the myth refers. The most skilful and prestigious practitioners of the structural analysis of myth have always recognised this principle.[31] Furthermore, most of them have recognised the need to cover a wide geographical area and utilise many myths in comparative analysis. On the other hand, few of these analyses are fully paradigmatic, Detienne's *Les Jardins d'Adonis* forming a fascinating, though cautious, exception with paradigms revealing hitherto unnoticed relationships among many levels of ancient Greek culture.

Detienne, like Lévi-Strauss in the Asdiwal myth[32] and elsewhere, appears to give some primacy to the level of social struc-

---

30 See *Anthropologie structurale deux*, pp. 301–15.

31 Examples are the works by de Heusch and Detienne cited above; also Edmund Leach, "The Structure of Symbolism." Multilevel analysis has often been wrongly interpreted as 'Hegelianism,' most oddly so by Percy Cohen in "Theories of Myth," *Man*, 7 (1969), 337–53, who forecast what structural analysis would do with the myth of the Tower of Babel. He was (unconsciously) controverted by de Heusch, who showed an actual multilevel analysis of that myth in Africa.

32 Reprinted in *Anthropologie structurale deux* (pp. 175–233), with an important postscript.

ture as determining structures at various other levels. This is in the Durkheimian tradition, but with a new twist: in the structuralist view, mythic paradigms reflect "fundamental structures" more accurately than the social level, which is distorted by environmental contingencies. Writers such as Harris, Rappaport, and Kirk, have argued that both paradigms and social structure are mere derivations, and that the real determining factors are to be found in the ecology, as modified by culture. Lévi-Strauss has countered that models based on the ecological levels alone do not suffice to account for the mythological data.[33] We should probably abandon attempts to find a single underlying cause of all cultural phenomena and build models including both ecological and paradigmatic forms of causality, distinct in practice though perhaps not in theory.

The problem whether literary works ought to be treated as 'myths' (in the Lévi-Straussian sense) springs from the ambiguity of our terms: it may not be useful for anthropologists and literary critics to try to use the same definitions. The anthropological student of myth, even when constructing paradigms, remains firmly anchored in the ecology. In literary criticism, the relationship between verbal structures and the actual objects and events they describe is usually far looser; verbal structures are paramount. Hence, *la logique du concret,* the bond between objects and events and verbal structures, is far more crucial in anthropological than in literary analysis.

This difference in perspectives does not prevent interpenetration between the two scholarly fields: the boundary has been crossed by Lévi-Strauss in his study on Baudelaire,[34] by Barthes in *Mythologies* and his later semiotic projects, by Northrop Frye in an essay in which he classifies fictional events according to their location in *world above* or *world below.*[35] He shows that mythic elements assigned to *world above* in one historical period have been assigned to *world below* in another, a transformation for which he seeks to account by introducing cultural levels quite distinct from verbal structures.

Nonetheless, it would be difficult to reconcile Frye's use of

---

[33] In "Structuralism and Ecology," quoted above.

[34] Roman Jakobson and Claude Lévi-Strauss, "Charles Baudelaire's *Les chats,*" in *Introduction to Structuralism,* ed. Michael Lane (New York: Basic Books, 1970), pp. 202–22.

[35] "New Directions from Old," in *Myth and Mythmaking,* ed. Henry A. Murray (New York: Braziller, 1960), pp. 115–31.

the terms 'myth' and 'mythos'[36] with an anthropological perspective. If myth is to remain embedded in *la logique du concret*, comedy, romance, tragedy, and satire cannot be mythic modes, though irony may be. Many works of literature, such as Gide's *Thesée*, or Sartre's *Les Mouches*, seem to correspond to Lévi-Strauss's canonical formula—but this need not indicate that we can usefully adopt his notion of myth in literary criticism.

Does Lévi-Strauss recognise the existence of myths in literate societies? In principle, it would seem he does, as he has thus classified both Freud's *Totem and Taboo* and his own *Mythologiques*. He has highly commended myth analyses conducted by scholars such as Dumézil, Vernant, Detienne, in (literate) Indo-European societies. Furthermore, he has described *la logique du concret* as "one of the major concerns of modern thought," giving as an example "so-called qualitative mathematics."[37]

As against this, Lévi-Strauss has cast doubt on the suitability of the Old Testament for myth analysis and has repeatedly emphasised that the age of mythology ended with the coming of literacy and class societies. One cannot survey the rich literature on contemporary 'myths' and the 'myths' of developing societies without recognising that few of them would satisfy the criteria of concrete logic, collective involvement, and unconscious content implicit in his method.[38] An exception would probably be Da Matta's interesting study of the transformation of an ancient fire myth[39] because this shows—as does de Heusch's *Le Roi ivre* —the shift from a reciprocity-based to an hierarchy-based society. I personally believe that there are vast possibilities for the structural study of contemporary myths, but these depend on the development of precise criteria as to what would be suit-

---

36 See *Anatomy of Criticism* (Princeton: Princeton Univ. Press, 1957).

37 See *Anthropologie structurale deux*, p. 83.

38 Though such tales present recent history in what appear to be rich mythic images, the question is to what extent these images do more than provide a language for the enunciation of ideological rhetoric. Some examples of the rich literature are: K. O. L. Burridge, *Mambu: A Melanesian Millennium* (London: Methuen, 1960); Freerk C. Kamma, *Koreri: Messianic Movements in the Biak Numfor Culture Area* (The Hague: Nijhoff, 1972); Alan Dundes, Edmund R. Leach, Pierre Maranda and David Maybury Lewis, "An Experiment: Suggestions and Queries from the Desk," in *Structural Analysis of Oral Tradition*, pp. 292–324; Shuichi Nagata, "The Pahana Legend," *The Journal of Symbolic Anthropology*, 1, No. 2 (1974); E. G. Schwimmer, "Symbolic Competition," in *Anthropologica*, 15 (Dec. 1972); and "Why did the mountain erupt?" in *Migrants and Exiles in Oceania*, ed. M. Lieber (Honolulu: Univ. of Hawaii Press, 1974).

39 Roberto Da Matta, "Myth and Anti-Myth among the Timbira," in *Structural Analysis of Oral Tradition*.

able texts—a question to which sufficient thought has as yet not been given.

Progress in structural myth analysis has so far been impeded by the extreme complexity of the methodology. The most hopeful (because rigorous) of the simplifying devices we have seen is computer analysis. Most of the work seems to have been done in France, where a programmatic symposium was published several years ago and work is continuing.[40] In Canada, this approach has been pioneered by Pierre Maranda. The documents are translated manually from the natural language to the analytical language. The computer assigns each term and each function to a specific analytical category, but these categories are not formed a priori; they rest on the data themselves. Not only is there an important saving in time, but many dimensions of arbitrariness are avoided, both by translation into computer language and by the way in which the computer establishes the categories from the data.[41]

It will be seen that an ethnographer wishing to use myths as a research tool still faces many grave difficulties. Yet, an increasing number of field workers will probably turn to them now, because of the incomparable richness of the insights they offer and because the general pattern of the inner logic of myths has become discernible through the work of Lévi-Strauss.

Toronto 1972–73

Postscript

When this paper was going to press, I happened to attend, in Paris, Professor Lévi-Strauss's course of lectures at the Collège de France 'Sur certains aspects du rapport entre cannibalisme et travestissement rituel' (1974–75). After rejecting the interpretation most commentators have given of his 'canonical formula' for myth, he presented a brilliant clarification of it. Though my own interpretation in this essay is perhaps closer than most, the reader may find an additional note useful.

---

40 See J. C. Gardin and R. Jaulin, eds., *Calcul et formalisation dans les sciences de l'homme* (Paris: Centre National de la Recherche Scientifique, 1968). Work is continuing at the Centre d'Ethnologie Française with the emphasis placed on methodological issues. The Centre maintains a liaison with Canadian scholars by means of biennial colloquia, of which the second was held in Paris in 1974 under the joint auspices of the French and Canadian governments.
41 See Maranda's essay in *Calcul et formalisation* and his contribution to the experiment reported in *Structural Analysis of Oral Tradition*.

This note is a development of my own thoughts based on what Lévi-Strauss said in his lectures. We should, says Lévi-Strauss, call a tale a myth if it satisfies four conditions. There must, first, be an irreconcilable contradiction. Let me supply an example from Maori mythology (I did *not* hear Lévi-Strauss lecture on it) : woman belongs to earthly life, man to sky life, and the two are separated, yet are necessary to each other.

Second, there must be a hero who acts as mediator in the myth, in this case Maui, who—in Maori mythology—taught humanity sexual intercourse. But that is not what he set out to do. He set out to become immortal. He was told that in order to become immortal he had to kill the Great Woman of Death. He decided the best way to kill her would be to climb into her vagina when she was asleep.

At this point, let us look at the formula, where x is woman, y is man, a is earth life, b is sky life. The left hand side of the formula poses no problem. $f_x(b)$ tells us that Maui wanted to achieve sky life through a female function, which is sex. This was his way of mediating, of transforming the original contradiction. We may say, in a general way, that a third condition of myth is that a tale should contain a transformation of this order.

Several interpreters of Lévi-Strauss's canonical formula have come as far as this. The problem lies in what follows. If man wants to achieve sky life through sex, what does woman do? She unsky-s the man or unmans the sky. Specifically, when Maui crawled up her vagina, she squeezed him to death—ignominiously for him, as he lost immortality in a ludicrous manner. Yet it was thus that man *learnt* sexual intercourse. The perfect solution is forever out of reach, but the original man-woman contradiction was reduced somewhat as a result of Maui's act; it was reduced enough to make life and momentary happiness possible.

In the expression $f_{a^{-1}}(y)$, we may read the function a^{-1} as 'the taking away of earth life'—from man. This is not a purely formal construction but corresponds to the meaning the Maori gives to the myth: when a man has sacred functions to fulfil—in ritual, war, etc.—he must keep away from woman for she will destroy his mana. When her femininity is especially strong (periods, childbearing, etc.) he should keep away from her altogether. Her sexuality is always potentially dangerous to him.

This final term, then—the fourth condition of myth—stands for a quintessential traumatic counteraction brought about by the hero's act of mediation, such that his mediation fails in its full intended result but reduces the original contradiction. This quintessential counteraction usually has relevance in many spheres of life simultaneously, as in this case, where the implications were not only ritual but also social and economic (woman's status) as well as sexual, i.e. psychological. Above all, the myth combines these levels in an integrated world picture.

It will be seen that this view of myth, though by no means identical with that of Jung, is somewhat similar in the way it distinguishes myth from non-myth. The difference between Jung and Lévi-Strauss lies partly in the latter's starting point, which includes very much the socio-political and economic relations between man and woman, and partly in its outcome, which again refers back to the empirically testable ethnographic starting point. Thus, structuralist analysis is concerned not only with universals but also with cultural diversity.

Paris 1975

"Mythomorphism" in Greco-Roman Historiography: the Case of the Royal *Gamos*

Douglas J. Stewart

Brandeis University

T HE rich array of publications by Georges Dumézil and his students and collaborators has given us a provocative new way of looking at myth. For instance, it is their contention that Indo-European (IE) myths, from Avestan and Vedic to Roman and Celtic, are remarkably at one in providing a kind of narrative "code" to original IE social structure, a tripartite division of peoples into a hieratic, a military, and an "economic" caste.[1] (Greek myth, oddly enough, is seen by adherents of the school as largely alien to this pattern, or "ideology" as Dumézil calls it.)[2] Too, in some instances the same school has given us an equally provocative insight into history and historiography as well. For instance, Dumézil has argued that in surviving records authentic Roman myth has been displaced "downwards"—perhaps by the creation of pure *fictions* in order to give envious Romans a pantheon parallel to that of the Greeks—and is thus turned into pseudo-history. The "true" divine system native to Roman thought and myth was the common IE triad—at Rome, Jupiter, Mars, Quirinus—and not a gaggle of Greek gods answering to Latin names like Venus, Minerva and Neptune.[3]

---

[1] See C. Scott Littleton, *The New Comparative Mythology* (Berkeley: Univ. of California Press, 1966) for a general account of the school's history and activities, as well as a Dumézil bibliography. See pp. 49–56 on castes.

[2] *Ibid.*, pp. 3–6, and 14.

[3] Georges Dumézil, *L'Idéologie tripartie des Indo-Européens*, "Collections Latomus," 31 (Brussels, 1958), pp. 48–54.

Thus the early "history" of Rome as recorded by Livy is really, then, the early mythology of the Romano-Italic peoples, not precisely forgotten, but remembered as a different category of reality, as a series of single facts, rather than a body of timeless observations upon the essential nature of society, as it once was seen. What fraction of these theories will withstand the test of time is not for me to say. What interests me here are the methods of observation and analysis practiced by the school of Dumézil because, theoretically, they seem equally applicable to research problems dealing with non-IE myth as well, especially where, as in the case of the Roman materials, myth which springs originally from anterior social structure but loses coherent contact with that same social structure (because society has changed, if not for other reasons) later returns disguised as history. In fact, the process can apparently take one more step: it seems possible for myth not only to return as disguised (past) history, but to return as an historical precedent, a paradigm or guide for *future* action, even well into literate times. For example, in a recent volume of essays by adherents of Dumézil, Professor Donald J. Ward[4] has suggested a further complication in the tangled relationship of myth and history. In his essay, Professor Ward notes that generally the ancient Germanic tribes practiced three different forms of execution: hanging, burning, and drowning. This practice, he infers, derives from an original tripartite system of sacrifice, which in turn can be traced to the fundamental IE ideology of a tripartite social function—three different forms of sacrifice, to the three classes of deity presiding over the three chief cncerns of the IE peoples—with three different forms of execution imposed upon those who seriously violate the aims and rubrics of the three functions and thus the prerogatives of their particular deities. Ward then goes on to discuss the persistence of these three forms of execution into historical times, including quite modern times, particularly execution by drowning. At this point, he then mentions the famous incident in which George, Duke of Clarence, imprisoned in the Tower, was secretly executed by drowning in a butt of Malmsey wine, apparently at the order of his brother, Edward IV. The incident is peculiarly apt for my purposes here, for, as Ward says, "Since the murder was performed

4 "The Threefold Death: An Indo-European Trifunctional Sacrifice?" in Jean Puhvel, ed., *Myth and Law Among the Indo-Europeans* (Berkeley: Univ. of California Press, 1970), pp. 123–46.

in secret, one will probably never know with certainty whether the drowning was the actual means by which the victim was killed. . . . Yet, one point is clear. Since the populace of London associated the murder of the Duke with the motif of drowning . . . it is evidence that this motif was, at that time, a part of the popular tradition."[5] That is, if I understand Ward correctly, *either* the event really occurred as reported and recorded, *or* the minds of contemporaries were predisposed to see and think of it as having occurred in that fashion. If the former, this seems to mean that historical agents—whether Edward IV, or Richard of Gloucester, or the gaolers, or all together—somehow fell under the spell of a mythic archetype, now of hoary antiquity, and saw fit to repeat it unreflectively. If the latter, it means that the thought and imagination of the "witnesses," i.e., contemporary gossip, were constrained to locate a given historical event in some preexisting archetypal mythic pattern, long after the *original* meaning of myth—say, to confirm preexisting social structure—had passed out of both reality and consciousness.

This then, can leave us in very serious doubt about the history of *any* period which has lain under the strong influence of myth, however disguised and detached from its original moorings.

First, in such cases one must speculate to what extent we can trust our witnesses and records, if indeed they *are* invincibly prone to assimilate to mythical patterns what they see or transmit as supposedly historical actions. And second, we must also ask how we can trust historical agents themselves. Can we be so very sure that they are acting with *some* sense of the particularity of their own situations, which is to say that they are both conscious and self-conscious individuals, in the sense that "history" assumes? In order to have history at all—we think—we need not assume that men always act wisely or decently, but we must assume that they are at least *awake,* and in sufficient command of their free will to make a personal choice of actions —at least among a reasonable range of mistakes and blunders. Now, even that minimal and modest assumption may be threatened for long and important stretches of history. I for one feel more than a little uncomfortable with a "history" of the era of Edward IV and Richard III that is so contaminated by myth that I am forced to think that either the witnesses have distorted the event to fit preexisting mythical patterns in their own

---

5 *Ibid.,* pp. 123–29.

minds, or that the principles were predetermined to act as they reportedly did, not out of any sort of policy shaped by a particular context of events, but because mythical archetypes overruled whatever private thoughts they had. I may still find this period of history fascinating for a variety of reasons, but I am not quite sure that it has, any longer, the characteristic we call "history."

II

"Royal *gamos*" in my title is my own makeshift term used to refer to a sexual connection between royal personages where the people involved are not married to each other; normally they meet on some sort of official or even diplomatic occasion; normally, too, the male partner of the affair is, at least for the moment, only a *would-be* king, a pretender, an adventurer, or an exile. In the total record of Greco-Roman civilization this pattern is nearly as frequent in history as in myth and leads me to suspect just what status it has as history. The suspicion is worth at least a second look. Considering for the moment only this one pattern (among many others, one or two of which are mentioned more briefly in part III), there is something altogether too pat about the way the reported history of the Greco-Roman world imitates myth so devotedly.

For instance, Xenophon's account of the expedition of Cyrus the pretender contains an item that, before my reading in the school of Dumézil, I had always put down to the rather predictable delight prudish authors take in scandal and gossip: "Cyrus, it was said, had sexual relations with the Queen of the Cilicians" (*elégeto dè kaì syggenésthai Kyron têi Kilíssēi*).[6] This event occurred, if it did, when Cyrus was negotiating a safe passage for his forces with King (Syennesis) of Cilicia through that strategically placed if otherwise unimportant principality. The modern, more or less pragmatic, view of political history as a series of calculated gestures in the direction of institutionalized self-interest might see the event so reported as a means used by Cyrus to gain the queen's favor so that she could, in turn, influence her husband in Cyrus' favor. But then again the modern view of human nature might equally see the event as fraught with political disaster for Cyrus, had the king been the jealous type. Yet, I suspect, neither modern reaction to the

---

6 *Anabasis* 1.2.12.

story has anything to do with its meaning, either for Xenophon, or for Cyrus and Epyaxa the queen. For, one notes, Xenophon himself puts no such pragmatic political interpretation upon it; in fact he fails to interpret it, in the modern sense, at all. For all we know, sexual relations *may* have been a form of diplomatic protocol between royal personages of different sexes in antiquity (or even of the same sex, as will be discussed below in the case of Caesar and King Nicomedes of Bithynia) and, indeed, sexual relations between a reigning queen and a male pretender to a *different* throne may have a *de facto* form of diplomatic recognition of the pretender's royal status and an important index or portent of the viability of his claims and ambitions. In fact, these last-mentioned interpretations of the event (which are, in themselves, simply guesses) are *more* likely to be true than the modern variety, given the text itself. For, one must notice, Xenophon does not himself vouch for the truth, in our sense, of the tale; he only certifies that it was spread publicly, and that he, and no doubt others, heard of it (*elégeto*). An important part of the event, possibly the more important part, is its dissemination among the many (one is reminded of the importance, in perhaps more ways than one, of *Fama* in *Aeneid* IV, discussed below). The *report* of the affair, to Xenophon, seems to suggest its own interpretation, and he no doubt expected his readers to grasp what it was. We no longer naturally respond to the signals Xenophon has relayed, and can only hope to ferret out its meaning with painful research. But I think the meaning can be found in Greek myth, and it is an almost perfectly clear answer.

If one compares the myths of Paris, Oedipus, Theseus, Jason, Odysseus, and Aeneas, not to mention minor myths, one will find several common motifs and indeed almost a common narrative pattern, even though the oldest or best sources we possess for these myths are of different dates and were composed for a great variety of purposes. In all cases the hero in question undergoes some sort of exile, usually early in his career. In all but the last case the hero's purpose is to find his way back home again and to assume some sort of rightful authority, normally the kingship, to which he is entitled by right of male primogeniture, even though in each case male primogeniture has been sidetracked and frustrated by circumstances. (This assumes that male primogeniture *was* the social reality contemplated by the myths—actually I think it was not; this particular development was embroidered into the fabric of these myths at a later date to account for a later shift to male primogeniture.) Oedipus, one might say, was not *trying* to get home again, but that is where the fates are taking him, regardless of his own actions. And Paris was trying, at most, simply to get parental recognition of his *noble* status, but not really a throne.[7] Yet one must conceive of the possibility that in an earlier version of the myth Paris was the first and rightful heir of Priam, as his ability to get Priam into trouble by courting Helen seems to hint even in Homer, though Homer's attention has shifted to Hector as the more interesting, because more warlike, Trojan hero, and perhaps has upgraded him for that reason. Aeneas, with no Troy to return to, was still trying to re-found Troy in a new location, and so his general conformity to type can hardly be questioned seriously. But in all these cases an additional element enters in. It becomes necessary, for a variety of *narrative* reasons suggested by *our* sources, but perhaps not important originally, for the vagabond, unrecognized, or uncrowned hero to go to bed with a royal female, either a queen or a bona fide princess with assured title to a throne, in order for him to assume or regain authority in his newly discovered or revisited kingdom. Oedipus becomes king of Thebes, *not* for destroying the Sphinx but because he married the queen, Jocasta, who, so far as he knows, is the queen of a different country from that of his origins, Corinth. Paris, in a special sense, proves his royalty to Troy and the Trojans by seducing Helen, the queen of an entirely different country.[8] Jason, who aims to be king *somewhere*—if his rightful city, Iolcos, is hostile, anywhere else will do, apparently —does little else throughout his career except court women of royal birth and title: Hypsipyle, Medea, and Glauce of Corinth. Circumstances simply play him false, unfortunately. Hypsipyle, on Lemnos, is eager enough to retain his sexual company, but,

---

[7] Evidence for this is primarily Euripides' fragmentary *Alexander*, esp. Nos. 49–51 and 58 (Nauck). See also Ovid, *Heroides*, ll. 16, 51–56, 89–102. But the idea that Paris was only a fickle playboy, a man of no authority, is implied in *Iliad* 3.391–94, where Paris is described as looking like a boy just home from a dance. See also *Troades*, ll. 928–32, 991–97; *Andromache*, ll. 280–300.

[8] See *Iliad* 3.16, *trosìn mèn promákhizen Aléxandros theoeides* ("For the Trojans, godlike Alexander [Paris] fought in the van"), which appears like a fossil from an earlier time when Paris was perhaps treated as Priam's *most important* son. At 3.146 ff. (the elders chirping like grasshoppers to convince themselves that Helen's beauty is worth a very bad war), we seem to have Homer's revised rationalization of the motives for the war; since, in his view, major dynastic considerations could not be attached to the effete person of Paris, a mere younger son and fashion-plate, it must have been the person of Helen—here, her beauty—which propelled Priam, and the city generally, into a risky war to keep her among them.

given the peculiar history of that particular polity, a mere husband could hardly count on the guarantee of life itself, much
less of authority.[9] Similarly, with Medea, her ability to help
him steal the golden fleece and save his life in doing so is in
inverse proportion to her ability to help him win a throne to
which she could conduct him by her own natural right; Medea's
favors were of no *political* use in Colchis, and she was perhaps
just a shade too foreign to be exploitable in Iolcos. And finally,
in sedate middle age, Jason tries once again in Corinth, and
attempts to *marry* the princess, with the well-known results.
In a sense one might say that Jason is a mythical character who
has deciphered at least a part of his own myth: he realizes that
for an unknown, unrecognized freebooter to gain a throne, he
must first win the bed of a real princess. What he seems to have
misread is the additional mythical requirement that normally
the pretender should remain a paramour of the princess or queen
of a country different from the one he desires to rule. His mistake, in a sense, was to marry. Theseus, on the other hand, won
official recognition as son and heir from king Aegeus of Athens,
and was never required, in the technical sense, to prove his le-
gitimacy by any special means; yet he did, and in very much
the same pattern. Each of his travels results in a "marriage"
with a foreign princess—Ariadne, Hippolyta, Phaedra—and not
just a foreign princess but an "enemy."

The pattern should now appear reasonably clear: for a young
hero to exercise a believable claim to a throne which he does
not own outright—although his own sense of himself, if not
divine oracles and other indications, tell him he has a higher
right to it—the *swiftest* credible means of making that claim
is his ability to point to a well-known sexual liaison with a recognized queen or princess of a *different* nation. Both factors
are somehow vital: the woman must be royal and the affair must
be public knowledge. Passion seems to have little to do with it.
A private love affair that remained a well-kept secret would
seem to have no value whatever in promoting the political ends
which dominate these accounts of so many heroic careers: to
acquire or regain a throne. Even Virgil, I think, sensed the underlying mythical "rule" of such stories, and his treatment of
Aeneas' strange affair with Dido—quite apart from the motives
of Venus, Juno, or Dido herself—seems aimed at proving Aene-

---

9 Apollonius Rhodius, *Argonautica* 1.609 ff., esp. 839–41, where Jason refuses
royal authority on Lemnos (having just heard the horrid story Hypsipyle tells
him) with the frigid and diplomatically vague phrase: *allá me lygroì epispérk-
housin áethloi* ("But hateful contests are driving me onward") .

as' royal status and his title to a new throne ruling over a new
state, a destiny that Aeneas is not altogether agreeable to. The
affair with Dido, one might say, has the effect of convincing
Aeneas himself, and not just the reader, of his kingly status. The
fact that Virgil abruptly drops the description of the actual
events in the cave to write the famous *Fama* passage (4.173 ff.)
is due, no doubt, partly to the poet's squeamishness. But it
also fits admirably the pattern under discussion here: an essential element in all these cases is the public knowledge that sexual congress has taken place between an acknowledged queen
or princess and an important pretender to a throne, who needs
this very sort of recognition to achieve his goal.

Odysseus, who of course is only returning home, does not
face the same pressure in making his own claim to a throne.
The throne—a rather minor and petty one, one might add—
was originally his. But to reassert his right to it, he must first
assert or win his right to the bed of Penelope, and after twenty
years he is, for all practical purposes, a different person. In effect, he must seduce his own wife and win her sexual acceptance
as though he were just one more freebooter or adventurer. Thus
the quarrel over the bed and its status in Book 23 of the *Odyssey* acquires a new status. Ostensibly, the quarrel is simply a
test of a factual memory, by which Odysseus will reveal himself as the true master of his house. But it is, as well, a test of
his ability to return from the limbo of his memories and try
occasions with a mortal queen whose sexual acceptance he needs
in order to regain his throne, but whose mood is suspicious if
not quite hostile because in her mind he has been entirely too
cautious and deceptive to be acceptable *tout court* as her husband.[10] Odysseus and Penelope face each other as almost com-

---

10 See *Odyssey* 19.309–16: Penelope, who begins her conversation with the disguised Odysseus (l. 89) in hopes that either *he* is Odysseus or may *know of*
Odysseus, 200 lines later rejects all consolation and declares that he will never
return. What has happened? In the intervening lines Odysseus has told two lies
about himself: that he, the disguised guest, met Odysseus years before in Crete
(172–202), and that he has *heard* that Odysseus is in nearby Thesprotia and will
return any day now (269–91). The lies, clearly, are told *in the wrong order:*
Penelope's first question was for fresh, not stale, information, and Odysseus should
have told the second lie first. This state of affairs seems to convince Penelope of a
paradoxical truth: that the stranger *is* indeed Odysseus, and that he is even more
heartless and deceptive than ever. One imagines her wondering whether Odysseus
will ever make the *moral* return to Ithaca to accompany his physical return, and
this seems to trigger her despairing outburst. Notably, after the slaughter of the
suitors and his revelation of his identity (23.174–78), Penelope pretends not to be
sure of him and says, in so many words that he is not the same man who left
Ithaca years before. With this we may contrast 19.163, where she had said that he
was not born from stone or oak, i.e., that he must have had a family; now she is
not so sure.

plete strangers, as foreigners (which his own lying tales help establish), who yet have a deep sexual attraction toward one another, such that it seems almost irregular. Thus their going to bed together is conditional upon their mutual acceptance of certain insecurities about one another. Odysseus could never be altogether certain, before the final risky moment of self-assertion, that Penelope was not treating him as just one more suitor, while Penelope could not be certain that Odysseus was anything more than another would-be paramour, though more clever and devious than the others (and who may also be divine)[11]—one who seeks some advantage from her, not in the form of material goods like the other suitors but, from the very fact of her sexual compliance, perhaps a throne somewhere else.

And thus we return to the question posed concerning Xenophon's account of the *amour* between Cyrus and Epyaxa. Is this not also a case where the benefit accruing to the pretender from this affair was nothing so utilitarian as the queen's influence over her husband to achieve a momentary strategic advantage, but the very act itself which, sufficiently publicized, should have helped convince public opinion (as well as Cyrus himself) of his own royal destiny?

The social reality behind these myths devoted to the vicissitudes of pretenders to royal status seems reasonably clear. True enough, the narrative rationalizations employed by the authors of *our* particular sources have in some cases blurred or rearranged the steps of the typical mythical story. But they must be regarded for what they are: attempts to regularize and harmonize odd-sounding details in the myths with the differing social reality familiar to the authors themselves, particularly the shift in inheritance customs to male primogeniture. Thus, for instance, it seems clear that the story of Paris was converted somewhere along the line of its transmission to Homer from a tale of royal succession achieved through "adultery" with a queen of a different kingdom to a tale of desperate romanticism involving not the heir to the throne, but a younger son whose achievements are limited solely to the boudoir and whose fate is to have, at best, interesting adventures but never any real authority. (Another example of how common mythical patterns are "disassembled" in literate times to serve the purposes

---

11 *Odyssey*, 23.174–78: Penelope's last-minute reluctance to accept Odysseus' self-identification contains an antique anxiety, common to many myths: he may be a god trying to deceive and seduce her.

of entertaining and plausible fictions, is discussed below in part III: the motif of the suppliant and infant.)

If my reconstruction of mythical clues is more or less correct, at some point in its development prehistoric Greek society seems to have passed through a stage that might be called— *sit venia barbarismo*—"feminilineal." That is, for a time, and it is impossible to guess how long a time, power and property seem to have descended through the female not to her son but to her husband. The husband could apparently come from anywhere and perhaps *had* to: this may also involve a taboo against endogamy. The important thing, so far as property and legal status were concerned, seems to have been who the daughter was and to whom she might turn a favoring eye. Men ruled, it seems, but their daughters determined who succeeded them. This form of social process is illustrated in a neutral fashion, among many examples, by the legends of the early Attic kingship. For instance, as Pausanias records the tradition,[12] of the four earliest kings of Attica, each, except for the first, is the son-in-law of his predecessor—Cecrops, Cranaus and Amphictyon— and each is an adventurer or interloper whose origins are elsewhere.

In the case of the Attic kingship, there is no question of adultery, or any other irregularity or scandal. It is simply the case that each successive king, passing over sons (if any—none are mentioned), bestowed his daughter in marriage upon his approved successor. The procedure is straightforward and neutral with respect to the *fictional* properties of the events described, which indeed have virtually no fictional properties we can discern. How then do we move from this state of affairs to the fictionalized and provocative cases where royal adultery is the path to a different throne? What has happened here, I think, is roughly as follows: with the disappearance of a social reality to which myth originally cohered in a close and efficient way, myth then became subject to wayward and exotic distortions, as is understandable enough, so that eye-catching if unimportant details were exaggerated as essence was lost sight of. Probably at one time there was a very large body of Greek myth repeating the same theme, which may once have been a social reality, that descent of royal or even lesser authority went from father to son-in-law through marriage with a royal daughter, as in the case of the Attic kingship. Much of this must have

---

[12] *Descriptio Atticae* 2.6.

been quite unremarkable material. But with the emergence of new social and political rules—male primogeniture, the dropping of exogamy, and even any concern for female heirs—only the bizarre cases which contained an irregular element, like adultery or an affair not leading to marriage because the man in question wanted to be king somewhere else, or perhaps of several places at once like Theseus, would retain the interest and attention of myth-tellers. And in the light of new social conditions, it would then appear necessary to discover new and more contemporary theories to explain the motives of such persons. Thus, it may be, a special class of amatory pretenders, adventurers, and exiles was conjured up from the ruins of an earlier socio-mythical pattern, and these were permitted to go their own way in a corpus of tales now totally unconnected with real social structure. This body of myth then floats vaguely over the lives of men in historical times and begins to influence their actions and their thoughts, not according to its original connections to social structure but precisely because of its failure to correspond to humdrum social matters. Thus, irregular sexual connections rather than routine marriages would tend to dominate one's attention, and such connections would be seen, more and more, no longer as *legal* proofs of a man's title to power and authority but as *symbolic* proofs of his title to authority *somewhere else.*

Turning from myth to history one finds, if anything, that this particular pattern is exaggerated and made more explicit. (By "history," I obviously mean, here, merely that which passes for historical fact with the reporting source.) The case of Cyrus the pretender has already been discussed. It seems clear that Xenophon, who is not otherwise interested in the sexual life of Cyrus or his other supporters, reports the affair with Epyaxa because, to him, it was a half-mythical token of royal destiny. Then there is the case of Gyges and the wife of Candaules, with which Herodotus opens his history: an unwarranted intimacy—seeing the queen naked—even if not an a priori sexual encounter, enables Gyges to win both the queen and the throne.[13] There is the case of Alcibiades' reported adultery with Timaea, queen of Sparta.[14] There are, of course, the notorious cases of both Caesar and Antonius with Cleopatra. (Here one might also add the case—or gossip—about Caesar's homosexual affair

---

[13] *Herodotus* 1.8.2–13.1
[14] Plutarch, *Alcibiades* 23.7; cf. also *Agesilaus* 3.

with Nicomedes, king of Bithynia, reported by Suetonius, who also adds that Caesar had a particular addiction for royal women.) [15] Finally there are the cases of the opposite form of behavior, examples of men who refused to sleep with certain royal females, though it was in their power, and apparently in the eyes of contemporaries their right, to do so, and who thus seemed to forfeit or weaken their title to royal status by the choice they made. Pompey's refusal to take Stratonice, the mistress of the dead Mithradates, to his bed—though his sexuality was more than robust—puzzled Plutarch's sources.[16] And Alexander's refusal to sleep with the relict of Darius III puzzled everyone.[17] It is perhaps in such negations that one can see most clearly the dominant effect of mythic patterns at work upon the ancient consciousness. To forego the right to sexual intercourse with the women of a defeated monarch seemed tantamount to resigning the fruits of victory one had gained by defeating him in the first place. Defeating a foreign king and sleeping with his women seem to have been the two more or less obvious ways of proving to the world at large that one deserved royal status oneself and in one's own place. In fact, perhaps defeating a king was *less* important than sleeping with his wife. Oedipus, Paris, Jason, and Theseus are among the least military of mythic heroes, and all must have seemed originally to be royal figures who gained that status primarily through exogamic, and usually irregular, sexual liaisons with royal women.

The affairs of Caesar and Antonius with the temptress of the Nile are of course the most intriguing on our list. It is remarkable if not actually incredible that eight centuries after Homer, when social life had changed in almost every conceivable way, leading men of the literate, cynical, and sophisticated capital of the world, which hardly believed in the literal truth of the myths any more (or are we so certain?—Antonius apparently did, as will be discussed below) could reenact so devoutly the perceived patterns of myths that were old when Homer was young. Or, rather, is it the case that historians and other sources reporting these events were themselves so enchanted by the patterns of myth that they reported historical events as though they were myths? Or, finally, is this distinction a real one? Is it not more likely that a kind of mythic cloud encircled both

---

[15] *Vita Divi Juli,* ¶'s 49 and 51.
[16] Plutarch, *Pompey* 2.2–3 and 36.2–7.
[17] Plutarch, *Alexander* 21.4–5.

historical actor and historical source, guiding them both to the same conclusions? What Caesar may have thought of his own actions is very hard to say. Supposedly diffident and skeptical, he may have seen through the mythical furbelows attached to historical action and reached to the "reality" beneath—assuming that *our* age has in fact caught at the "reality" of history in some way both superior to, and revelatory of, other ages—but then again he may not have. Caesar, after all, is somewhat like Socrates in the modern imagination: his life and career are considered public domain, and anyone who wishes can write and theorize about him as though he were an all-purpose symbol available to any age to help it explain its own woes to itself. The twentieth century, I suspect, has more or less accepted the image of Caesar as a benign, world-weary Shavian rationalist. It may be that his affair with Cleopatra was mainly what Shaw saw in it. But it might have been something else, too. If Caesar was the gargantuan sensualist that Suetonius portrays, then, at most, we might conceive of him as pretending to fulfill the old mythical pattern with Cleopatra, while really caring only for his private pleasures, and knowing full well that his military prowess was what really made him a candidate for royal status. But this presumes too much: first, that Cleopatra was a woman naturally attractive to him, regardless of her power and position, which we do not know to be true; and second, that Caesar, by some unaccountable accident, was a pragmatic rationalist in the modern sense, interested simply in a rational and viable political solution of socio-economic problems on the one hand, and on the other, attracted to Cleopatra, if he was, in some personal sense. Neither notion, it seems to me, avoids serious anachronisms. First, one may doubt that Caesar, however cynical he was on other occasions, necessarily saw policy considerations in everything he did, including his liaison with Cleopatra. (It seems, in fact, to have caused him serious and unforeseen practical political problems back in Rome.) [18] And second, one may doubt that deep personal feelings affected either Caesar or Cleopatra, since both were in a position to command purely physical gratification any time they chose. A much more reasonable hypothesis, it seems to me, is the idea that Caesar, like the ancients generally, guided as they were by the

---

[18] *Vita Divi Juli*, ¶'s 49–51 (The scurrilous pamphlets, verses, and speeches Suetonius reports on could not have helped Caesar's career and plans); Plutarch, *Caesar* 28.3–4.

precedent of myth, regarded a sexual affair with a reigning queen as an important token and portent of his own dreamed-of royal status.

All the foregoing is speculative, of course. It is very hard to pin Caesar down. But with Antonius, the situation is much simpler. It is quite clear that he, and he alone, was the cause of his own historical record and the mythical elements therein. He really saw himself, according to Plutarch, as a mythical figure. As a self-proclaimed descendant of Heracles he saw himself as the new Heracles with a divinely sanctioned mission to father an innumerable brood of dynasts throughout the world. We may draw the momentary conclusion that at least in his case, if not in others, the thesis of this paper is more than sustained. Marcus Antonius, given his remarkable sexual charm, had countless women at his beck and call.[19] Therefore his affair with Cleopatra had little or nothing to do with private passions. It was seen, both by him as well as others, as an arrangement which would somehow guarantee him a throne and an enduring effect on history because of the deep influence of myth upon his character and imagination.

III

The purpose of this paper has been mainly aporetic and cautionary. It has been to suggest, unenthusiastically, that our own fundamental perceptions of ancient history just may be so ineradicably colored by a mythical warping and bending of events that we are effectively denied even a surface comprehension of what it was ancient historical figures were doing or even what they *thought* they were doing. In fact, it may not be proper to assume that they thought at all, in any sense that our era could quite appreciate or comprehend. The thinking of Antonius, at any rate, would seem incomprehensible to a Machiavelli, an eighteenth-century rationalist, a capitalist individualist, much less to the "social consciousness" of a Marxist. It may well be that mythic patterns were so readily available to ancient man *to think with,* that he rarely forewent the temptation to let myth do his observing, thinking, and planning for him. If this is the case, much of what we hope we possess of ancient history may turn to mystery or vapor in our hands.

My use of the *gamos* as the case in point was dictated not

---

19 Plutarch, *Antonius* 4.2–4, 36,2.

because of its scandalous ring, to our ears, but because it is so very peculiar a phenomenon according to our conception of politics; because it seems to be linked, at an early stage, to an important item of social structure; and finally because this item seems to have been very old, antedating both recorded history and even the socio-political arrangements of late prehistoric times.

What I am suggesting, in effect, is that in times of strong mythical influence, it was perhaps much more difficult than Thucydides imagined to purge *tò mythôdes* from history; indeed, I am suggesting that, just perhaps, it may have been impossible. For the royal *gamos* is not the only case in point I might have chosen to illustrate the peculiar shakiness which infests our records of antiquity. Here let me sketch more briefly other instances where myth seems to have doctored our received evidence of historical events, in some cases by influencing the conduct of an historical figure; in others, by influencing the historian, or observer, or passer-on of the story; and in still others, where it may have influenced both, or at least where we are unable, as I see it, to decipher which it may have been.

An example of the first case may be—surely must be—Thucydides' tale of Themistocles' flight from a decree of outlawry, and his device to get the protection of Admetus, king of the Molossians, by crouching on the king's hearth while cradling the king's infant son in his arms.[20] A. W. Gomme, on this passage, discusses the possibility of *literary* influence upon Thucydides from Euripides' *Telephus*, if only to reject it.[21] But if one thinks, rather, in terms of myth, to which literature per se often supplies only indifferent and clouded testimony, it would appear that what we have here is the influence of a very general and widespread mythical motif, *represented* by the myth of Telephus as dramatized by Euripides but hardly exhausted by it. And, we have an influence upon either Themistocles, or upon the wife of Admetus, who, according to Thucydides, actually

---

20 Thucydides 1.136.3–137.1.
21 Historical Commentary to *Thucydides* (New York: Oxford Univ. Press, 1959), I, 438–39. Gomme notes that there is a suspicious parallel here with Euripides' lost play *Telephus,* which presented a similar scene known to us from extensive parody in Aristophanes' *Acharnians* (ll. 326 ff.). Somewhat arbitrarily, Gomme decides "I do not myself see Thucydides uncritically accepting well-known stories from tragedy and attaching them to historical personages." Neither do I, but what I suggest is the serious possibility that neither Thucydides nor Themistocles is an entirely free agent here, and that the basic background myth, not a particular literary representation of it, has exercised a degree of control over the reported events which neither ancient historian nor modern scholar can ever completely assess.

devised the scheme; or, at the outside, an influence upon Thucydides' sources. (I would agree with Gomme that Thucydides
was not likely to be influenced by merely *literary* parallels.)
Suppliants nursing, fostering, holding, blessing, and otherwise
granting special boons to the children of their hosts, are relatively common in our surviving records of the Greek myths.
One thinks of Phoenix, Demeter, even the tale of Odysseus and
Nausicaa, and perhaps even that of Adrastus and the son of
Croesus. Though our *literary* sources, in all cases, have their
own aims to pursue and axes to grind—which are seldom coex-
tensive with myth itself, and are sometimes in serious conflict
with it—and though they routinely engage in what I have called
the disassembly of mythical details in order to recompose them
in a more particularized narrative—still the fact remains that
in all the cases noted a figure who is banished, hunted, or lost,
seeks asylum from strangers by entering their houses, and usually by sitting on their hearths. Beyond that, the children of
the unwitting patrons are *always* involved, in some way, even
in surviving fictions, though in the fictions their roles are not
univocal (yet they probably were at one time). Phoenix,
of course, does tend to and foster the infant Achilles, though
Homer tells the tale as simply that of a princely older resident
of the house of Peleus who happens to like children, and whose
acceptance as a suppliant, years before, was not originally con-
ditioned by his future service as a male nurse for Achilles.[22]
Demeter's service to the son of her hosts is portrayed by the
Hymn as a spontaneous act of gratitude for their hospitality;[23]
but one must not neglect the ever present hearth, spectacularly
employed in this case, as well as the parents' understandable fear.
The sixth book of the *Odyssey* gives us, perhaps, the furthest
stage reached in the disassembly of a myth. In this case, Odysseus *is* a suppliant, and he *does* crouch on the well-worn hearth.
But in this case, the plan to do just that is thought up by the
child Nausicaa herself, though she is hardly a child at all any
more. But even here the basic outlines of the anterior myth are
still visible: a child, to whom the interloper might in some way

---

22 See *Iliad* 9.436–38 (Phoenix is the guardian of Achilles even in adulthood);
448 ff. (the reason for his exile); 479 ff. (he came to Peleus in Phthia and was
received as an honored guest); 485 ff. (he was a special, if irregular, tutor to
Achilles); and 492–95 (Achilles has become, in effect, his special obligation, or
ward, apparently as a *quid pro quo* for Peleus' original kindness in accepting him
as an exile and suppliant).
23 *Hymn to Demeter*, 192–274.

be dangerous,[24] is critically involved with the interloper in his approach to her parents as a landless and friendless suppliant seeking refuge, comfort, and a new direction in life. The net effect of all such myths, with their converging similarities, regardless of special literary variations, must have exercised a profound effect upon *any* refugee or suppliant in the ancient world, even in historical times. Indeed, for any man who found himself in that condition, the mythical pattern must have been that to which his mind turned most swiftly and naturally. If the incident of Themistocles and Admetus actually occurred in something like the form reported by Thucydides, I would think it likely that the prevailing mythical climate simply induced either Themistocles, or the queen herself, to adopt this strategy because myths, when strong and vital, tend to persuade men that they represent important *general* truths of existence, which are substantially repeatable time after time, and to which men would be wise to pay heed. At least on the surface, myths, far from being tied to a peculiar set of social and historical situations, *seem* to carry forward essential paradigms for human action over an indefinite, and perhaps an infinite time scale.

Examples of the reporter or recorder of historical events falling under the spell of myth might be the remarkable similarity of certain events in Herodotus' account of Persian *history* to those in Greek *myths*. For instance, the circumstances surrounding the birth, parentage, and treatment of the infant Cyrus are suspiciously similar to the myths of Oedipus and Paris.[25] Again, the remark of the wife of Intapharnes to Darius, when he was planning to execute her husband, is disturbingly similar to Antigone's statement in Sophocles' play: that she could always get another husband, but not another brother.[26] On the other hand, this sort of problem is, in a sense, the least of our worries. If historians *alone* labored under the spell of myth, from which all other important witnesses were free, it would be very little trouble to disentangle their mythical lapses from the otherwise truly individualistic record. And to the extent that Herodotus may be guilty of forcing Persian history into the mold of Greek myth, he is relatively transparent. Moreover, in cases like this the historian is reacting, most likely, to *literary* repre-

---

24 See *Odyssey* 6.130–32 (Odysseus approaches Nausicaa *os te léon* and "with eyes blazing"); 138 (the girls are afraid, and bolt); 138–41 (Nausicaa only manages to stay and confront him because Athena gives her an extra dose of boldness).
25 Herodotus 1.107 ff.
26 Herodotus 3.119.6; see *Antigone* 905–15.

sentations of myth and not to the deeper influences of myth itself. The putative influence of Sophocles' *plays* on Herodotus, as distinct from the totality of the mythical experience, is rather easy to discount in Herodotus or any ancient historian.

Finally, let me mention two examples where it seems quite impossible to discern exactly *where* the influence of myth has fallen, whether primarily on the historical agents themselves or only on their historians. I, for one, would speculate that in these cases there is no meaningful distinction between the two. Both cases come from the gamey history of the Diadochi. The essential mythical model is the Phaedra-Hippolytus story, as told by Euripides: these are tragedies of incestuous feelings between a step-parent and step-child.[27] One "historical" parallel is the love of Arsinoe, wife of Lysimachus, for her step-son, Agathocles, as recorded by Pausanias. Pausanias, interestingly enough, in opening his narrative first offers some half-hearted opposition to the incest story: namely that Arsinoe *feared* Agathocles from the first and wanted to destroy him to protect her children and assure their succession upon Lysimachus' demise.[28] Yet in the next breath, and in an excess of vagueness, he goes on, "Historians have already related that Arsinoe. conceived a passion for Agathocles, and upon her failure to win him over, arranged his death."[29] Taking Pausanias' *two* versions together, this is the Hippolytus-Phaedra legend down to the last detail, including the younger wife's not altogether consistent fear for the fate of her children.[30] If this romantic tale seems out of place in the *Realpolitik* of the Diadochid empires (as it does to Pausanias himself, who emphasizes the authority of others for the tale: *égrapsan, légousin*), it is all the more important as evidence of the power of myth to affect the telling of history, such that a reasonably worldly author like Pausanias would interrupt and confuse an account of events to which he himslef ascribes by interjecting a "mythical" version of those same events with which he does not himself seem to agree but which he seems helpless to criticize or even to expunge from his own text. The second example is from Plutarch's life of Demetrius the Besieg-

---

27 Except that they are not legally related, the tales of Bellerophon and Anteia (*Iliad* 6.160 ff.), and Joseph and Potiphar's wife (*Genesis* 39.6–20) are essentially parallel.

28 *Descriptio Atticae* 10.3–4.

29 *ede dè égrapsan kaì hos Agathokléous aphikoito es érota he Arisinóe, apotygkhánousa dè epì tôi bouleúsai légousin Agathokleî thánaton.*

30 Euripides, *Hippolytus* 305–10 and 716–17 (yet, at 313–15, Phaedra seems to deny an overriding concern for her children).

er, namely the tale of Antiochus, son of Selecus, and his nearly
fatal passion for Stratonice, his father's new wife, and his decision to settle the problem by starving himself to death.[31] Except for a reversal of the sexes, the tale is éxactly parallel to the
Hippolytus-Phaedra legend, down to the starvation motif,[32] as
well as the role played by the kindly and indulgent court phy-
sician, Erasistratus, reenacting the role of the nurse in the
Hippolytus. Admittedly, Plutarch seems more relaxed in dealing with such material, and, unlike Pausanias, does not even
struggle to match his own perception of these events with the
mythical paradigms which clearly fostered them in *someone's*
mind. We can hardly know what he thought of this tale, except
to mention in passing that the symptoms of Antiochus' stifled
love were similar to those noted in Sappho's famous poem about
ringing ears and tingling skin.

In the second book of the *Republic* (377b–378a) Plato has
Socrates observe that in actual practice it is mothers and nursemaids who "administer" myths and their effects to children under their care. It is at *this* stage and level of consciousness that
myths make their entrance into the soul and produce their far-
reaching and profound modulations of the mind and personali-
ty. This function[33] he would hope to see sophisticated by linking
to it the function of a professional and politically accountable
body of myth-makers, poets under state license, as it were, or
even direct state control. Otherwise, the implication is, poets
will simply devise and revise myths as fancy strikes them and
then inject their results into the common stream of social awareness, from which mothers and nursemaids draw indiscriminately
to feed the minds of their charges. Here Plato indicates he realizes the crucial point: myths *never* simply appear as neutral
accounts of behavior in the far past. Nor indeed do their true
origins, even if known or guessed at by a few intellectuals, necessarily comprehend or explain the hold of myth on the minds
of the mass of society. No matter what myths may have been
originally—e.g., accounts of prehistoric social structure, *à la*
Dumézil—the fact is that they outlive, at least some of them,
the social or ritual routine and humdrum to which they may
once have been connected; and *some* form of them, however
poorly understood and however garbled by literary second-

---

31 *Demetrius,* Chap. 38.
32 *Hippolytus,* 135–40.
33 *pláttein tàs psykhàs autôn toîs mythois poly mâllon e tà somata taîs khersín.*

guessing and other *writers'* strategies, comes to exert a special force which is prompt and efficient at dictating human conduct along the lines of their superficial details if not their deepest meaning, which may quite probably have been lost in the flurry of social and institutional change. (Plato, one must observe, was *not* simply a crotchety reactionary trying to peddle a program of literary censorship and "thought control," in the style of modern totalitarianism; he was, in fact, trying to rebel against an unplanned but enormously effective form of thought control which already existed in the prepotent body of myth with which, to him, Greek thought and society were sorely burdened. He is concerned with *myth,* not with literature per se, and with myth's almost uncontrollable power to prescribe both paths of conduct and styles of thought.)

That myth exercised something like this degree of control over the majority can in a sense be "proved" by consulting the minority which did not acquiesce in this situation. There is a thin, but continuing, tradition in Greek thought and letters which has left us a record of dissent and demurrer against the total surrender of the mind to myth. Hesiod begins it, not by attacking myth directly, perhaps, but by insisting that myth does not dictate action but *demonstrates* truth and by showing that myths could be put to almost anyone's conscious educational purposes as when he says, in effect, that one myth may be as good as another in order to make the same intellectual point; i.e., to Hesiod both the tale of Pandora *and* the myth of the Ages are useful demonstrations of his theory about the sickness of history, though obviously both could not be literally and simultaneously true.[34] Xenophanes quarreled directly with myth— or with its most famous purveyors, Homer and Hesiod—accusing them of corrupting human morals and blaspheming deity with their tales of the gods' misbehavior.[35] (Xenophanes, I would have to say, missed the real differences in approach to myth used by Homer and Hesiod.) The point here is merely that Xenophanes recognized the prescriptive nature of myth and thus the dangers certain myths held, both for private morals and the social order. Plato, in addition to his direct polemics against the content of traditional myth in the *Republic* and elsewhere, precisely because of its educative power, its ability to

---

[34] See Hesiod, *Works and Days* 106–08; also my essay, "Hesiod and the Birth of Reason," *Antioch Review*, 26 (1966), 226–47.
[35] Xenophanes, DK.B.11, 12, 15, 18, 23–24.

make one reenact its details, paid myth the reverse compliment of trying to steal it, and to surround the figure of Socrates with a mythical halo of his own so that Socrates becomes the hero in a rival myth which attempts to *displace* rather than simply assault traditional myths of "immoral" heroic careers, an intellectual substitute for the physical heroism of Achilles and Heracles.[36] Here too, like Hesiod, Plato gives recognition to the didactic quality of myth and suggests that as a means of moral training, myth must be looked at and supervised by those who have conceived of a particular moral end for society in general and for individuals within it. Thus a loud if minority voice which struggled to fight its way out of mythic consciousness, or at least to regularize and purify that consciousness and put it to productive and moral ends, testifies to the prevalent condition, the dominant status of myth and its power to guide men's conduct according to its perceived patterns, and perhaps even to influence observers of such conduct so that their subsequent reports of that conduct were themselves tailored to fit the selfsame patterns. At least that is my very great fear, because of what it implies for our understanding of ancient history.

The aim of this paper has been to present to what I have come to view as a serious problem involved in the way we think about allegedly historical events in antiquity, and to invite further speculation and research in this area. I am afraid, as a result of my own research thus far, that we may be facing certainly not a total disintegration, but perhaps a considerable contraction of what we have heretofore assumed was real knowledge about the behavior of historical personages in ancient history. If their actions were so totally dominated by mythic patterns as to become quite impersonal, if not irrational, by the standards we use to judge such things today, what becomes of our total record of that era? Where can we find the historical *terra firma* that we demand of private, individualized, and rationalized (if not rational), human behavior? What will become of our deeply fixed convictions, derived more or less equally from Adam Smith, Comte, and Marx, that a mixture of

---

36 See *Apology* 41b, where Socrates compares himself with Palamedes Ajax as yet another hero who was unjustly condemned. Plato, I think, has quite deliberately taken the step of trying to replace traditional heroes with the sainted figure of Socrates. One may note, moreover, "Socrates'" labored reference to his own personal vocation as though it was tantamount to the labors (*pónoi*) of Heracles: *hosper pónous tinàs ponoûntos* (22a). Plato was obviously attempting to claim for Socrates the mythical status of Heracles, the greatest of heroes, and premier cultural benefactor of mankind known to traditional myth.

economic self-interest, a concrete sense of here-and-now personal needs, and class consciousness, play the truly determining
role in what we call history? Or, to delve even deeper, what
will become of our apparently still serious belief, perhaps derived ultimately from Augustine, that history is going somewhere, that it is a linear progression in *some* direction, even if
not toward some end designed by Providence, and that truly
new events, institutions, and historical aims actually appear on
the horizon of time? As the details studied above tend to suggest, it is not at all clear that Greco-Roman civilization had any
firm sense that its own historical record answered to any such
definitions, however loosely applied, of a *history*. If, to the ancient mind, history was, sometimes clearly and sometimes con-
fusedly, a replay of mythic patterns, what are we, who think
so differently, to do with that history? To take the extreme case,
if Marcus Antonius actually thought of himself, even intermit-
tently, as the reincarnated Heracles, *how* precisely are we supposed to effect entrance into his mind, much less assess, in terms
intelligible to us, the plans and behavior which we assume issued
forth from that mind?

Very little changes when we turn our attention toward historians and away from major historical agents. How can we
possibly trust them to provide us with the unique and discrete
character which today we must insist real historical events possess? If even over a selected range of cases we find some doubt
that in those cases historical events, as we understand them,
actually *occurred*—because we cannot be sure how historical
agents viewed their own actions—we face even steeper difficulties in supposing that ancient historians and record keepers
could possibly have rendered those events with the *particularity*
which we demand.[37] (Whether ancient historians operated with
objectivity and care are eighteenth- and nineteenth-century
questions, products respectively of the Enlightenment and positivism, one supposes. From our perspective, it may now appear
that these questions were posed too naïvely. It now appears

[37] I am not saying that we know nothing about ancient history, of course. Obviously, at the very worst, we know a great deal of overt fact and simple details:
the birth and death dates of important people (if known at all); the rise and fall
of dynasties; major institutional changes (though not all details, and much less
about the causes thereof). What I am really saying is that we know a great deal
more about ancient myth, both as an inventory of tales and details, and as a style
of thought, and that our knowledge of the latter should make us prudently suspicious
about the recorded history of group and individual behavior within the very largest
movements of ancient history until they are tested for their possible contamination
by myth.

necessary to ask whether this or that ancient historian, or even the historical figures he describes, possessed the epistemological tools to observe or perform what *we* call historical acts at all.)

With this paper I have merely posed a problem. I have hardly begun to delineate its dimensions, much less provided a method of solution. It is far too complex and grandiose for any one man, *hoîoi nyn brotoi easi,* to comprehend in its fullest extent, I imagine, or even to produce a definitive survey of all the pertinent phenomena. What I propose here are simply provocative cases, and insights drawn from them, to invite a co-operative venture among philologists, historians, philosophers, and students of myth, to work toward a much more sophisticated understanding of the effect of ancient myth on ancient history than we now possess.

Psychoanalysis, Structuralism, and Greek Mythology

Richard S. Caldwell

University of Texas

F REUD'S "discovery" of the unconscious, the dividing line between nineteenth- and twentieth-century theories of myth interpretation, is also the source of a common denominator in both major twentieth-century theories—the psychoanalytic method, as found in the works of Otto Rank and Géza Róheim, and the structuralist method identified with Claude Lévi-Strauss. For both psychoanalysts and structuralists, myths are a product of the unconscious, generated by unconscious psychic mechanisms, and for both the impetus of myth is a contradiction or conflict inaccessible to consciousness or "somehow inconsistent with conscious experience."[1] In one sense, of course, the stress on unconscious function in both methodologies is no accident, for to deny its importance would mean a return to the rationalistic and allegorical interpretations of a pre-Freudian world, as much a *temps perdu* as the time of Greek myth itself. In another sense, however, chance did play a part, at least originally, in the eventual affinity of psychoanalysis and structuralism; as Lévi-Strauss records, it was acquaintance with psychoanalysis which caused him to leave the study of philosophy by revealing to him that "those actions which seem most purely affective, those results which seem least logical, and those demonstrations which we call prelogical, are in point of fact precisely those which are meaningful in the highest degree."[2] And if psychoanalysis had a formative and enduring effect on the leading exponent

---

1 Edmund Leach, *Claude Lévi-Strauss* (New York: Viking Press, 1970), p. 57.
2 Claude Lévi-Strauss, *Tristes tropiques*, trans. John Russell (New York: Atheneum, 1971), p. 59.

of structuralism, so also has structuralism become a part of psychoanalytic theory, especially in France and particularly in the increasingly influential work of Jacques Lacan.

One wonders how much Freud's deep knowledge of classical mythology influenced his own thinking and, through it, the eventual shape of psychoanalytic theory. References to myth continually recur in Freud's writings; myth served both as a kind of sanction for empirical findings and also as a fertile field for the application of these findings. As Freud said, he had "long been haunted by the idea that our studies on the content of the neuroses might be destined to solve the riddle of the formation of myths, and that the nucleus of mythology is nothing other than what we speak of as 'the nuclear complex of the neuroses.' "[3] At any rate, the early psychoanalysts, especially Karl Abraham, Rank, and Ernest Jones, applied the new science to the interpretation of mythology so brilliantly that there remained, it seemed, little for subsequent analysts to add save in a quantitative dimension. If the psychoanalytic study of mythology has continued to be sporadically productive, it is due largely to the work of specialists in other fields, such as the psychoanalytic anthropologists Róheim, George Devereux, and, most recently, the sociologist Philip Slater.

For a variety of reasons (which in themselves invite speculation), the psychoanalytic explanation of myth is being increasingly supplanted, at least among nonanalysts, by the structuralist methodology of Lévi-Strauss. Based on the linguistic theory of Ferdinand de Saussure and Roman Jakobson, structuralism regards myth as a coded language, a system of signifiers whose meaning is found in the relationships between signifiers, or structure; since, in Roland Barthes' explanation, the signifiers of myth are the "signs" of language, myth is a "second-order semiological system."[4] Various structural properties follow from the status of myth as a semiological system. Just as language can be viewed, in de Saussure's terminology, as *langue* (its structural aspect, or formal rules) or as *parole* (its statistical aspect, the unconscious utilization of grammatical rules in actual speech), myth may be viewed synchronically (the structure revealed by isolating common or repeated elements in disre-

---

[3] Sigmund Freud, "Letter to D. E. Oppenheim," in *Dreams in Folklore,* by Sigmund Freud and D. E. Oppenheim (New York: International Univ. Press, 1958), pp. 13–14.
[4] Roland Barthes, "Myth Today," in *Mythologies,* trans. Annette Lavers (London: Jonathan Cape, 1972), p. 114.

gard of the chronological continuity of the mythical tale) or diachronically (the irreversible chronological sequence of the mythological tale). Second, just as language (in the sense of *parole*) is composed of lexical units chosen from a paradigmatic series and arranged in a syntagmatic chain, myth uses paradigmatic (metaphoric) and syntagmatic (metonymic) associations to establish homology between systems of differences; the variations in one system may be seen as algebraic transformations of the variations in the other system. The basic homology is between Nature and Culture, and the purpose of establishing homology is to mediate a logical contradiction (e.g., in the customs governing the exchange of women in primitive societies, the contradiction between women perceived as homogeneous *qua* women and as heterogeneous from the viewpoint of culture). Thus myth is a means by which men organize the natural and social universe as a coherent totality; "the mythical system and the modes of representation it employs serve to establish homologies between natural and social conditions or, more accurately, it makes it possible to equate significant contrasts found on different planes: the geographical, meteorological, zoological, botanical, technical, economic, social, ritual, religious, and philosophical."[5]

Third, just as structural linguistics is concerned with the organization of constituent units (morphemes, phonemes, etc.), the structuralist interpretation of myth analyzes the selection and arrangement of more complex constituent units, or *mythemes*. Fourth, individual mythic elements, like phonemes on another level, have no meaning in themselves; as the meaning of a word depends in the first place on the choice and sequence of phonemes, the meaning of a myth depends on the arrangement of elements in a structure which differentiates myth from ordinary discourse by revealing its synchronic dimension. It is these synchronic groupings of related elements which make up gross constituent units, or mythemes.

It has been pointed out that it is simply an error to treat a context-free system of oppositions between the acoustic characteristics of distinctive features in language as if it were isomorphic with myth, which is a system with a context.[6] This is also a point at which structuralism seems to depart markedly

---

[5] Claude Lévi-Strauss, *The Savage Mind* (Chicago: Univ. of Chicago Press, 1966), p. 93.

[6] See Anthony Wilden, *System and Structure* (London: Tavistock, 1972), pp. 8–11.

from classical psychoanalysis; as Lévi-Strauss continually stresses, meaning inheres only in the structure of relationships:

> appeal must be made to form and not content. The substance of contradictions is much less important than the fact that they exist . . . the form contradictions take varies very much less than their empirical content . . . It accounts for the fact that men have so often had recourse to the same means for solving problems whose concrete elements may be very different but which share the feature of all belonging to "structures of contradiction."[7]

The killing of Laius by Oedipus, in Lévi-Strauss's well-known example, has no meaning other than that conferred by a structure which groups it with other instances of the "underrating of blood relations"; this mytheme is in opposition to another which represents the "overrating of blood relations," and the contradiction between underrating and overrating mediates by analogy a contradiction between theoretical belief in autochthony and experiential denial of this belief.[8]

Finally, the debt owed by structuralism to the concept of binary opposition in Jakobsonian linguistics is seen not only in the basic opposition between nature and culture, the synchronic /diachronic axes, and the paradigmatic/syntagmatic associations, but also in the categories which determine the relationship between mythemes in a given structure, e.g., high/low, dry/wet, male/female, raw/cooked, symmetry/asymmetry, alternation/repetition, life/death, silence/noise etc.

Despite the ascendancy of structuralist methodology in the study of myth (and in other fields as well), there are reasons to think that the interpretation of mythology by psychoanalytic methods is not yet exhausted. One of these reasons is the vast new area of psychoanalytic research that has been opened up in recent decades, particularly the study of pre-oedipal child psychology. Another, more germane to our purposes, is the way in which psychoanalytic and structuralist methods tend to complement one another, a complementarity which has proven fruitful in the work of Lacan but still awaits application to the study of mythology. I will therefore describe briefly some of the more important similarities and differences between the psychoanalytic and structuralist methods of myth interpretation, and then attempt a demonstration of how a kind of psychoanalytic struc-

---

7 Lévi-Strauss, *The Savage Mind*, p. 95.
8 Lévi-Strauss, *Structural Anthropology*, trans. Claire Jacobson and Brooke Schoepf (New York: Basic Books, 1963), pp. 214–16.

turalism might be applied to the interpretation of a specific Greek myth.

Certain key similarities are readily apparent, based, as I noted earlier, on the presupposition of both theories that myth is a product of the unconscious and a reflection of unconscious thinking processes.

Dream theory is, of course, the basis of the psychoanalytic interpretation of myth, in accord with Freud's definition of myth as "the secular dreams of youthful humanity,"[9] and the metaphoric (paradigmatic) and metonymic (syntagmatic) associations which, according to Lévi-Strauss, govern mythical thought are equivalent, in Lacanian analysis,[10] to the "primary processes" of condensation and displacement, the principal mechanisms of unconscious discourse and the formation of dreams. To return to a linguistic analogy, in Barthes' semiological description of the dream the signifier is manifest content, the signified is latent content, and the sign is the dream itself as functional union, or compromise, between signifier and signified.[11] As applied to myth, signifiers are the literal constituent units, signifieds are the concepts determined by the membership of a mythemic set, and the sign is the myth itself, a structure which unites signifiers and signifieds.

> All that I claim to have shown so far is, therefore, that the dialectic of superstructures, like that of language, consists in setting up *constitutive units* (which, for this purpose, have to be defined unequivocally, that is, by contrasting them in pairs) so as to be able by means of them to elaborate a system which plays the part of a synthesizing operator between ideas and facts, thereby turning the latter into *signs*. The mind thus passes from empirical diversity to conceptual simplicity and then from conceptual simplicity to meaningful synthesis.[12]

In Lévi-Strauss's analysis of the myth of Oedipus, for example, the killing of Laius by Oedipus is, like the mutual fratricide of the Spartoi, one of several signifiers whose underlying signified is the underrating of blood relations. The sign is the myth it-

---

9 Freud, "Creative Writers and Day-Dreaming," in *The Standard Edition of the Complete Psychological Works of Sigmund Freud*, ed. James Strachey (London: Hogarth, 1958–74), IX, 152. In subsequent footnotes the *Standard Edition* will be abbreviated as *SE*.

10 Jacques Lacan, "L'Instance de la lettre dans l'inconscient ou la raison depuis Freud," in *Écrits* (Paris: Seuil, 1966), p. 511.

11 Barthes, pp. 113–14.

12 Lévi-Strauss, *The Savage Mind*, p. 131.

self, the structure which determines that these signifiers will be united with this signified.

The structuralist notion of the "superabundance of signifiers"[13] means, on a linguistic level, that language makes meaning possible before that meaning is known; that is, the structure of language provides us with signifiers instantaneously (whose meaning can only progressively be learned). On a mythological or psychoanalytic level, this is simply "the admission that there is always something more meant than (or in) what we say; the mode of insistence of the unconscious in the conscious."[14]

In the structuralist interpretation of myth by Lévi-Strauss, "it cannot be too strongly emphasized that all available variants should be taken into account." The myth is defined "as consisting of all its versions . . . therefore, not only Sophocles, but Freud himself, should be included among the recorded versions of the Oedipus myth on a par with earlier or seemingly more 'authentic' versions."[15] Not only all versions but also all details of each version are regarded as potentially important, for it is not contents but only forms which convey meaning. This methodological principle has an obvious affinity with the psychoanalytic theory of displacement, which would regard any detail in the manifest content of dreams or myths, no matter how apparently insignificant, as the potential bearer of displaced affect. A psychoanalyst, presumably, would not share the incredulity of the anthropologist Leach at the ease with which Lévi-Strauss brought a report of a myth in which honey is a metaphor for semen into relation with his prior theory of the analogy between honey and menstrual blood.[16]

The structuralist emphasis on isolating the synchronic dimension which cuts across the diachronic axis, while on one level a parallel to the atemporality of the unconscious and the temporality of consciousness, may also be compared with the concept of secondary revision in dream theory. The diachronic axis gives coherence to the mythical tale, while the synchronic axis reveals the structure of the myth. Similarly, in a dream or a myth, the function of chronological sequence, a product of (usually secondary revision, is to provide coherence, often at

13 Lévi-Strauss, "Introduction à l'oeuvre de Marcel Mauss," in Marcel Mauss, *Sociologie et anthropologie*, 3rd ed. (Paris: Presses Univ. de France, 1966), p. xlix.
14 Jeffrey Mehlman, "The 'floating signifier': from Lévi-Strauss to Lacan," *Yale French Studies*, 48 (1972), 24.
15 Lévi-Strauss, *Structural Anthropology*, pp. 218, 217.
16 Leach, p. 127.

the expense of distorting the underlying meaning; disclosure of this meaning, then, involves "undoing" the distortion caused by diachronic sequence and isolating synchronic similarities.

There is a remarkable similarity, with one very important difference, between the structuralist and psychoanalytic explanations of the phenomenon of duplication in myth. In the view of Lévi-Strauss, duplication is a necessary antecedent of the presence of a synchronic axis:

> the question has often been raised why myths, and more generally oral literature, are so much addicted to duplication, triplication, or quadruplication of the same sequence. If our hypotheses are accepted, the answer is obvious: repetition has as its function to make the structure of the myth apparent. For we have seen that the synchro-diachronical structure of the myth permits us to organize it into diachronical sequences (the rows in our tables) which should be read synchronically (the columns). Thus, a myth exhibits a "slated" structure which seeps to the surface, if one may say so, through the repetition process.
> However, the slates are not absolutely identical to each other. And since the purpose of myth is to provide a logical model capable of overcoming a contradiction (an impossible achievement if, as it happens, the contradiction is real), a theoretically infinite number of slates will be generated, each one slightly different from the others. Thus, myth grows spiral-wise until the intellectual impulse which has produced it is exhausted.[17]

Now let us compare this to the psychoanalytic view of Rank and Hanns Sachs, in which duplication is defined as:

> a means of wish fulfillment and gratification of instinct, which can never take place in reality on the original object of desire, but only after corresponding compensations in the sense of a continued series. Just as many dreams seek to fulfill as adequately as possible always the same wish motive in a series of successive situations in different disguise and distortion, so also the myth repeats one and the same mental constellation until it is exhausted to a certain extent in all its wish tendencies.[18]

With this we come back to the "superabundance of signifiers"; but whereas for the structuralist an interminable series of duplications is due to the reality of the underlying contradiction, for the psychoanalyst it is due to the impossibility of gratifying

---

17 Lévi-Strauss, *Structural Anthropology*, p. 229.
18 Otto Rank and Hanns Sachs, "The Significance of Psychoanalysis for the Humanities," in *Psychoanalysis as an Art and a Science*, ed. Harry Slochower (Detroit: Wayne State Univ. Press, 1964), p. 44.

the original desire or resolving the original conflict. The obvious and important difference between these two theories is that in the former it is an *intellectual* impulse which is "exhausted," while in the latter an *emotional* impulse is "exhausted." This is an essential difference between the psychoanalytic and structuralist theories of myth. For psychoanalysis the function of the unconscious is the elaboration of a motive impulse or conflict by the mechanisms of the primary process; the manifest content of a myth is a reflection of unconscious wishes and fears, to which it is related as the manifest content of a dream is related to its latent content. For Lévi-Strauss, on the other hand, the unconscious is a cognitive faculty, and the manifest content of the myth is the product of the unconscious structuring of an intellectual problem.

> A good deal of what Lévi-Strauss regards as basic, Freud would no doubt have dismissed as rationalization. Most of what Freud regards as basic, Lévi-Strauss would dismiss as a failure to be truly human. Yet both are psychological reductionists. Freud reduces to the power of the instinctual processes, and Lévi-Strauss to the power of logical processes. For Freud the world of Nature is something onto which man can project his emotions: for Lévi-Strauss it is a source of metaphors for social thinking.[19]

Now this is clearly an exaggerated dichotomy, for few structuralists would deny the importance of the instincts and emotions, and few psychoanalysts would deny the presence of some kind of systemic logic in the unconscious. It would perhaps be better to view the problem in this way: both agree that representation, or inscriptions, occur in the unconscious and are subject to certain laws of unconscious discourse; the difference lies in identification of the energizing origin of these inscriptions, whether it is to be regarded as instinctual or experiential—or, perhaps, to a confusion of the unconscious and the preconscious systems. Yet it is, I would think, his unswerving determination to regard both myth and the unconscious as cognitive phenomena that leads Lévi-Strauss to the disappointing analysis which he gives of the myth of Oedipus, that it is ultimately an attempt to mediate the contradiction inherent in experiential denial of theoretical autochthony. As I have discussed both the myth of Oedipus and its interpretation by Lévi-Strauss elsewhere,[20] I will add only this: One has the impression that the question of

---

19 Robin Fox, *"Totem and Taboo* Reconsidered," in *The Structural Study of Myth and Totemism,* ed. Edmund Leach (London: Tavistock, 1967), pp. 161–62.
20 "The Misogyny of Eteocles," *Arethusa,* 6 (1973), 197–231.

autochthony in Greek myth, like the animals which appear on occasion, is a residue of an earlier stage of myth formation, or perhaps of a fusion between the myths of the Indo-European invaders of Greece during the second millennium B.C. and those of the indigenous peoples, for whom autochthony would presumably be of greater interest. At any rate, autochthony, animals, or, for that matter, the opposition between nature and culture do not seem to be of paramount concern in Greek mythology, and it may be for this reason that Lévi-Strauss has studiously avoided the discussion of either pre-Hellenic or Indo-European myth. From a psychoanalytic point of view, in fact, the distinction between nature and culture as homologous systems of differences would perhaps not be found in the global totality of natural and social conditions, but could be located specifically in that mythical moment, occurring in the first year of every individual's life, when the symbiotic presubjective universe gives way to the differentiation of self and other; that is, that point at which the biological existence of the human being is complicated by the introduction of a historical dimension.[21]

We may now turn to an application of these theories to a specific Greek myth, and in particular to instances of duplication or repetition, that property of myth which seems to encapsulate most clearly the similarities and differences between the two methods of interpretation. For the purpose of demonstration, we will examine a familiar myth, that of the descendants of Tantalus, and we will aim at a structural clarification of a single event within this myth, the killing of Clytemnestra by Orestes, an episode which has received considerable attention from a psychoanalytic point of view. The mythical background of the matricide is quite complex, but its salient aspects may be summarized as follows, paraphrasing the account given in the *Library* of Apollodorus (*Epitome* 2.4–6.25).

Oenomaus, the father of Hippodameia, was in love with his daughter (or had received an oracle that he would be killed by whoever married her);[22] he therefore proposed to her suitors a contest, with marriage to Hippodameia as the prize. The contest was a chariot race between Oenomaus and the suitor, and twelve suitors had already lost both the race and their heads, which Oenomaus nailed to his house. When Pelops came to

---

[21] See Heinz Lichtenstein, "Identity and Sexuality," *Journal of the American Psychoanalytic Association*, 9 (1961), 244, 252.

[22] A fine example of the function of oracles as projective rationalizations of the unconscious wishes and fears of the subject who receives the oracle.

court Hippodameia, she fell in love with him and secured the assistance of Myrtilus, the charioteer of Oenomaus, who, like father and suitors, was also in love with her. While preparing Oenomaus' chariot for the race with Pelops, Myrtilus deliberately failed to insert the pins in the wheel-naves, and Oenomaus was killed, tangled in the reins and dragged to death. As he was dying, Oenomaus realized the truth and cursed Myrtilus, to the effect that he would be killed by Pelops. Myrtilus, Hippodameia, and Pelops escaped together, and when Pelops left the other two to search for water, Myrtilus tried to rape Hippodameia. She informed Pelops of this and he threw Myrtilus into the sea.

Atreus and Thyestes were the sons of Pelops. Atreus was married to Aerope, the daughter of Catreus, but Aerope and Thyestes were in love with one another and conspired against Atreus. A golden lamb having appeared in the flocks of Atreus, he had killed it and hidden it away, but Aerope gave it to her lover Thyestes. In a contest between the two brothers over the kingship of Mycenae, Thyestes told the people that whoever had the golden lamb should be king. Atreus agreed, thinking that the lamb was still in his possession, but Thyestes produced it and became king. With the help of Zeus, however, Atreus recovered the kingdom and banished Thyestes. Learning later of the adultery, he invited Thyestes to a supposed reconciliation supper; having cut up and boiled the sons of Thyestes, he served them to their own father, who unwittingly ate his children.

The sons of Atreus were Agamemnon, king of Mycenae, and Menelaus, king of Sparta. The two brothers married sisters; Agamemnon married Clytemnestra and Menelaus married Helen. Paris came from Troy to be the guest of Menelaus, and on the tenth day of his stay Menelaus went to Crete to bury his maternal grandfather. Paris persuaded Helen to run off with him to Troy, and the result, of course, was the Trojan War. Twenty years later, Paris was killed by Philoctetes and Helen was recovered by Menelaus and Agamemnon.

While Agamemnon was off to war, Clytemnestra and Aegisthus, the son of Thyestes, fell in love. They sent away Orestes, the son of Agamemnon, and killed Agamemnon himself on his return from Troy. Some years later, Orestes returned from exile and killed Clytemnestra and Aegisthus.

Orestes' murder of his mother was the subject of extant plays by all three major Greek tragedians and seems to have been the focal point of a myth whose ultimate message may be viewed as the upholding of the oedipal taboos against parricide and incest. Orestes, who kills his mother in order to avenge his father, is diametrically opposed to Oedipus, who kills his father and marries his mother. The myth of Orestes is an inversion of the myth of Oedipus, and the two great myth figures are situated, it seems, at opposite poles of the series of transformations of familial relationships which constitute the entire system of Greek mythology. Several psychoanalytic studies of the myth of Orestes, however, have discussed matters which may indicate that Orestes and Oedipus are not so very different after all; an implied incestuous content of matricide has been suggested, on the basis of cross-cultural comparison of matricidal myths,[23] or as a component of ambivalence in a mother-son relationship so intense as to compel an extreme solution.[24]

If there is in fact an incestuous element concealed under the act of matricide, we might expect that this will emerge from a structural analysis of the myth, in the same way that Lacan's "subject," which is constituted by its repetition, is to be sought as a "lost object."[25] Repetition, or duplication, is apparent in the genealogical and episodic nature of the myth itself, but can be seen more clearly in the following outline, which is arranged on both diachronic and synchronic axes:

I	IIa	IIb	IIc	III	IV
Oenomaus loves Hippodameia	Myrtilus loves Hippodameia	Pelops loves Hippodameia	Hippodameia loves Pelops (and not Myrtilus)	Myrtilus and Hippodameia kill Oenomaus	Pelops kills Myrtilus (cursed by Oenomaus)
Atreus marries Aerope	Aerope and Thyestes love one another			Aerope and Thyestes deceive Atreus	Atreus regains kingdom, kills children of Thyestes
Menelaus marries Helen	Helen and Paris love one another			Helen and Paris leave Menelaus	Menelaus regains Helen, Paris is killed by Philoctetes
Agamemnon marries Clytemnestra	Aegisthus loves Clytemnestra		Clytemnestra loves Aegisthus (and not Orestes)	Aegisthus and Clytemnestra kill Agamemnon	Orestes kills Aegisthus (to avenge father)
		Orestes kills Clytemnestra			

---

[23] Henry Bunker, "Mother-Murder in Myth and Legend," *Psychoanalytic Quarterly*, 13 (1944), 198–207.

[24] Philip Slater, *The Glory of Hera* (Boston: Beacon, 1968), p. 187.

[25] Lacan, "Of structure as an Inmixing of an Otherness Prerequisite to Any Subject Whatever," in *The Languages of Criticism and the Sciences of Man*, ed. Richard Macksey and Eugenio Donato (Baltimore: Johns Hopkins Univ. Press, 1970).

This outline tries to avoid the charge sometimes brought against Lévi-Strauss, of having deliberately selected those elements which will confirm his interpretation, by being simply an enumeration of the positive and negative relationships in the myth, listed chronologically in such a way that instances of repetition are arranged in vertical columns. Reading the myth diachronically, it appears as four miniature oedipal dramas, in each of which the desired woman is won from her husband or father by a hero who then is punished for his deed. Reading synchronically, the father-figures are Oenomaus/Atreus/Menelaus/Agamemnon, the mother-figures are Hippodameia/Aerope/Helen/Clytemnestra, and the son-figures are Myrtilus/Thyestes/Paris/Aegisthus. In answer to the objection that none of these "son-figures" is in fact the real son of his respective "father" and "mother," I would agree with the structuralist philosopher Jacques Derrida: "It is obvious that, if by *mother* one understands *real mother*, the Oedipus complex no longer has any meaning."[26]

The first column contains the relationships between mother and father, the second those between mother and son, the third is the successful conspiracy of mother and son against the father, and the fourth is the punishment of the guilty son. The pattern is quite straightforward, with these two complications: the variations of punishment in Column IV, and the doubling of the son-figure, with resultant complexity of Column II, in the first and fourth horizontal series. To understand Column IV, we should recognize that in each of the four instances the son is indirectly punished by the father. In the first and fourth series (which the structural outline reveals as clearly opposed to the second and third series), the father is dead but still an efficacious agent; Myrtilus is killed in accordance with the curse of Oenomaus, Aegisthus is killed in order to avenge the memory of Agamemnon. In the second and third series, the father, having been only betrayed, lives on to regain his lost possession but punishes the son indirectly nevertheless; either the son is killed by someone other than the father, or the father kills someone other than the son. Displacement of father or son occurs in all four instances: Oenomaus to Pelops, Thyestes to his sons, Menelaus to Philoctetes, Agamemnon to Orestes. To continue the clear parallelism of the first and fourth series, in each the

---

26 Jacques Derrida, Discussion of: Jean-Pierre Vernant, "Greek Tragedy: Problems of Interpretation," in *The Languages of Criticism and the Sciences of Man*, p. 194.

son (Myrtilus, Aegisthus) who has killed the father (Oenomaus, Agamemnon) and thus usurps his position is killed by a second or alternate son (Pelops, Orestes) who, by carrying out the father's will and by eliminating the pretender to the father's position, wins the father's position for himself. Myrtilus and Aegisthus, then, are scapegoats; having killed the father at the instigation of the mother, they turn out to have done this on behalf of Pelops and Orestes, who thus are freed from the onus of parricide. But how, it may be objected, can Orestes be connected with parricide? The answer to this question depends on the answer to the question with which we began, the possibility of an incestuous element in Orestes' act of matricide, for parricide is simply the necessary antecedent of incest; if an incestuous wish can be shown in Orestes' case, and he is then seen playing a role exactly equivalent to that of Pelops, there should be little doubt that a parricidal impulse is concealed beneath the murder of Aegisthus.

The solution is, I think, to be found in Column II. Myrtilus and Aegisthus love Hippodameia and Clytemnestra, just as Thyestes and Paris love Aerope and Helen. But at this point the situation is complicated by the entry of Pelops and Orestes, the alternate sons, who will play exactly identical roles in Column IV but precisely inverted roles in Column II. Pelops desires and wins Hippodameia, but Orestes kills Clytemnestra (IIb), and the reason is immediately given: Hippodameia loves Pelops but not Myrtilus (whom she accuses), while Clytemnestra loves Aegisthus but not Orestes (whom she exiles—IIc). The oedipal desire of Pelops is fulfilled in the reciprocal love of Hippodameia, but that of Orestes is frustrated by Clytemnestra's choice of Aegisthus. Myrtilus, despite his intentions, simply did Pelops' work for him, but Aegisthus did Orestes' work too well; by killing the father and winning the mother as well, he has usurped the oedipal project of Orestes. For this he is killed and for this yet another cause is added to the overdetermined aetiology of matricide: Clytemnestra chose to bestow her favors on the false rather than on the true son.

The postulate of incestuous content in matricide having been strengthened by structural duplication (Orestes = Pelops), other reasons for its presence, in addition to the previously mentioned views of Bunker and Slater, may also be adduced: (1) Overcompensation reveals an urge which is the opposite of the apparent emotion; the matricidal act may, in this light, be seen as

a compulsive denial of, or defense against, incestuous desire.
(2) By the same principle, a defense against parricidal impulses
or, alternatively, against guilt for such impulses in the past may
be seen in Orestes' resolve to avenge his father. We may note,
in this respect, that the fantasied rescue of the father is regarded
by Freud as an expression of defiance and of a wish to be rid
of the father[27] and is seen by Abraham as equivalent to parricide.[28] (3) Like the seemingly irrelevant details in dreams, apparently insignificant details in the retelling of a myth may
sometimes hint at its repressed meaning. Parricide is the last
thing we would expect Orestes to be charged with, and yet in
the *Marmor Parium* account of his trial he is charged not with
the murder of Clytemnestra, as in the usual version (e.g., Aeschylus' *Eumenides*), but with the killing of the father of Erigone
(the daughter of Aegisthus and Clytemnestra), whom he then
married (Apollodorus, *Epitome* 6.25,28). A psychoanalytic
interpretation would see in this account the thinly disguised
suggestion of parricide (displaced from the first husband of
Clytemnestra to the second) and incest (displaced from Clytemnestra to her daughter). Such instances of the "return of
the repressed" occur elsewhere in Greek myth, as, for example,
in the statement found in ancient scholia that Oedipus cursed
his sons not only for mistreating him, as in the usual version,
but also for the attempted rape of their stepmother. Another
example is a variant of the myth we have been examining, in
which Pelops, not Myrtilus, is named as the slayer of Oenomaus,
or that variant in which Agamemnon has by Cassandra a son
named Pelops.

With the association of murder and desire, matricide and
incest, in the myth of Orestes, we seem to be in the sphere of
Freud's Eros and Thanatos, the sexual drive and the death drive,
concepts which occupy an important position in the formulations of Lacanian theory.

In one of his latest statements of the duality of the instincts
(or drives), Freud described Eros and the death drive, concepts which he traced back to Empedocles of Acragas, as that
"which strives to combine existing phenomena into ever greater
unities" and that which "seeks to dissolve these combinations

---

[27] Freud, "A Special Type of Choice of Object Made by Men," *SE*, XI, 163–75.
[28] Karl Abraham, "The Rescue and Murder of the Father in Neurotic Fantasy-
Formations," *International Journal of Psycho-Analysis*, 3 (1922), 467–74.

and destroy the structures to which they have given rise."[29] A major concern of French psychoanalysis, in comparison with the predominantly American dismissal of the myth of the death drive, has been the study of the mechanisms by which both drives, constant somatic forces, are "inscribed" in ideational representations of the unconscious. The inscriptions of Eros appear as the ideational metonymy of desire, i.e., the metonymic chain of unconscious signifiers of desire which receive the free flow of libidinal energy. Among the endless varieties of displacements and symbolisms of unconscious desire, we might locate two examples from Greek mythology: the transformation of the castrated phallus of Ouranus into Aphrodite, a metonymic displacement from instrument to object in which both signifiers are prime emblems of desire, and the metonymic symbolism by which a golden fleece bears the desire of Jason and the Argonauts as well as that of Atreus and Thyestes. Both representations are parts of a metonymic chain in the unconscious, a chain which might be pictured either as a metonymic circle whose center is manifest only by its absence, or as a linear syntagmatic sequence of which only the first member is subject to repression; as Freud says, "each single derivative of the repressed may have its own special vicissitude . . . if these derivatives have become sufficiently far removed from the repressed representative, whether owing to the adoption of distortions or by reason of the number of intermediate links inserted, they have free access to the conscious."[30]

But "if it is easy to represent the domain of the sexual drive energy—in other words, the libido—it is surely not the case for the realm subject to the . . . indescribable, ungraspable fact of the death drive."[31] We might expect a similar metonymic chain representing death, limit, frustration, absence, void, negation; but how could this be the case, if the unconscious cannot negate and, furthermore, if metonymy itself is the instrument of the erotic drive? Where might death appear, in an unconscious

[29] Freud, "Analysis Terminable and Interminable," SE, XXIII, 246. I should stress at this point that I myself do not regard the "death drive" (or, for that matter, the "aggressive drive") as an actual instinct; as employed by certain French psychoanalysts, however, the concept is a valuable heuristic metaphor in the analysis of desire.

[30] Freud, "Repression," SE, XIV, 150, 149.

[31] Jean Laplanche and Serge Leclaire, "The Unconscious," Yale French Studies, 48 (1972), 142–43.

which seems to know only the marvelous proliferation of desire? The answer, for Leclaire, is that the death drive appears precisely on the circumference of desire, not as a state or goal but as "catastrophic instantaneity." The ideational representation of the drive, if there could be such, would seem to be castration: not as a state but as the moment in which desire ends and the simultaneous moment in which desire is born anew. The unconscious, in its imperious and insatiable striving for the gratification of desire, simultaneously admits and denies its castratory limits: the "original castration" which makes desire possible and the "final castration" which is equivalent to satiety, seen most clearly in the most intense experience of instinctual gratification, the simultaneity of orgasm and the death of erection and desire (*la petite mort*).

Eros unites; and the phallus, which unites one body to another, is the signifier of desire. The death drive (an "anti-instinct," in Jeffrey Mehlman's phrase) separates; and castration, which severs the uniting organ and dissolves combinatory union, is its expression. Thus the phallus, "the signifier *par excellence* of desire,"[32] signifies desire not-yet-achieved, and castration signifies the instant at which the gratification of desire introduces death. And thus the orgasm can only end in castration. The dissolution of the Oedipus complex is usually ascribed to fear of castration at the hands of the father, but if the total gratification of desire in itself is castration, one can see, first, that the father is a symbolic function (in Lacanian terminology, the *Nom-du Père*); second, that we might better name the Father, rather than castration, as the inscription of the death drive; and third, that dissolution of the Oedipus complex results from fear not of castration by the father, but of the castration which is satiety, a castration fled through the infinite metonymic byways of desire.

If the end of orgasm is equivalent to castration, one might think that genital sexuality would bear a high quotient of anxiety and be easily subjected to repression. Psychoanalysis has shown that this is indeed often the case; that it is not always the case (that is, that fear of castration does not invariably result in repression of genital sexuality) may perhaps be explained

---

[32] *Ibid.*, p. 174.

by the postulate that absolute castration depends on absolute satisfaction, possible only in the fantasied incestuous relationship for which all subsequent sexual acts are inadequate substitutes. Thus the ultimate and inescapable dissatisfaction which mars every act of intercourse is the price demanded by the possibility of freedom from castration and repression.

In myth and in the unconscious, death and castration are in general synonymous. This can be seen most clearly in a myth such as the one analyzed previously, in which all six male deaths are directly associated with sexual rivalry. In one instance, however, that of rivalry between Atreus and Thyestes, it is not the rival who is killed (i.e., castrated) but his children. But to kill the children of oneself or of another is to render impotent, and is therefore also a means of castration. By killing the children of Thyestes, Atreus castrates Thyestes just as Medea castrates Jason through the murder of Mermerus and Pheres. To be castrated is to have no children, and to have no children is to be castrated. But also, to have children is to be castrated, both because the orgasm which (for the male) is necessary for procreation is, as we have seen, a castration, and also because the mythical orgasm is, by Poseidon's Law of Mandatory Fruitfulness (*Odyssey* XI. 249–50), the beginning of the son, the castrator-to-be. The closing off of escape locates the death drive at the beginning as well as at the end of desire.

The paradigmatic myth of castration is, of course, the mutilation of Ouranus by his son Cronus, a myth which contains many similarities to the story of Tantalus, Pelops, and their descendants. Ouranus, recognizing, in effect, that to have a son is to be castrated, attempts both to rid himself of sons and to undo the sexual act of procreation, by reinserting his children as they are born in the *keuthmon* (secret hole) of their mother Earth. But this is no solution: by having children or depriving himself of children, by engaging in intercourse as well as by attempting to annul it, Ouranus incurs castration, symbolized in the richly over-determined instant of Cronus' attack. But it is the law of *talion*, as well as of structural synchrony, that the castrator will be castrated, a law which achieves beautiful complexity in Herodotus' story of Hermotimus who, having been castrated by Panionius, then compels Panionius to castrate his own sons and to be castrated in turn by them (Herodotus 8.

105–06).[33] Thus Cronus, like Ouranus, will try to get rid of his children, not, however, by forcing them back into their mother but by swallowing them himself, as his own son Zeus will swallow Metis (and like Tantalus, the cannibal father of Pelops, and Thyestes, who eats his own sons). And, as Devereux has shown, the castration of Cronus is assured, as much by the structure of the myth as by its inclusion in numerous variants.[34]

In the canonical accounts, however, Cronus is not castrated, but rather is deceived, subdued, and eventually reinstalled as ruler over a kingdom, the Islands of the Blest. Ouranus, on the other hand, *is* castrated but retains a measure of efficacy, predicting the punishment of his sons. A parallel may thus be drawn with the four father-figures of the myth diagrammed earlier. Oenomaus and Agamemnon, the father-figures of the first and fourth series, which are structurally paired, resemble Ouranus, the primal father, in that they are killed but retain their efficacy. In the second and third series, Atreus and Menelaus are, like Cronus, not killed but deceived; Atreus then recovers his kingdom, while Menelaus recovers his wife and, as a direct result of his relationship with her, will live after death in the Islands of the Blest, the realm of Cronus.

With Pelops we arrive at Zeus and the third generation of theogony: 1) both Pelops and Zeus are the (intended) victims of paternal cannibalism; 2) both survive through the intervention of Rhea, who substitutes a stone to be swallowed instead of Zeus and who restores Pelops, according to Bacchylides and the scholiast on Pindar, by returning him to the cauldron; 3) both are ultimately victorious.

Orestes also may be compared to Zeus, not in his role as swallowed but as swallower. Whereas Zeus swallows Metis, the predicted mother of his potential castrator, and thus gives birth himself to Athena, the masculine woman (or castrated man), Orestes kills his own mother, revealing the potential castrator to be himself; he makes himself a castrated man, establishing a congruence with Athena which is made clear when she comes to rescue him in Aeschylus' *Eumenides*.

Thus the castrator is identified as ultimately oneself, either as begetter of the actual executor of the deed, or as bearer of

---

[33] George Devereux, "La naissance d'Aphrodite," in *Mélanges Lévi-Strauss*, ed. Jean Pouillon and Pierre Maranda (The Hague: Mouton, 1970), II, 1241.
[34] Devereux, pp. 1238–40.

the desire which begins from, and ends at, the moment of absence, lack, limit, castration, death.

In killing Clytemnestra, Orestes kills his own desire by killing the object of desire; this is not the "liberating" murder of the murderous self[35] but is rather the self-castration which marks the eruption of the death drive, a parallel both to the self-mutilation of Attis and to the swallowing by Zeus of Metis, the dangerous object of desire. The result is absence of tension, lack of conflict, complete discharge of affect—in other words, the goal of the death drive.

In a sense, Orestes' solution to the problem of desire may be seen as springing from the same source as the age-old myth of seminal retention, based on the premise that if one never has an orgasm, one will never die. It is this sort of wisdom which prompts the oracular advice of Apollo to Orestes, paralleled by the famous oracle to Laius; the former kills the object of desire (Clytemnestra), the latter avoids the object of desire (Jocasta), each thereby castrates himself (is this then the Delphic maxim?). And to be castrated is to be, like Teiresias or Attis, turned into a woman or, alternatively, to be homosexual, which figures manifestly in the relationship between Laius and Chrysippus, latently in the relationship between Orestes and Pylades.

Let us recall at this point the symbolic function of the Dead Father, the *Nom-du-Père,* for it is in the name of his dead father Agamemnon that Orestes kills his own desire, repeating by matricide the words and actions with which he began Aeschylus' *Choephori,* the invocation to his dead father (and to Hermes *psychopompos*) and the symbolic offering of a lock of his hair on the grave, an act recalled in the later song of female treachery by the story of Scylla, who killed her father by cutting off his hair and now lives with Hermes in the Underworld.

Once again we may perceive, from a different angle, the libidinal (incestuous) component of Orestes' matricide, in terms somewhat similar to Bunker's explanation. For castration, which brings an end to desire, is, as we have seen, equivalent to the fulfillment of desire; both orgasm and castration bring an end to desire, an equivalence apparent in the ecstasy, climaxing in castration, of Attis, or in the castration of Ouranus, at the precise moment of orgasm, by the severing slash of the jagged-

---

[35] Herbert Fingarette, "Orestes: Paradigm Hero and Central Motif of Contemporary Ego Psychology," *Psychoanalytic Review,* 50 (1963), 437–61.

toothed sickle which marks the appearance of the death drive.

The orgasm and castration of Ouranus are simultaneous and produce simultaneous issue: from the semen of orgasm are born the Phaeacians, from the blood of castration are born the Giants, the Meliad nymphs, and the Furies. From the phallus itself, as instrument and signifier of desire, comes Aphrodite, the object and signifier of desire. From death, as castration, comes desire, the phallus which becomes Aphrodite. Thus death generates desire which ends in death, and the myth graphically portrays Leclaire's statement of "the gap through which desire originates and into which it perpetually plunges, on the bedrock of the death drive."[36]

In Lacan's formulation, the phallus is the metonymy of desire; but metonymy itself—extending, joining together, combining, grappling—is the phallus. And metaphor—a process of selection which excludes other members of the paradigmatic set —or better, as the mechanism of repression, by which any connection between a repressed signifier and its substitute is denied —is the severing, separating sickle of Cronus. Metaphor, the modality of repression and denial, is an act of negation; and negation, the "successor to expulsion,"[37] belongs to the death drive.

Metonymy, or desire, both masks and reveals the death drive; is there not a reciprocal process by which metaphor performs a similar function in regard to the sexual drive? Matricide, in its metaphorical function, would then reveal the shape of repressed desire: in the first place because as a paradigmatic signifier (in the diagram above) it is limited and defined by the other signifiers, all associated with desire, in the paradigmatic set; and second, because as the negation of desire it expresses desire. "Negation is a way of taking cognizance of what is repressed."[38]

In the case of Ouranus, there is no repression, castration is inflicted from without (whereas repression is self-inflicted), and thus the penis maintains itself as Aphrodite who is, in Devereux' phrase "le phallos lui-même,"[39] a metonymic displacement of

---

36 Laplanche and Leclaire, p. 151.
37 Freud, "Negation," *SE*, XIX, 239.
38 *Ibid.*, p. 235.
39 Devereux, p. 1248.

desire. In the case of Orestes, there is repression, castration is self-inflicted (in the denial of desire and in the offering of hair), and the survival of the phallus as woman and object of desire is negated.

For Clytemnestra, by metonymic displacement of desire to desired object, is as much the phallus of Orestes as once Aphrodite was the phallus of Ouranus. And from the blood of Clytemnestra, as once from the blood of Ouranus, spring the Furies: spirits—as Apollo tells us so forcibly in the *Eumenides* (in the lurid vocabulary of decapitation, slitting throats, gouging out eyes, loss of semen, ruin of virility)—of death and castration.

Perhaps the best way to summarize what the psychoanalytic and structuralist methods of myth interpretation have in common is to regard both as concerned with a *principle of redundancy*. For the psychoanalyst this means, essentially, that complex mythic structures will be generated by a kind of repetition compulsion (as found, clinically, in children's play or in dreams during traumatic neurosis).[40] We should also note that the "overdetermination" of an element in a myth or dream, or of a symptom, may be regarded as virtually equivalent to the notion of "redundancy" in information theory.[41] For the structuralist, redundancy is implicated in the emphasis on synchrony and in the location of meaning only in the relationship between repeated and opposed events (or functions), never in the isolated event. This emphasis on the priority of structural relationships, on the relation between relationships, is analogous to Freud's insistence that the "meaning" of a dream element is not to be found in a "dream-book," or one-to-one code, but rather must be sought as a function of the complex of relationships in which the event occurs; as Freud says of dream symbols, "as with Chinese script, the correct interpretation can only be arrived at on each occasion from the context."[42] And yet far more radical than this contextualism (which is, after all, striking only in the light of typical misconceptions concerning Freud's theory of dream interpretation) is a little-known footnote in *The Interpretation of Dreams,* a footnote in which Freud proleptically aligns his theory with structuralism by arguing that the "code" is to be

---

40 Freud, "Beyond the Pleasure Principle," *SE*, XVIII, 18–23.
41 Wilden, *System and Structure,* pp. 5, 35.
42 Freud, "The Interpretation of Dreams," *SE*, V, 353.

found not in symbols but in processes, not in the *dream-thoughts* but in the *dream-work*:

> I used at one time to find it extraordinarily difficult to accustom readers to the distinction between the manifest content of dreams and the latent dream-thoughts. . . . But now that analysts at least have become reconciled to replacing the manifest dream by the meaning revealed by its interpretation, many of them have become guilty of falling into another confusion which they cling to with equal obstinacy. They seek to find the essence of dreams in their latent content and in so doing they overlook the distinction between the latent dream-thoughts and the dream-work. At bottom, dreams are nothing other than a particular *form* of thinking, made possible by the conditions of the state of sleep. It is the *dream-work* which creates that form, and it alone is the essence of dreaming—the explanation of its peculiar nature.[43]

---

43 Freud, *Ibid.*, pp. 506–07.